'I love this book. A clear, concise, and wonderfully engaging introduction to the pluralistic approach to therapy. The book conveys a deep understanding of the philosophical roots of pluralism, along with clear guidance on how these principles can be applied in practice. Research findings are integrated throughout to develop a compelling, contemporary perspective. This is a goldmine of information on how to think and practice pluralistically – if you've got questions on the pluralistic approach to therapy, this is the place to come.'

Mick Cooper, *Professor of Counselling Psychology, University of Roehampton; co-author of* Pluralistic Counselling and Psychotherapy *and co-editor of* The Handbook of Pluralistic Counselling and Psychotherapy

'This is an intelligent, well written and accessible book that beautifully captures the essence of pluralistic therapy. By addressing the kinds of questions that are often in the minds of students and practitioners who encounter this approach, it offers a valuable introduction to what we know about pluralistic therapy so far, illustrated by case examples from the practical experience of the authors. It is a "must read" for all pluralistic trainees and practitioners who want to defend and explain their practice to colleagues, wish to develop a deeper understanding of what they do with clients and why, and are committed to working in ways that deliver an ethical and competent service to their clients.'

Julia McLeod, *Lecturer in Counselling, Abertay University*

'I really appreciated the ability of these authors to capture and convey the growing edge of pluralistic practice, as an approach that has always been grounded in a willingness to be open to dialogue and new ideas. An invaluable addition to the growing theoretical, research and practice literature on pluralistic counselling and psychotherapy.'

John McLeod, *Visiting Professor of Counselling, Institute for Integrative Counselling and Psychotherapy, Dublin*

'Interest in pluralistic therapy has grown steadily over the last couple of decades as practitioners have moved away from a "one size fits all" approach to working with clients, instead building on true collaborative relationship informed through inclusivity and the context of social justice. Frankie Brown and Kate Smith, in an engaging and accessible way, provide a perfect gateway into pluralism that values and respects the unique contribution   same time, exploring how they can be woven into the therapeutic process informed by client preference. From the curious, to those who have embraced pluralism into the heart and soul of their work, this book is compelling and essential in equal measure that will inform thinking for years to come.'

Professor Andrew Reeves, *Professor in Counselling Professions and Mental Health, a BACP Senior Accredited Counsellor/Psychotherapist and Registered Social Worker*

'This book is a comprehensive, concise and considered exploration of the key tenets of Pluralistic Therapy. It is an accessible read for the beginner as well as a primer and refresher for the more advanced student. It is an engaging text and an important source of philosophical and clinical information, with valuable insights and explanation into this cutting edge approach. It will evoke and encourage critical thinking and questioning of important facets of theory and practice. In addition it will add to the ever-expanding body of knowledge and promote further debate and deliberations as the pluralistic approach to therapy widens its reach and applicability. As a higher education institute that teaches a masters in Pluralistic Counselling and Psychotherapy, we will definitely place this on the required reading list for our students.'

Marcella Finnerty, PhD, *President, IICP College, Dublin, Ireland*

Pluralistic Therapy

Pluralistic Therapy provides answers to the most important and common questions asked about the origins, principles, and practice of pluralism.

Written in an accessible style by experts in the field, the book provides the reader with a comprehensive understanding of the pluralistic approach in theory and practice, and builds on the contemporary developments in the field. The questions cover five areas, including an overview of pluralism, pluralism in practice, client factors, pluralistic developments outside of individual therapy, and critical questions about pluralism. The questions also cover some of the key challenges posed to the approach.

This book will appeal to a wide range of audiences, including therapeutic practitioners, researchers, and professionals interested in the application of the approach within mental health contexts. It will also serve to help professionals from non-therapy backgrounds, such as mental health services, education, and social care, understand the nature of pluralistic work.

Frankie Brown, M.A., is a pluralistic counsellor and psychotherapist. Having previously lectured in pluralistic therapy at IICP, Dublin, she now works in private practice and as a school counsellor providing individual therapy and teaching inputs for students, teachers, and parents.

Kate Smith, PhD, is a professor of Counselling at the University of Aberdeen, UK, and a pluralistic therapist. Having trained in 2007, she led the pluralistic practice steering group until 2021. Kate is the co-author of *The Pluralistic Therapy Primer* (2021).

Edited by Windy Dryden, the *50 FAQs in Counselling and Psychotherapy Series* provides answers to questions frequently raised by trainees and practitioners in a particular area in counselling and psychotherapy.

Each book in the series is written by experts based on their responses to 50 frequently asked questions, divided into specific sections.

The series will be of interest to practitioners from all orientations including psychotherapists, clinical, health and counselling psychologists, counsellors, psychiatrists, clinically-oriented social workers and trainees in these disciplines.

Windy Dryden PhD is Emeritus Professor of Psychotherapeutic Studies at the Goldsmiths University of London. He is an international authority on Rational Emotive Behaviour Therapy and is in part-time clinical and consultative practice. He has worked in psychotherapy for more than 45 years and is the author and editor of over 250 books.

Single-Session Therapy
Responses to Frequently Asked Questions
Windy Dryden

Pluralistic Therapy
Responses to Frequently Asked Questions
Frankie Brown and Kate Smith

For more information about this series, please visit: www.routledge.com

Pluralistic Therapy
Responses to Frequently Asked Questions

Frankie Brown and Kate Smith

Routledge
Taylor & Francis Group
LONDON AND NEW YORK

Designed cover image: © Getty Images

First published 2023
by Routledge
4 Park Square, Milton Park, Abingdon, Oxon OX14 4RN

and by Routledge
605 Third Avenue, New York, NY 10158

Routledge is an imprint of the Taylor & Francis Group, an informa business

© 2023 Frankie Brown and Kate Smith

British Library Cataloguing-in-Publication Data
A catalogue record for this book is available from the British Library

ISBN: 978-1-032-30570-7 (hbk)
ISBN: 978-1-032-30567-7 (pbk)
ISBN: 978-1-003-30573-6 (ebk)

DOI: 10.4324/9781003305736

Typeset in Bembo
by Apex CoVantage, LLC

Contents

Section 1

An overview of pluralistic counselling and psychotherapy

1. What is this 'thing' called pluralistic therapy?
2. What is the underlying philosophy behind pluralistic practice and why is it important?
3. Did we really need another approach?
4. There are lots of ways of integrative therapy – how is pluralism different?
5. What are the fundamental principles that guide pluralistic therapy?
6. Is pluralistic therapy an evidence-based practice then?
7. I'm confused between a pluralistic perspective and pluralistic practice, can you help?
8. How can someone trained in a single approach adopt a pluralistic stance?
9. Can you explain the language of pluralism?
10. What is the role of the therapist as a person in pluralism?
11. Why do pluralistic therapists focus so much on collaboration?
12. What knowledge is appropriate to use in the therapy room?

DOI: 10.4324/9781003305736-1

1 What is this 'thing' called pluralistic therapy?

Pluralism, at a philosophical level, is the belief that there are multiple truths and a variety of plausible, yet conflicting, responses to any one question. In contrast to monism (a single truth) and relativism (neither right nor wrong; it depends on the context), it allows the parallel existence of more than one answer to any question. In alignment with this philosophical perspective, pluralism in therapy is based on the belief that there are multiple ways of undertaking therapy and, within each therapeutic encounter, more than one effective way to respond to client needs. The approach builds on a body of research in therapy that challenges the either/or position – for example, that a single school of therapy is more effective than another or that there are consistently 'best' ways of responding to client experiences and distress.

Pluralistic therapy was first articulated as a framework for therapeutic integration in 2007 by Mick Cooper and John McLeod as a result of the large number of available and effective therapeutic schools and modalities. Developed as an open and discursive practice, more recently it has become common to differentiate ways of thinking about the approach. In practice, a pluralistic *stance* or *perspective* reflects a position where a practitioner of one modality can fundamentally value other approaches to therapy, without it necessarily impacting how they undertake their work. Pluralistic *practice*, or pluralistic *therapy*, involves using a set of guiding principles as a reference point for how therapy is undertaken and allows for the integration of methods and change pathways. The most common way of integrating methods in practice is through the pluralistic *framework*, which is supported by a series of founding principles (see Chapter 5 for more) and entrenched in a humanistic perspective, valuing the individual, recognising personal striving, empowerment, and the need for equality. More recently, an ethic of social and epistemic justice has been influential in supporting the drive for pluralistic therapy

DOI: 10.4324/9781003305736-2

to champion an equality and inclusivity agenda in mental health and society more broadly.

There are multiple ways that a client can experience problems in living, how they understand and interpret this experience, and what they would like to do about it. To respond to this, the pluralistic framework serves to structure flexibility into therapy. It also assumes that clients will desire, and benefit from, different therapeutic activities and interventions and that their preferences might change over time (Cooper and McLeod, 2011). Indeed, evidence points to a degree of flexibility (and non-adherence to a core model) occurring in practice for practitioners across the profession, with therapists increasingly identifying as integrative (Castonguay et al., 2015). However, with over 400 therapeutic approaches in existence (Norcross, 2005) and a therapist's desire to respond to clients' preferences and needs, there can be confusion (which therapy model and why?) and tension (how do I integrate two theories that hold opposing positions?). Pluralistic therapy offers a framework in which these theoretical tensions can be managed (O'Hara and Schofield, 2008). Therefore, taking a pluralistic perspective and undertaking pluralistic practice allow the therapist to draw upon multiple sources of knowledge (see Chapter 12) as well as elicit the client's perspective and knowledge about their preferences and expectations in order to understand what is helpful to them.

The pluralistic framework, which guides the work of therapists to apply pluralistic therapy in practice, grew from empirically evidenced factors that are shown to positively impact on client outcomes. Primary interest is given to the 'common factors' on which all useful therapy approaches rely and include therapist alliance, feedback and treatment effects, general and specific model/technique effects, and client contributions/factors (Duncan et al., 2004). In practice, the framework is conceptualised around the domains of goals [what the client wishes to achieve], tasks [or subgoals], and methods [the processes used in undertaking the tasks] (see Chapters 16–19). The therapist and client creating a shared understanding and collaborating (see Chapter 11) on these domains is central to the approach, and this in turn is an important component of a successful therapeutic alliance and outcomes for clients (Cooper and McLeod, 2007).

Central to a pluralistic practice is the development of effective collaboration, open dialogue, and feedback (within the conversation but also through process and outcome monitoring; see Chapter 20), and this focus on responding to the client allows therapists and clients to be creative with what they do in practice. The ongoing dialogue with each client, with particular attention on therapy direction and progress, is called *meta-therapeutic communication* and encompasses the ability to discuss multiple perspectives about the client's presenting problem, their inter-relational experiences, the impact of learning styles, and their strengths and resources. Alongside this, it is used to facilitate the client through a series of change processes and aid them in acquiring strategies for life (McLeod et al., 2013).

A pluralistic approach allows therapy to progress in a coherent and highly client-centred way and is said to *take the therapy out of the therapist's head in order to share it with the client.* Grounded in a set of principles and deploying meta-strategies (Finnerty et al., 2018) to tailor therapy, it allows therapists to draw on the huge evidence base for effective therapeutic interventions from across a range of schools of thought. Whilst the approach is relatively new, and research is in its infancy, early signs are promising (Antoniou et al., 2017; Cooper et al., 2015; Morgan and Cooper, 2015). The community of practitioners training in and aligning with the approach is growing, lending support to the ambition that a pluralistic stance on therapy can unify counselling and psychotherapy for the benefit of all clients.

2 What is the underlying philosophy behind pluralistic practice and why is it important?

Whether the client is aware of it or not, all approaches to therapy rely on being embedded in some form of philosophical belief. This is rarely discussed in the therapy room, but having a foundational set of beliefs concerning what life is about, what being human involves, and how a person might strive to live is surprisingly influential. Cooper and McLeod (2011) propose that pluralistic therapy emerged as a philosophical construct rather than a psychological one, and it is this position that enables therapists to understand the nature and construct of 'problems' within the context of what it means to be a person, rather than simply through schools of psychological understanding. By avoiding the restrictions imposed by strict psychological interpretations, it instils the capacity for understanding the life of the client in a variety of meaningful ways. To understand pluralistic practice, it is therefore useful to understand some of the philosophical approaches that are influential for a therapeutic encounter and, importantly, provide some degree of stability in the ways we go about understanding it.

Pluralism is defined by Rescher (1993) as *the doctrine that any substantial question admits of a variety of plausible but mutually conflicting responses* (p. 79) and was first suggested as a basis for psychological theory and practice by William James, one of the founders of modern psychology (Slife and Wendt, 2009; Woody and Viney, 2009). The recognition of a theoretical and methodological dissensus within counselling and psychotherapy underlies the notion that practice, and practitioners, can respond to different clients with different approaches at different points in time because the 'answer' to the question of how to help can result in *a variety of plausible but mutually conflicting responses* (Rescher, 1993). Within this statement is a clear challenge to how we think about therapy, suggesting that *there's no one answer to how to respond to a client*, and so the pluralistic therapy framework supports and encourages a therapist

DOI: 10.4324/9781003305736-3

to work with ambiguity, that *we can't know everything nor do we need to*, the absence of objective truth, *we will never converge on a single optimal 'truth' as a profession or across our clients*, and the inherent scope for creative flexibility because, *if all things can be true, we need to use different reference points to guide our work*. Ultimately, this allows for an effective therapy to be constructed with the client by using the client's experience as the reference point.

Because of its philosophical approach, pluralism allows us to align with the idea of using a 'working model' of the truth that reflects aspects of experience important to the individual, so the answer to the question 'how can I help this client?' can be adaptive and responsive. Rarely would this working model have to be complete because the purpose of therapy is not truth-seeking and instead seeks the resolution of distress and a response to client needs. In practice, the ways that therapy is understood and the choices made by the client for what helps can be based on this partial co-construction of 'reality'. This in turn allows the work to focus on what is helpful in rendering changes in the way that the client wishes them to happen – a therapeutic 'frame of reference'. Fundamentally, this sits in contrast with how, traditionally, therapists train in individual models that have wide-ranging and complex explanatory structures to make sense of client problems. In pluralism, each client and therapist will be drawing on things they know (see Chapter 12), have experienced, and the moment-to-moment process of therapy, to build meaning in the room. This means that both clients and therapists will have ideas of their own, which need to be captured in the encounter, and that there are an infinite number of combinations of client, problem, theory, experience, and therapist. Therefore pluralistic therapy cannot help but understand that there is not one distinct and superior truth which spans all clients, rather each therapeutic encounter will need a slightly (or very) different explanation and focus, hence the plurality!

The adoption of pluralism in counselling and psychotherapy reflects the situation within the profession in the 20th and 21st centuries, which has been beset by 'schoolism'. Historic contrasts, and in some cases conflicts, between approaches have led to patterns of allegiance to some schools of thought and derogation of others. This can be witnessed within differing psychoanalytic groups: the emergence of behaviour therapy in sharp contrast to the Freudian traditions, the evolution into cognitive-behavioural therapy and its subsequent 'third wave', and the emergence of humanistic therapies rooted in the tradition of experiential over mechanistic or subconscious human design. Patterns of research endeavour to follow the 'truths' of therapy schools over the 20th century, resulting in a competitive culture attempting to prove comparative effectiveness, but on review, what we find time and again is that all therapies are (across the board) as effective and ineffective as each other. What is perhaps insufficiently attended to is that some are more beneficial for some clients than others (Cooper, 2008). It is also worth noting that the majority of contemporary therapists draw not solely on the practices available from their own schools but respond to what the client wants in the best way they can (e.g. Owen and Hilsenroth, 2014; Stiles and Horvath, 2017). Therapy, it seems, was already conceptually pluralistic before pluralistic therapy got its name!

The emergence of pluralistic therapy in the cultural context of late 20th and early 21st century Europe means that it is heavily influenced by schools of thought such as post-modernism (Aylesworth, 2015), social constructionism (Berger and Luckman, 1966; Gergen, 1994, 1999; Lyotard, 1984), existentialism (Cooper, 2021; May et al., 1958), meta-modernism (Storm, 2021; van den Akker et al., 2017; Kraft, 2020), and feminist ideas (e.g. Brown, 1994, 2018). This means that there are many useful philosophical ideas that aid us in understanding how pluralism emerged. The most influential is a group of philosophical ideas stemming from post-modernism, in particular the concept of *social construction*, which relates to the belief that we are, as a society and as humans, so highly embedded in the systems of communication, understanding, and information that we cannot realistically expect to sit outside and garner any objective truth about what is going on. This is unlike the approach to objectivity and discovering truth used in, for example, scientific inquiry, or firm and immovable beliefs, which are often seen in religion, and pays more attention to the processes under which possible 'truths' are constructed. *Feminist therapy* approaches (Brown, 1994, 2018) recognise this post-modern notion of construction but place particular emphasis on the gendered nature of how society is understood, and work to deconstruct the embedded assumptions around power, identity, and equality. *Meta-modernism* (Storm, 2021) is an approach for understanding the ways that, in thinking about the world, we tend to pivot between a belief in objective and constant truths and the more nebulous construction of meaning. Whilst *existential philosophies* used in therapy (van Deurtsen et al., 2019) demand us to think in terms of the meaning and purpose of life, in practice, existentialism ensures that we recognise that the purpose of life must be created by the person themselves and is not 'given' at birth. Two things are important here for a pluralistic practitioner, one is that these ideas allow us to recognise the nature of humanity as fluctuating and contextual, and, whilst we and our clients may hold beliefs and ideas that originate from structured belief systems, these are heavily influenced by society and not fixed. The other is that it opens up thought around how we live a 'good life' within this flexible environment whilst recognising the impact of power relations and perceived immobility of 'the world'.

Beyond these ideas, one of the most important philosophical approaches for pluralism is humanism, partly because of its intellectual and practice origins (Cooper and McLeod both align to person-centred, humanistic beliefs), but also because pluralistic therapy uses a set of guiding principles which stem, by and large, from a humanistic view of the world. Within the therapy world, the term humanistic is used to define a particular group of therapies, but humanism is a much broader school of thought that developed as a rational alternative to deism (believing in an interventionist God or Gods). The disjoint between pluralism being humanistic and pluralistic practitioners drawing on theories and methods from 'non-humanistic' schools relates to this. Humanism is a broad collection of beliefs that emphasise the importance of empiricism, experience, and knowledge over belief, and is surprisingly contemporary as a way of looking at the world (Royce and Mos, 1981). The influence of humanism on pluralistic therapy is that it emphasises the need to think of a person holistically and not, for example, prioritise a focus on one aspect of experience (such as cognitive function). Alongside this, humanism values the ability of people to be free thinking, able to understand, to choose, and importantly, live their lives in a way which is regarding and reflective of their potential – overall a very positive way of thinking about people (Maslow, 1954).

Maintaining a philosophical, rather than a psychological, frame of reference is evident in practice through the variety of methods that can be undertaken in therapy (there are many ways to help a person along their journey), but it is also key to the justification of this undertaking – that the world, experiences, and problems of living can have limitless explanations and justifications. In a plural world, there is an acceptance that 'truth' is overall contextual and transient but may be fundamental and fixed for an individual.

In practice, a therapist and client can locate, share, develop, and deploy their own understandings and meanings in therapy alongside more formal ideas to help the client with what they are facing. In some cases, this creation of meaning is the most prevailing outcome of therapy, it's empowering, exploratory, insight-building, and relational all in one. Interestingly, and something we will explore more in this book, the explanations are also what justify the therapeutic interventions and methods used.

3 Did we really need another approach?

Talking therapy works in a range of contexts, for a range of people, and for a range of problems in living. Each approach is based on particular values, ways of conceptualising the therapy process and client-therapist relationship, and methods for undertaking it – but with hundreds of models in existence (Norcross and Neman, 2003), the question could be asked, do we need yet another way of doing it? The answer to this is both simple – we don't, because there seem to be plenty of helpful aspects to therapy and lots of effective interventions, and more complex – we do, because we need a reliable means of matching the therapy to the client, the context, and the problem. Although pluralistic therapy in some ways does represent a 'way' of going about therapy, because it has its own set of principles and values that guide how therapy is undertaken and what is drawn into consideration by practitioners, it is not another school. Rather, pluralistic therapy could be viewed as a framework that encourages and supports therapists in thinking about the decisions and actions they take to fit the therapy to the client. Some aspects of pluralistic practice are structured, whilst others ask for creativity and responsiveness in the moment; however, unlike other approaches to therapy, none of it is compulsory! What it does is invite clients and therapists to consider the range of options available and to optimise the depth of their understanding of what is possible, how it might help, and how to go about it.

Whilst there are plenty of studies to support the use of a single therapeutic modality (Cooper, 2008), there are limitations and drawbacks to sticking to only one.

• Schools of therapy are 'belief-based', and the beliefs of the therapists might not match the beliefs of the client. Even when we know what

DOI: 10.4324/9781003305736-4

works for one client (or even most clients), there's no guarantee it will work for the next one.

- If the method of undertaking practice is assumed within the school, there is no real need to ask the opinion of the client. Fixed track therapy will have fixed track ways of responding to the client, both in terms of activities and relationship characteristics, and these might not be the right ones for them.
- Schools might make implicit assumptions around what changes will happen for the client and why – and these don't necessarily match the client's experience or goals.
- Schools might impose silencing of useful knowledge stemming from both the therapist and client – so being instructed in a particular approach might mean a therapist is primed with a wealth of potentially helpful things they should not be doing!

If we add to this the principles of humanism and contemporary recognition of the potential of 'otherness' in terms of how people experience that world, how we understand problems in living, and how we respond to these, then we hit upon a problem. Although we might acknowledge that people seeking help will be informed, able to make active choices, and have the capacity to decide their own way forward, what we tend to have is a therapist who will have been trained within a particular approach (or approaches) and who is likely to hold beliefs around the ways that therapy can help, complete with the drawbacks outlined earlier. A further, somewhat troubling reality is that despite the ambition of all therapists (apart perhaps from a very few who are in the wrong job) to aid the client for the *client's* benefit, history speaks of antagonism between schools of thought and structures of care delivery, which has created barriers for clients accessing what they may need. In a multicultural society, people seeking help will be informed of the variety of options available, through experience and open knowledge systems like the internet and education, and once again, the evidence points to the best way of responding to this being that the clients' worldview and preferences are taken into account. The belief is that maintaining a single perspective on how therapy is done, and how the client will change psychologically as a result, is clearly unsustainable, and pluralism was designed to respond to this contemporary issue.

Pluralism has the effect of zooming out the lens from a single therapy and setting aside some of the associated 'schoolist' beliefs, to establish some key features of effective therapy in order to better meet the needs and expectations of the client, which subsequently aims to avoid disengagement, rupture, and poor outcomes. In order to move towards the idea that therapists are flexible and want to respond to the client in the best way possible, it is worth turning therapy on its head and starting with the things that clients tell us about their therapy experiences, beneficial change, and more specifically their reports of 'helpful events' (McLeod, 2013b; Timulak, 2007, 2010). For example, some clients report the helpfulness of the development of awareness, gaining insight and self-understanding, and being able to explore emotions and emotional experiences, whilst others report behaviour change and finding solutions to their problems, gaining empowerment and as a result relief. Furthermore, clients experienced a sense of being involved in therapy, being reassured, supported, and personal contact in the therapy relationship and beyond. Forming an overview of the kinds of things clients want in therapy, McLeod (Cooper and McLeod, 2011) developed the idea of a therapeutic task-taxonomy that analyses tasks and subtasks to classify them into a logical framework, thus enabling the therapist and client to undertake therapy methods as appropriate to complete the task (see Chapter 18).

The final, and possibly most important, driver towards reframing therapy within the pluralistic approach draws on the findings that therapists and clients reliably differ in terms of what they consider to be helpful and what they consider to be significant events in therapy (Timulak, 2010). No matter what the therapeutic school, clients appear to be deferential to the therapist, and this sits neither with the philosophy of empowerment nor the drive to make therapy effective. Rennie (1994) found that even when clients were concerned that the direction the therapy was taking was not suitable, they were reticent in letting the therapist know. They were concerned that their feedback might be perceived as critical, that they would not challenge their therapist and would strive to understand the therapist's frame of reference whilst working to meet therapist expectations (not necessarily vice versa) and accept their limitations, and that much of this was a result of feeling indebted to the therapist. These issues arose as part of a subtle dance between therapist and client (see Chapter 31 for discussions on power in the therapy room), and whilst what the client experienced is unlikely to have been intended, the list still makes disturbing reading for those wishing to create a safe space for the client where they are facilitated to work on their problems! The proposed resolution to this was meta-communication (see Chapter 28, for example), but subsequent work has indicated that this can only happen when certain relational standards are met (von Below, 2020). Pluralistic therapy is unique in directly addressing these barriers for the client, purposefully creating a collaborative space, and developing practitioners who approach their clients with a balance of humility and knowledge.

So, whilst it is vital that the client experiences therapy as something that makes sense to them and aims to address their particular needs, this is done in the context of a multitude of understandings and activities available. The pluralistic framework is a way to work with this complexity without the creation of a new way of understanding problems and client experiences; it is not 'another approach' but a means of navigating therapy to find what fits the client.

4 There are lots of ways of integrating therapy – how is pluralism different?

Therapists tend to differentiate between single-model approaches to therapy and approaches that draw on multiple models. Integration in therapy is the latter. It involves the active combining of theories and interventions in order to meet the needs of clients and achieve better outcomes. Pluralism is both a way of integrating therapeutic activities and a way of justifying working within one single model whilst accepting that other models exist and have equal merit. The difference can be explained through the language (see Chapter 9) used by the pluralistic community and is an important distinction for those learning about the approach. A pluralistic *stance* or *perspective* reflects a position where a practitioner can fundamentally value other approaches to therapy without it necessarily impacting how they undertake their work. Pluralistic *practice* or pluralistic *therapy* involves using a set of guiding principles as a reference point for how therapy is undertaken (see Chapter 5), in terms of things like shared decision making, preference accommodation, a focus on client resources, and an underlying ethic of care, and allows for the integration of methods and change pathways. The pluralistic framework, as provided by Mick Cooper and John McLeod (2011), is one way of operationalising pluralistic practice, which both enables and encourages collaborative integration and acts as a platform for creativity in how therapy is carried out.

Pluralistic practice is an integrative approach but it is also unique in the way integration happens. This is because it uses the knowledge, strengths, and expertise of the therapist and client in a shared decision-making process to guide how and what takes place in therapy. It also results in therapy potentially looking very different for different clients (even with the same therapist). It is worth comparing this idea with the ways other integrative approaches function, as, at their core, all integrative models seek to use research and practice evidence (to varying

DOI: 10.4324/9781003305736-5

degrees) to create new approaches to therapy by harnessing effective factors (Norcross and Lambert, 2019). Such approaches include the *common factors* model, which aims to focus therapy on aspects that are found to be commonly effective for all therapy approaches. These factors might be considered the 'active ingredients' of therapy, for example, the instillation of hope, establishing desired outcomes, articulating a process of psychological change, the development of a way of making sense of life difficulties, and the development of a connection with a trusted and culturally valid 'healer' (Laska et al., 2014; McLeod, 2018b). *Eclecticism* (Lazarus and Beutler, 1993; Lazarus et al., 1992) is largely focused on the methods and interventions provided to the client according to the therapist evaluations of the problem at hand, and entails the use of techniques from different approaches without too much concern for the research evidence supporting the approach, nor integrating the diverse theories that underlie them (i.e. it tends to ignore the psychological explanations of why they work), so therapy involves doing things with the client that have been shown to help others with similar presentations. Contrastingly, *theoretical integration* involves the merging of the theories and techniques of two or more psychotherapies into a new therapy approach (Prochaska and DiClemente, 1982; Stiles et al., 1990; Wachtel, 2014) with a new or amended explanation of why it works. Whilst *assimilative integration* involves keeping a single theoretical orientation and thoughtfully integrating techniques and principles from other orientations (e.g. Safran and Muran, 2006). Table 4.1 offers some practice examples to distinguish between these levels of integration in pluralistic therapy.

The pluralistic framework for counselling and psychotherapy is an evolution of these models, in that it does not serve to articulate a 'new therapy' or a new psychotherapy theory, nor does it support the idea that a therapist can determine the best interventions to use in therapy (see Chapter 3). Rather, it provides guidelines which ensure that practitioners can ethically draw on different aspects of therapy approaches and interventions to create an individualised therapy which is flexible and aligned to clients' needs and preferences so that they each get a unique integrative therapy.

Similar to the common factors model of integration, pluralistic therapy draws directly on aspects of therapy that are shown, through evidence, to make a difference to the individual client. One such aspect is the therapeutic alliance (Bordin, 1979), with agreement on goals and tasks, and the effectiveness of the therapeutic relationship, along with the availability of many effective methods to create change (Muran and Barber, 2010). It privileges the prioritising of individual needs and

Table 4.1 Examples of integration levels

Integration focus	Practice example		Therapist response	Therapeutic activities
	Presentation			
Theoretical	Client talks about their problematic relationships with a number of different people, which indicates that they have a pattern of responding with an assumption that they are being criticised.		Therapist proposes and explains the concept of cognitive filters – stemming from core beliefs, and prompts the client to consider if this is a useful explanation for their reactions.	Therapist and client work together monitoring client thoughts associated with the events, to test for 'goodness of fit' of the idea of cognitive filters and evaluate how helpful the idea is for future work.
Evidence-based	Client presents with alcohol addiction and has indicated that previous therapy has aided them by allowing them space to contemplate the changes thoroughly before planning and undertaking action.		Therapist provides a description of the cycle of change (Prochaska and DiClemente, 2005), which has been shown to be effective with addiction recovery, and suggests how this might be weaved into the work together.	Cycle of change is used as a reference point for the activities in therapy in the subsequent sessions. Decisions on how to progress and what to talk about are based on the intervention model. Feedback on how helpful this is, and whether other aspects of the experience should take precedence, is checked regularly.
Methodological	The client presents with high stress levels and indicates that they would like to undertake activities to reduce their current anxiety experience.		Therapist offers the client a session on managed breathing techniques and shares an understanding with the client on the purpose and process of the technique.	The outcome of the intervention method is evaluated, and the client is invited to suggest when the technique is offered again.

(Continued)

Table 4.1 (Continued)

Integration focus	Practice example		Therapeutic activities
	Presentation	*Therapist response*	
Relational	The client indicates that they prefer thinking about their relationship patterns, and that they tend towards wanting to be given guidance and instruction.	Therapist suggests that it might be helpful to consider 'trying out and observing' their experiences of adjusting the patterns of guidance and challenge in the therapy.	After four sessions, the therapist and client reflect on how they have interacted, the client discloses that they feel most 'safe' when they believe the therapist is in charge – this then is used to target developing client confidence in taking the lead and retaining a sense of safety.

preferences of the client and structures the deployment of the therapist's skillset accordingly. The key to this is that the decisions on how a therapy should be undertaken and what might be done are made with the client, whereas other integrative models tend to be centred around therapist judgements.

The guiding rationale for integrating activities in pluralistic practice is neither a particular fixed theoretical understanding nor particular manualised activities. Instead, shared decision-making and active client involvement in the integrative process is key. What happens in therapy is decided by the client and therapist together – with an equity of decision-making – which pools their knowledge and skills to meet the client's needs. In terms of expertise, both the client and therapist will have ideas and experiences that can be used, and each client will be provided with a therapy that allows the potential to integrate a range of activities drawn from therapeutic approaches alongside cultural resources.

5 What are the fundamental principles that guide pluralistic therapy?

As with the underlying philosophy of any therapeutic approach, there tends to be a set of principles that are treated as reference points for the way therapy is undertaken. These tend to align quite strongly with the therapist's internal philosophy of life, and many pluralistic therapists will say they have adopted the approach because it 'makes sense' to them. The guiding principles of a pluralistic approach to therapy are enacted through the pluralistic therapy framework and relate to beliefs about the nature of personhood, the ethical stance of practitioners, and the chief considerations of how therapy can be carried out. Ten principles for pluralistic practice, were outlined by Smith and de la Prida in 2021:

An ethic of care

Underlying all therapy is a deep and genuine care for others. This stance reflects a sense of equality within a personal and relational meeting of two people but is underlined in pluralism by an explicit respect for the other, and for clients, this means that the therapist is responding directly to their experience, preferences, and needs. Expanding this out from the relational and therapeutic experience, pluralism encompasses a relational ethic, which means that clients' context, beliefs, perspectives, and feelings (Gabriel and Casemore, 2009) are respected and incorporated into the therapy. As a result, pluralistic therapy is characterised by flexibility in responding through communication, collaboration, and a drive to understand and respond to the otherness of the other.

The primacy of the client

Beyond the ethic of care, which drives the scope of the therapeutic encounter, is the principle of ensuring the client is central to the

DOI: 10.4324/9781003305736-6

therapy; this ensures that aspects such as the therapeutic model, beliefs of the therapist, and assumptions about socio-cultural factors are not privileged when deciding what can and does happen in therapy. Pluralistic therapy holds the client perspective as central to the therapeutic process. This overtly incorporates the client lens, their lived experience, and ways of responding to it, their knowledge and understanding, and their socio-cultural beliefs and preferences.

This principal is particularly pertinent when considering the stage of developing a shared conceptualisation or formulation of the client situation (see Chapter 14) but also as the collaborative relationship develops and evolves. The therapist may impact on the client's perspective in several ways and must sustain reflective insight into this to ensure candour and dynamic sharing of position. The issues around power and the management of the power dynamic are discussed in Chapter 31 and develop the idea of how the primacy of the client is sustained whilst insight, empowerment, and choice are supported.

Recognition of diversity

This principle leads on from the need to recognise the primacy of the client and furthers the emphasis on the strengths to be found in the recognition and bridging of differences. This principle resonates with the belief that there are two experts in the room striving together for the betterment of the client.

Recognition of the diversity in the room, and acknowledgement of this, is managed with congruence and respectful curiosity of the client lifeworld. Beyond this, recognising the impact of the social justice and diversity agendas across society provides a capacity to understand and work with the client experience within these contexts. Finally, beyond the therapy room, there is a growing social justice agenda (Cooper, 2023) (see Chapter 35) within the profession of counselling and psychotherapy, and this is being furthered by pluralistic approaches, for example in pluralistic research (see Chapter 41) (Smith et al., 2021).

Multiplicity of approaches

It is well established that, on a population level, there is no one globally effective or superior model of therapy, but that many approaches, techniques, and methods can help if they are suitable for the client. This principle overtly emphasises not just the plurality of effective ways of undertaking therapy but also that the decision on the 'best way' sits with the individual client and not the therapist. If the primacy of the client is to be respected, then the task of the therapist is to first understand their experience and needs and then find the best way to respond to them. The ways that this is done are discussed in later chapters. Core to this is understanding that knowledge is a resource that can be shared; that empowering clients to make judgements and choices enables therapy to fit but is in itself likely to provide a skill which can take them forward in their lives, and that methods and approaches to therapy can themselves be deployed, amended and evolved to create a therapy to fit the uniqueness of the client.

Uniqueness of experience

This principle reflects the belief that all people are subject to and respond to fluctuating and developing experiences, and change occurs throughout life as a result of context and learning. It means that at any one-time, clients will be different from all other points in their lives, and thus, what they need and what might help them in therapy will also change – different people need different things at different points in time. This is a welcomed and accepted aspect of the process of therapy, allowing it to develop according to the client perspective, and directionality at the point of contact, but also in understanding past experiences and envisaging the future.

Knowledge

This aligns with the idea that all understandings may be helpful and welcome, and that pluralistic therapists should value multiple forms and sources of knowledge. In practice these can be understood as *common knowledge* – knowledge that is generally available about various ways of helping or understanding experience; *client personal knowledge* – which includes insight, ways of being, experiences, resources, and preferences; and *therapist personal knowledge* – all that a therapist has learned and developed through training, practice, and life experience (see Chapter 12). The role of the therapist is to help the client build upon their knowledge in helpful ways, not through informing and correcting, but rather through a reflective broadening of the potential ways that change can occur, such as insight, learning, and reframing. Important in this is the balance that must be sustained by both therapist and client in tolerating tensions between their own and other knowledge, and between knowing and not knowing, with judgements being made by both to authentically recognise and build what is most useful to the client.

Individualisation

The primary goal of pluralistic therapy is to develop a unique therapeutic experience for each client based on their lived experience, directionality, and goals. The process and outcome of therapy are unpredictable at the outset, and the foundation of the work together is a shared and evolving understanding and navigation based on the client feedback and responses to the process. Individuation relies on the therapist's ability to respond and adapt to 'getting it wrong' and allowing and supporting a space to try things out with the client and reflect on the experience. Importantly, individualisation avoids the impact of applying or encouraging (even when well-meaning) therapeutic activities that are not helpful to the client.

Relationship

There is no doubt that clients find the nature of the therapeutic relationship one of the most important factors in 'good' therapy (Norcross and Lambert, 2019). The characteristics of the relationship can include not only a fundamental sense of safety, trust, and hope instilled by the therapist, but also interactive factors such as balance of influence and decision-making, empathic responses and mutuality of experience. The collaboration required in pluralistic therapy must itself be flexible, as well as the pace, focus, and adaptability of the interaction. As discussed in Chapter 11, the dynamic of the collaborative relationship may shift as a result of the purposeful engagement of the client through their developing understanding of their situation and the nature of the therapy itself.

Therapist reflexivity

To enact a non-manualised, flexible, responsive therapy, pluralistic therapists need a high degree of self-knowledge about their own beliefs, assumptions, and preferences about therapeutic change. This is needed to make the best use of their knowledge, but also to avoid misreading or neglecting their clients' perspectives (Cooper and Dryden, 2016). Alongside this commitment is the need, in pluralistic therapy, to seek client empowerment, build shared understanding, and sustain the ability of the client to choose. This self-awareness (see Chapter 10) and capacity to both be in the relationship as therapy unfolds and maintain a perspective over the process is an ethical commitment requiring ongoing work in supervision (see Chapter 38), combining humility and self-compassion.

Flexibility

This final principle is one that is essential to allow the client's needs to be met. Therapy should have some level of flexibility in terms of how it is carried out on a variety of dimensions as well as clearly communicating what is on offer to the client – choices can refer to the structure, process, communication style or platform, and characteristics of the relationship. Flexibility is further seen in the ability of the therapy to adapt to the unpredictability and fluctuations of the ongoing process, so whilst preferences and choices may be made, the way these can change is also responded to flexibly. This provision of an open space for exploration and creativity, as well as direction and stability, requires trust in the co-creative process, which in turn places a demand on the therapist to be both 'in their head' understanding the therapy, alongside being 'in the room' with the client process. Hopefully, this means that therapists become more responsive in their practice.

6   Is pluralistic therapy
an evidence-based
practice then?

Pluralistic therapy is focused on the individualisation of practice for each client, the primary lens therefore starts with the client themselves, whilst drawing on the skills and experience of the therapist, their shared knowledge of research, and other information available. The balance between the knowledge streams available depends very much on how we interpret evidence in practice.

A common misconception exists that 'evidence-based practice' is an approach that provides interventions and activities that have been shown through empirical research to be the most effective for particular diagnoses, experiences, and groups of clients, that is, the 'evidence' results in the 'practice'. This is perhaps the result of practice guidelines being more focused on published research than other factors such as delivery context, intervention palatability, therapist competence, and client choice. In many areas of healthcare, a more complex model of *evidence-based practice* is used, drawing on these areas to deliver interventions most effectively. The knowledge streams that are considered in this broader model are *empirical research evidence*, *practitioner knowledge* (see Chapter 12), and *patient or client preferences* (see Chapter 22). This model for evidence-based practice favours different lenses depending on the context – for example, a funding body who is trying to best deploy services that are effective for a particular group of people would rely more heavily on research knowledge when providing recommendations for what therapies are carried out for based on an 'average' client in this group, this is seen in things like the NICE guidelines in the UK NHS (NICE, 2022). In practice, a therapist might refer to their knowledge, experience, and training with a range of service users and have a sense of what might be helpful for the clients they see, drawing on different aspects of these to best fit the client. For example, someone trained in Dialectical Behaviour Therapy might deploy this approach when

DOI: 10.4324/9781003305736-7

a client presents with a diagnosis of borderline personality disorder (Shearin and Linehan, 1994), but will adapt and amend their approach according to the client presentation. Influencing this is the fact that the individual client may have particular strengths, preferences, and ideas about what they want to focus on and how they wish to progress. Whilst in some cases this drift in delivery from the 'research-supported' manualised treated is seen as a failure on the part of the therapist (Waller and Turner, 2016), it is precisely this position of valuing client preference and ideas which takes primacy over the others in pluralistic practice. Of importance, however, is the recognition that even when options on therapy can vary, and client preferences may differ, the therapist is also likely to have a stance on the options available and how helpful they are likely to be. There is no denying the influence of the therapist in providing an interpretation of the cause of problems, by rendering 'evidence-based' explanations, and 'knowing' about therapeutic activities, but in practice these can be made explicit and discussed with the client. A further consideration is that of practice-based evidence, which is to some extent the corollary of evidence-based practice, and aligns with the idea that if we draw evidence from what we do in practice, this can impact our actions and influence the system of knowledge that is applied. When we gather data from our clients on their experiences and well-being, we obtain evidence for what is working for them and what is not (see Chapters 20 and 48).

Despite the complex nature of undertaking an 'evidence-based practice' and the challenges of drawing flexibly on research in practice, the justification for this client-focused approach is (somewhat ironically) embedded in many years of empirical work. This includes research focusing on client experiences and evaluations of these experiences, which overall indicate the importance of collaboration, that different clients benefit from different things at different times, and that no one therapeutic approach is better than another for everyone (Cooper, 2008; Laska et al., 2014; Levitt et al., 2016; Norcross, 2005). This includes the nature and effectiveness of the Working Alliance (Bordin, 1979), the impact of client empowerment on the therapy process, and the concept of the heroic client (Duncan et al., 2004), alongside the evidence that points to the effectiveness of flexibly matching therapy to client intervention preferences and relationship styles (e.g. Perren et al., 2009). So, the framework within which pluralistic work is carried out is heavily influenced by research even if the practice itself is not necessarily directed by empirically evidenced interventions.

Dryden (2012) and McAteer (2010) have both highlighted the conflict between using scientific evidence to guide practice whilst respecting the phenomenological experience of clients. Dryden (2012) asked how a pluralistic therapist might decide between disparate knowledge streams and find a balance between the preferences and needs of the client with the research evidence and knowledge of the therapist. The response to this challenge, in pluralistic therapy, is complex and relates to meta-modernist thinking; theoretically, it holds a position on the objectivity and usefulness of research evidence but challenges the tendency to assume translation between research evidence and individual clients (this is discussed further in Chapter 41). Pluralists recognise that research must be understood in terms of its usefulness to practice rather than being of over-riding importance. The problem of translation is therefore addressed in pluralistic practice through research being most usefully deployed as an information stream feeding into the decisions made by the client and therapist – a source of 'ideas' rather than providing guiding principles for the work. Pluralism does not create the route-map using research and expect the client to undertake the journey along the pre-decided route, but rather allows the therapist and client to use the navigation system flexibly to get where the client wishes to go, metaphorically choosing their own roads and vehicles and whether or not they wish to travel economically or avoid tolls!

Whilst the pluralistic therapy framework is based on research evidence, since its inception it has evolved in terms of how it is understood and how it is undertaken. It is, by definition, pluralistic and therefore conceptualised as a dynamic system that influences and is influenced by practice and research. Whilst empirical work has been carried out in the context of this early evolution, compared with other approaches, such as CBT, pluralistic therapy is relatively under-researched. The key areas of understanding that have grown in relation to pluralism have included ideas around client goals in therapy (Cooper and Law, 2018), with evidence pointing to the use of goal setting (see Chapter 16) and goal-monitoring as enhancing but complex in practice (Di Malta et al., 2019) (see Chapter 48). Idiographic outcome measures pertaining to goals, where the client can define the outcomes and report their movement towards them, are often considered more suited to the personalisation (Sales et al., 2022) and flexibility of pluralism. For example, the goals form developed by Cooper and Xu (2022) was found to be helpful for clients and reliably sensitive to change. Pluralistic therapists are encouraged to work specifically with goals to map their work alongside the client, and these forms aid personalisation and move away from the generic population-based measures of well-being often used in mental health practice and may relate more to the meaning-making process in therapy (Adler et al., 2013).

Another body of work is growing around how to best accommodate preferences in practice (Swift et al., 2018). In their work, focusing on the ways that therapists might flex according to client preferences, Cooper and Norcross (2016) have developed the Cooper-Norcross Inventory of Preferences (C-NIP), which provides a platform for feedback and a dialogic tool for collaboration with clients. The C-NIP, whilst not exclusive to pluralistic therapy, is designed to meet the meta-communicative priority of empowering clients to express their needs in the domains of: directiveness on the part of the therapist and client; emotional intensity and reserve; past- and future-orientation; accepting warmth and focused challenge.

Other research directly examining the process and outcome of pluralistic therapy has included the results of a pilot for pluralistic therapy for depression (Cooper et al., 2015; Antoniou et al., 2017), indicating the effectiveness of the pluralistic approach and emphasising the importance of a safe therapeutic environment, appropriate challenging, and client empowerment. Pluralistic therapy was also perceived as helpful when beliefs about the potential for change were supported by the therapist through reassurance and non-intrusive guidance (Antoniou et al., 2017). More recently, the outcomes of pluralistic therapy in a community practice for adults with a range of difficulties have shown it to be equivalent in effectiveness to other interventions (Murphie and Smith, submitted). The use of the pluralistic therapy lens has led to work on understanding the therapeutic process in long-term health conditions (McLeod, 2013c; Thurston et al., 2013), whilst other work has driven an emphasis on cultural resources as therapeutic methods (Stevens and McLeod, 2019).

Additionally, research has provided an initial indication of the utility of pluralistic therapy in different contexts, for example, Al-Roubaiy's (2017) work on the potential role of pluralism in responding to the needs of Iraqi immigrants/refugees suggests that the capacity to apply the model and emphasise compassion as an action-based stance (over Rogerian core conditions) and the addition of a consideration of the social justice lens on practice would be beneficial. Whilst McLeod and colleagues (2021) evidenced the utility of training in pluralistic practice to enhance ability of practitioners to work in different contexts.

In their 2011 book, Cooper and McLeod proposed a range of important research areas that would support the development of pluralistic therapy, and there has not been substantial progress in this area. The limited body of evidence for the effectiveness of taking a pluralistic stance on practice in terms of outcomes, can impact perceptions of therapist identity and confidence in the approach (Lowndes and Hanley, 2010; Thompson and Cooper, 2012) and within the profession, as some key questions remain unanswered. McAteer (2010) refers to these as 'pluralistic dilemmas', and outstanding but significant questions remain to be explored. For example, how can a therapist know which strategy or actions to offer to the client, how do they develop a sense of the explicit and implicit client needs, and how flexible do they need to be? It is anticipated that these questions will be answered as the practice moves forward.

So, the answer to this question is complicated because, whilst, in empirical terms, pluralistic therapy is not something that has been tested in a rigorous sense (partly because the practice is so wide-ranging that it has been hard to articulate specific measurable features and partly because it is so new that practice is still being understood), it is evidence-based in its development and is fundamentally an evidence-based practice.

7 I'm confused between a pluralistic perspective and pluralistic practice, can you help?

The answer to this question relies on an ability to understand that there are numerous and conflicting beliefs and perspectives about how problems in living arise, and how therapy might be understood and undertaken, whilst what one does about them in practice might appear to rely on one single perspective. Knowing and accepting this is a pluralistic perspective, whilst a pluralistic practice is about the therapist undertaking therapy in a way that works with the plurality of truths available.

Counselling and psychotherapy have proceeded through four to five waves/forces; Psychoanalysis, from which psychodynamic therapy has its origins, behavioural, humanistic, cognitive-behavioural, and integrative/pluralistic, with many training programmes originally grounding students in a single tradition. Today, therapists typically train with two or more key explicit, or formal, theories, but Jones-Smith (2012) highlights that during this time and throughout their careers, they also form implicit theories based on their personal assumptions about how therapy 'should' best be conducted. In practice, research indicates that many practitioners who broaden their offering beyond their core school of training subsequently consider themselves to be practicing as integrative therapists (Mahoney, 1991 cited in Newman et al., 2004) being dissatisfied 'with single-school approaches and . . . desire to look across school boundaries to see what can be learned from other ways of conducting psychotherapy' (Norcross, 2005, p. 4). More recently, as lecturers in the field, we have seen a growth in therapists who identify as pluralistic, and we are often asked about the difference between a pluralistic perspective and pluralistic practice. To explain the difference, it might first be helpful to contemplate a pluralistic perspective outside of the counselling tradition.

In society, and in the interplay between members of society, it is easy to find examples of dissensus and opposing views based on beliefs,

DOI: 10.4324/9781003305736-8

ethics, politics, culture, and science, even within an individual's own perspective (Yumatle, 2015). Typically, in the Western world, we try to amalgamate or battle these diverse and seemingly contrasting objectives into one single 'truth', operating out of a 'win-lose-compromise' model (Douglas and Bushardt, 1988), which is characterised by debate and hierarchal-instruction forms of communication (McLeod, 2018a), a 'what you must do' or 'what you must believe' perspective. There can be a sense of pseudo-safety in having clear external reference points and 'the' map, soothing the conflict and turmoil that lies within us as individuals and societies. Pluralism, however, contends that there is no one universally valid reality (Rescher, 1993), different people require, experience, and believe different things at different points in time, and therefore there is potential value in other 'truths'. In recognising the other, pluralism steps away from the language of either/or and moves towards a both/and position (Cooper and McLeod, 2012) characterised by dialogue; each party is interested in the other's perspective, you can hold your truth *and* I can hold mine and *both* might have value. Taking a pluralistic perspective requires openness and flexibility, a tolerance of thoughts and beliefs that might clash with our own, and a willingness to try to understand the other. We apply this perspective within the counselling tradition (although we could extend this thinking to health-care and social care), when people seek help for what we would term as 'problems in living'. These problems in living form through unique internal and external stressors throughout an individual's life, comprising aspects of biology, psychology, and social contexts, and as such are complex. Helping clients to navigate their distress requires an ability to understand their unique circumstances and consider how *I*, as a practitioner, and *they*, as a client, might be able to help alleviate the distress. Purist/monist therapeutic traditions understand distress through the set 'rules' or 'principles' of their dominant theory, whereas a pluralistic therapist would concern themselves with understanding the client through multiple ways of knowing (see Chapter 12) acknowledging that there are always things that they do not know. To hold a pluralistic perspective is to consider that there are potentially many different things that might be helpful to this client at this point in time.

When speaking with students and clients about their own therapy journeys, and indeed reflecting on our own, few of us would answer that the therapy we needed or wanted in the past is still exactly the therapy we need or want today. Our preferences change, as does our understanding of ourselves and the unique stressors that created our problems in living, and how we make sense of the world around us. Almost certainly my understandings are also different, or diverge in some ways, to my family, friends, or you. The therapist's ability to reflect on their own journey can be a useful starting point in helping them to understand the importance of holding a pluralistic *perspective*.

Having a *pluralistic practice*, however, means having the ability to use one's own multiplicity of resources in addition to investigating and utilising the client's extensive knowledge, strengths, and resources. A pluralistic therapist will be able to consider the client's problems in living from plural viewpoints, incorporating theory, ethics, and science as well as personal, practical, and cultural knowledge, in addition to eliciting the client's perspective and knowledge about their understanding of the problems they face, including their preferences and expectations, in order to understand what is helpful to them at this moment in time. Questions that might guide a pluralistic therapist to apply these ideas in practice might be:

• What does my client think are the main factors in their distress? What do I think they are?
• How do I and my client understand their problems in living through therapeutic traditions [such as psychodynamic, humanistic, cognitive-behavioural, and systemic]?

    • Of these, would anything be helpful in alleviating distress now?

• How do I and my client understand their problems in living through non-therapeutic traditions [such as sociology, culture, and biology]?

    • Of these would anything be helpful in alleviating distress now?

• What ethical codes do I adhere to that are important when working together?
• Do the client or I have any research that helps us understand either the cause or what might help this problem at this time?
• Have either of us had personal or practical knowledge of this problem that might help us now [exploring strengths and resources]?

Some of these questions can be explored by the therapist alone, thus supporting a pluralistic perspective however, a pluralistic practice is the meeting point of 'both/and' between client and therapist; I as a therapist have my unique set of beliefs, understanding and skills born through life and education *and* you as a client have a unique set of beliefs, understanding and skills born through your lived experience and education. Undoubtedly the perspectives will diverge and converge but how we negotiate these and utilise this difference in practice to alleviate client distress is a highly dynamic, active, and collaborative event characterised by a high degree of reflection and communication by both parties. Therapists who practice pluralistically have skills in meta-therapeutic communication, case conceptualisation (see Chapter 14), and monitoring outcomes (see Chapter 20) as well as eliciting client goals, preferences, strengths, and resources, all of which will be discussed in more detail through this book.

Practicing pluralistically can be challenging, there can be a discomfort in navigating without 'the' map and instead making a conscious decision to plan a route forward with another to their destination, incorporating their own knowledge of the terrain and preferred mode of transport. Some therapists may find themselves blocked in the action of a pluralistic practice due to a lack of training, knowledge, or skills, the discomfort of working with multiple truths and the dissensus that ensues, or because of the client's desire to have a directive therapist or manualised therapy. In these instances, it is quite possible to hold a pluralistic perspective but practice through a monist or 'pure-form' theory or integrative process.

8 How can someone trained in a single approach adopt a pluralistic stance?

Whilst many universities and colleges in the United Kingdom, Ireland, and globally, offer integrative counselling and psychotherapy training in at least two key and competing modalities, there are still many single approach courses available. Even those trained in an integrative manner may benefit from this chapter to aid them in adopting a more pluralistic stance, should they so wish. As those who have come through integrative or pluralistic training will attest, it can be challenging to hold and assimilate two or more conflicting therapy models with equal regard, especially as we are often drawn to certain theories that make the best sense of our own lives (Ward et al., 2011).

The first step to adopting a pluralistic stance is an openness to, and welcoming of, 'otherness' – other truths, perspectives, and theories without reducing this 'other' down to a familiar theme or object (Cooper, 2009). We believe this to be the cornerstone of adopting a pluralistic stance, regardless of whether you are working in a single, integrative, or pluralistic approach. Whilst theoretically it is relatively easy to come to terms with the idea that other truths exist, and that one's own truth may be subject to change, or be considered as a 'working model', it is somewhat harder to apply this in practice. As a result, following this recognition, there is a need for self-reflection on the nature of a therapist's own beliefs about therapy and the ability to take a light touch and critical perspective about one's own practice [e.g. Why am I drawn to that theory/intervention over another? What skills and knowledge might I be missing? What is the relationship between me and my client?] as well as a philosophical position [e.g. How do we know what we know? What does it mean to be human? What is the interplay between society and values?]. It is when we become dogmatically entrenched in our beliefs, and rigidly hold on to them, that we can struggle to be open to otherness. Whilst few groups are ever truly closed, as new people (complete with

DOI: 10.4324/9781003305736-9

values and perspectives) enter a group new sub-groups emerge, pluralism actively strives to remain an open system – this poses a challenge to retain some structure *and* stay open. Thus, to move from an 'us and them' position, where diversity and difference is often seen as anything 'outside' the group, towards an appreciation of otherness, it can be useful to consider diversity 'inside' – such as within a group (Person Centred Therapy, for example, Cooper, 2020, or within oneself).

A practitioner wishing to adopt pluralism can recognise that even within a monist theory it is possible to examine multiple ways of knowing (see Chapter 12), considering a theory through the six domains of knowledge (McLeod, 2018a), and we have posed some initial guiding questions to provide examples of how somebody might critique their knowledge of any particular theory:

- Ethical – In which ways does this theory lend itself to ethical practice? Are there any ethical risks to this theory?
- Scientific – What evidence is there to support this theoretical orientation, and with what presenting issues/cultures, etc.?
- Theoretical – How do the theoretical concepts understand this presenting issue/person, and are there any areas that cannot be explained or understood?
- Cultural – Is this theory culture-specific? Which culture did this theory develop in? Are there any cultural groups that may not work well with this theory?
- Personal – Why am I personally drawn to this theory, and are there any aspects of this theory that do not sit well with me?
- Practical – What is my practical experience working with this theory? What works well for people, and what has not worked so well?

Starting with a critical appraisal of knowledge adopts a strengths-based perspective to the purist theory, or personal style, whilst also enabling the practitioner to identify gaps in their knowledge. Adopting a pluralistic perspective requires the therapist to be able to build an understanding of both their own personal philosophies and ways of intervening, as well as those available outside of their practice. Furthermore, the framework of knowledge allows the therapist to begin to consider and assimilate competing approaches or styles into their knowledge. For example, a CBT therapist may have experienced an aunt 'just' being present and listening without directing, which was experienced as helpful to them (*personal*); they may have come across research advocating the use of attachment-based therapy for working with adolescents (*scientific*), or they might have noticed that their clients seemed more empowered when they were given options as to how they could work (*practical*).

In considering our own personal and practical experience, it can also be beneficial to identify the strengths and cultural resources we draw from in life to assist in the broadening of a pluralistic frame of reference (McLeod, 2018a; McLeod and McLeod, 2014). Through our reflective inquiries, we develop knowledge that can shape our understanding of the communities our clients live in, including their available resources (or lack thereof) (McLeod, 2018a) and will allow for an appreciation of, and belief in, the importance of these for our clients, potentially expanding our work with the client to include their cultural resources and strengths. Additionally, practitioners rely on a variety of methods (and resources) in order to self-care for both clients and themselves as practitioners (Norcross and James, 2013). A further useful tool for examining a multitude of theories and one's own therapy style is Cheston's Ways Paradigm (2000) which is organised around three principles: Way of Being [who am I and how am I present, in the room?], Way of Understanding [what is my knowledge of personality theories, human development, and change processes?], and Way of Intervening [which techniques and interventions can aid a client in achieving their goal?] (Appendix I). It supports the therapist in compiling a tool kit, where competing models and interventions can co-exist, thus enabling the therapist to draw from an array of theories when conceptualising a case and a plethora of interventions when working with clients or their problems in living.

This critical openness to knowledge and otherness can also aid in recognising the diversity of discourses that exist around the concept of mental health and healing (Cooper and Dryden, 2016). This is important because, whilst a therapist may hold one core perspective on how a problem in living may manifest (and therefore be treated), clients may present with alternative perspectives. For example, depression can be thought to come from chemical disruptions in the brain, an underlying medical condition, adverse childhood experiences, the parent's responsiveness to the child, errors of thinking and behavioural changes, and more. Having a familiarity of these various understandings of problems in living can better aid us in supporting our clients, identifying gaps in our own knowledge, and the times we may need to refer clients on.

This chapter has discussed two key themes, a recognition of current knowledge and strengths as well as the identification of gaps in knowledge, of which the latter can be identified through deliberate practice (see Chapter 37) and serve as the catalyst to upskill or engage in development outside of one initial modality. Although continued professional development (CPD) is a requirement of accrediting bodies, it is a critically important aspect of a pluralistic approach. More than just a 'tick-box' exercise to fulfil an external requirement, it is a commitment to lifelong learning – striving towards building the skills and knowledge necessary to be responsive to a diverse range of needs that our clients present. There is a wide range of CPD and further education available that can support therapists in building a repertoire of counselling skills, including that of communication and dialogue, an expansion of theoretical knowledge, and presenting issues, and cultural topics such as trauma, diversity, and mindfulness. Of course, it may also be helpful to have some formal training in pluralism to aid the development of a pluralistic perspective, and there is also a growing resource of pluralistic courses in addition to informal methods of learning such as discussion groups, blogs, and reading material with which to engage (see Chapter 43).

9 Can you explain the language of pluralism?

The language of pluralism provides a framework for collaborative working which has the potential to incorporate a range of different therapeutic approaches and practices, thus serving as a bridge between modalities, capturing contrasts and commonalities. However, this language, and indeed the language of other theories, can be a sticking point for many practitioners, and it can take time to first learn and assimilate the terminology before identifying how this exists within a therapist's own vocabulary and that of their clients. What we are increasingly finding is that therapists substitute theoretical words for 'layman' terms in order to share information, and we actively encourage tailoring language to fit the therapy room. A prime example of this is in the research by Murphie and Smith (in preparation), which spoke with therapists about the terminology of 'goals, tasks, and methods', and found that, whilst most therapists could conceptualise their work in these terms, very few used them in practice. This appeared to relate to the way that pluralism was prized as a therapeutic approach within which practitioners felt they could 'make it their own'. So, whilst we might imagine many clients understand the language of goals, therapists, who believe it does not fit with their style, find other ways of talking about it with their clients (which is expanded on in Chapter 17). A further example is of the use of the word 'treatment', which is a widely used term within academic, research, and theory language to denote interventions, therapy, or methods employed, but can portray a more medicalised model which pluralistic practice strives to move away from.

The first step in understanding the use of language in pluralism is remembering that words mean what they mean to the people who use them so, in practice, as long as both the therapist and client know what they are talking about, they don't need to know that it matches a theoretical understanding or definition. In essence, words are metaphoric,

DOI: 10.4324/9781003305736-10

and we might not trouble ourselves with getting the meaning matched to some abstract idea, as long as the therapist, client, and possibly also the supervisor, knows what they are talking about. But this idea of flexibility causes problems when we try and understand and describe the therapy process to others in the field, and this necessitates the use of a terminology which describes parts of therapy, so that we can define the ideas and operational aspects of the therapy to other like-minded therapists. So, whilst pluralism is aimed at unifying understanding in therapy and simplifying the ways things are described, there are terms which need defining because they provide structure and, in some cases, can be misunderstood or misinterpreted.

Being a research informed approach, drawing from the appreciation of many truths both within psychology and other disciplines including health, philosophy, social and education, means that the language you encounter might sound familiar. For example, McLeod's concept of a 'task taxonomy' is a term used to categorise (taxonomy) common activities (tasks) which occur in therapy and represents a cross-modality description of therapeutic work. This task taxonomy (see Chapter 18), whilst not all-encompassing, serves to communicate to both therapists and clients what therapy is about, and also what it has to offer. However, the term was used in therapy relationship literature in the 1990s, and as early as 1967 Miller discussed task taxonomy which has been developed within the fields of manufacturing, science, technology, engineering, maths (STEM), human behaviour, and performance. Akin to this is the 'borrowing' and adapting of terms already in existence, for example, meta-therapeutic communication which Papayianni and Cooper (2018) credit Rennie (1994) who examined '*moments where participants in the therapeutic dyad discuss what actually has been said or done*' (Papayianni and Cooper, 2018, p. 1). Whilst the addition of 'therapeutic' emphasises this interplay, the term meta-communication originates from Reusch and Bateson (1951, p. 209), who were both interested in communication and psychiatry (Balbuena Rivera, 2018; The International Bateson Institute, 2018), to describe the process of communicating about communication in order to develop mutual awareness. Understanding the definitions and origins of terms, and how concepts and language developed, can provide the reader and therapist with a greater depth of knowledge, and therefore ability, to be able to both utilise the terminology, and adapt it to fit the work with their client, and we would encourage practitioners to make their own enquiries into terms they struggle with.

An experienced practitioner might also recognise that the practical concepts of 'competing' schools might closely align with each other and yet the language of one school of therapy might use one term, whilst a second uses another! Think, for example, about the idea of 'self-schema' (CBT drawing from psychodynamic therapies), which might be compared to 'self-concept' (Person-centred), which is very similar to 'identity' (used more broadly in society). Underlying these terms are school-based conceptualisations of meaning, but if in pluralistic therapy we are to construct a shared understanding, rather than impose one on the client, the concepts become flexible within the therapeutic dialogue. Yet some terms do have differences which need to be explored, because they give guidance as to how therapy is approached, rather than what is done with a single client, for example, the difference between holding a pluralistic stance versus a pluralistic perspective, which has been discussed in Chapter 7. There are also terms that we use which can be confusing, for example, some practitioners, and many trainees, are new to the concept of having a 'philosophy' of counselling. Unless it feels compelling, this doesn't mean you should apply the thinking of Satre, Descartes, or even Aristotle to your practice – it means that therapists should possess a secure base on the foundational meaning and purpose of therapy and the ability to question this knowledge and reality both for themselves and their clients.

In essence, whilst some may be very comfortable with language, especially theoretical and scientific language, others may find it takes a little longer to process. This is normal and unique for all of us. Yet, it is important to have a good comprehension of the material you engage with in, order to be clear when communicating with others, both when talking with clients, and, perhaps less important but more likely to be in contention, is the discussion of your practice approach with others. However, there are some useful strategies to improve your comprehension if you are somebody who struggles with reading, particularly academic texts. The guidelines offered by Pourhosein Gilakjani and Sabouri (2016) indicate that initially activating and using background knowledge available and generating questions prior to, and during, reading is an important part of comprehension. Making inferences, drawing conclusions and summaries, creating visualisations and predictions about what the text is about, can also aid the creation of meaning. Lastly, it is important to monitor comprehension, checking if you understand the text, and, if not, repairing this through activities such as re-reading, looking a word up in the dictionary, reading ahead, or asking for help. The same could be said of client work, in which we need to continually work at, and check, our understanding with the client.

In our bid to aid you understanding the work of pluralism, this book aims to offer explanations of the key theoretical language you will encounter as you journey through (or dip in and out of) this book, and so we have incorporated explanations, metaphors, and examples as to how language might translate in the therapy room. You will also find that we use a mix of terms to describe the helping role including 'therapist', 'counsellor', 'pluralistic therapist', and 'practitioner'. We did this consciously in recognition that people identify with different terms, and, in some cases, the material may be of benefit to professions outside of counselling and psychotherapy such as teaching, healthcare, and social work. A final point to note about the language of pluralism, and indeed this book, is that it is tentative, particularly in comparison to other texts within this series. This is partly a stylistic variation of the authors but is also embedded within the notion that there is no single truth, and that knowledge is fluid. Therefore, whilst some theories are more inclined to cement strategies and understanding into concrete statements, pluralism at its very heart allows, and is open to, the other that might exist. That being said, to the best of our knowledge, this is our understanding, drawn from the common understanding, of pluralism at this time!

10 What is the role of the therapist as a person in pluralism?

The importance of the relationship in therapy should not be underestimated, and, despite a perception that pluralistic therapy is the operationalisation of techniques and methods, none of this can happen without the collaborative relationship (see Chapter 11). This relationship is the foundation of the therapeutic alliance (Bordin, 1979), and none of the other aspects of pluralistic practice function without it. We know that what clients want from therapists is congruent responsiveness, recognition, insight, and safety (Norcross and Lambert, 2019), but that this alone may not be enough to render change. Whilst clients want to meet us as people, and we strive to hold the client in a person-to-person relationship, the role of the therapist in pluralism is subject to dualism, as we also coordinate and facilitate the process of therapy. As a result, we are fundamentally ourselves within the process of change whilst holding oversight of it, and each combination of therapist and client in collaboration is unique. Because of this, we need to consider who we are as people, the impact we have on the therapeutic environment, and recognise when this can be enhanced and when it causes problems.

When viewing the role of the therapist in the relationship from different schools of thought, there are a range of approaches. In some therapies, the role of the therapist is to be the container for the client's story and theirs alone, leaving the therapist's life at the door. Other therapies involve the therapist applying experience, knowledge, and judgements to facilitate the use of techniques with the client to help them re-think, re-act, or re-feel in order to render change. Sitting as a meta-theory, pluralistic therapy utilises and acknowledges both the benefit of techniques and the cathartic, growth-inducing, nature of a client telling their story, and it also transcends these by engaging the client in a human-to-human relationship. To some extent, the use of self within a collaborative relationship allows pluralistic therapists to offer a

DOI: 10.4324/9781003305736-11

relationship to the client based on this human-to-human interaction, offering psychological safety, intimacy, and depth, which forms the basis for therapeutic activities and change. Furthermore, the use of self allows for the negotiation and sharing of power and responsibility for the therapy process and aids in its navigation (see Chapter 31). This use of self allows the sharing of ideas, perceptions, and interpretations, and, most importantly, a positive stance on the client process, thereby co-creating and offering the client a relational crucible, from which the client can understand their own role in relationships.

The ability to incorporate all these things goes beyond operational competence (for example, being able to offer choice or express empathic understanding), it also requires a therapist to exist within the therapeutic frame as a robust, yet flawed, individual. When we, as therapists, connect with others in a genuine and human way we cannot pick and choose the aspects of our humanity that we include or leave at the door. '*If I remove my values, beliefs, experiences, and responses, am I still human (Aponte and Kissil, 2012)?*' In fact, it is precisely these human aspects, and the indelible marks or the 'wounds' we carry, that lead people into helping professions, often having endured, or witnessed, adversity in their families, community, and society. These aspects of ourselves can both enhance our practice, having a deep knowing about the impact of difficulties faced, including the change and growth that can emerge from them, and allow us to recognise and relate to client difficulty whilst endowing therapy with hope, knowing as we do that '*Even the darkest night will end, and the sun will rise*' (Victor Hugo).

In order to have this ability we need to have recognised our flaws and be willing, able and skilled to use them in order to understand and relate to our clients. It is perhaps understandable that some, like Freud (1959), argue that we should resolve our difficulties or 'wounds' prior to working with others. Imagine a nurse mending your broken arm with their own arm broken! Whilst the notion of being healed before helping is one to aspire to, humanistic therapists advocate for a wounded healer model; pragmatically speaking, our clients get who we are today, flaws and all, and not who we aspire to be when our issues may no longer be 'issues' for us (Aponte and Kissil, 2012, p. 4). A colleague who has taught for many years has a clever way of explaining this to trainees, stating that in order to work as a therapist we will need to '*dust the cobwebs in the cellar*' and locate and deal with the '*unexploded bombs*' (Thurston, personal communication). Ultimately, a pluralistic therapist must take a therapeutic approach to themselves and have insight and self-knowledge, not just for their own benefit but because of the impact of this on their ability to 'be real' for the client.

Ways our difficult experiences can help or hinder the client's process

Navigating our wounds whilst in the service of helping others takes care and awareness, and aligns to the principle of therapist reflexivity (see Chapters 5, 10 and 37). If we are currently wounded or in psychological distress, we may miss the client's bid for help as we focus on ourselves or, at worst, we may seek help from our clients through, for example, subtle bids reassurance, which leads to the erosion of boundaries. Yet ignoring our own wounds can result in us becoming detached from our client's experience and unresponsive to seeking help for our own wounds if they require attention. It is therefore important that, when helping a client, pluralistic therapists are alert and open to their own reactions and personal knowledge, as a way of understanding the client's world in order to co-construct a shared understanding. It takes courage to enter this vulnerable space and allow access to, sometimes painful, experiences and information in the service of the client. However, blind 'openness' is unhelpful without the tether of logic and discernment.

Ways of monitoring and subjectivity

Pluralistic therapists, often as a result of their own experiences, tend to balance openness with scepticism; simultaneously open to new information, learning from the client whilst using their own wounds as a point of reference, as well as sceptically questioning and querying this information in a pragmatic manner (McLeod, 2018a). A simplistic example might be, that during a depressive episode the client might speak of a desire to withdraw from human interactions in order to 'self-care'. Many of us have had similar feelings during periods of overwhelm, but through past experiences (clients and ours), research, and theory, we might query if disconnection strategies, whilst comforting short-term, may cause long term pain. This allows us to empathise in a genuine human way whilst also avoiding collusion with unhelpful strategies. In doing so, therapists can become more aware of the areas that might be of benefit in helping the client and where they might be blocking the client's journey. A more nuanced example can be found in 'Eleanor' Chapter 28.

As a pluralistic therapist, understanding helpful and unhelpful aspects of therapy requires two key skills, communication and reflexivity, which exist in tandem. Reflexivity is the ability to 'turn back' on oneself to examine values, beliefs, and cultural understandings, along with an acute awareness of reactions including thoughts, feelings, behaviour, and embodied responses. This is vital, because, when hearing information and trying to make sense of it – inextricably entwined processes – a pluralistic therapist will rely on many forms of knowledge (see Chapter 12), including personal knowledge, all of which will impact on their meaning-making process. Yet, filtering information through an internal frame of reference produces a *subjective* reality, one version of the truth, whilst a pluralistic therapist will strive to create a shared reality with the client. The degree to which they are influential as a result of their filtering requires careful monitoring, reflexively questioning this reality, looking for evidence to support and contend it, which aids us in generating a deeper understanding of the topic, both cognitively and emotionally. For example, a client discussing being verbally abused by their wife and wanting a better relationship with them, may produce the frame of reference of fear, that abuse is 'bad', and we must act to get the client to safety. Challenging our emotional and cognitive reactions, our understandings about the context, and our wish to rescue will be paramount – whilst there is nothing wrong in wanting to protect our clients, we must be careful that we do not take ownership of their reality.

Ways of recognising and responding to relational problems stemming from our own process

Reflexive self-examination can also be the base from which to question and illuminate concealed motives and drives behind interventions, a process that Thorpe terms 'psychological reflexivity' (2013, p. 37), that is, the ability to reflexively investigate internal processes, which takes a great deal of skill and development. Pluralistic therapists demonstrate a commitment to reflexive practice and openness to understanding and 'hearing' parts of themselves which they may wish to deny or ignore. As such, personal development tools can greatly aid practitioners in expanding their awareness. Whilst some opt for more formal techniques such as courses, supervision, and personal therapy, there are also many informal practices such as journaling, art, poetry, and reading, and these can aid pluralistic therapists in deciphering their responses to clients, and their work as a whole (McLeod and McLeod, 2014). Gaining confidence in the use of subjective realities and constructed meanings also influences the use of intuition (discussed in Chapter 25).

Ways of sharing self-hood in therapy

Whilst our role as pluralistic therapists requires continued reflexivity, it is also important in practice that we have the availability to be open and articulate what we uncover through meaning-making, congruence around interpretation and experience, and meta-communication. The ability to 'find the right words' to do this is not simply about recognising the purpose and impact of our communications, but also that we need to adjust our ways of communicating to suit the client. Sometimes this is intuitive, for example, adjusting the complexity of what we say to manage understanding or a perception of expertise, whilst sometimes communication is more purposeful and considered in order to develop meaning or aid the facilitation of activities. Although reflexivity is paramount in helping us become more aware of our reactions and motives, and in aiding us in sense-checking our interpretations of verbal and non-verbal cues with the client, it also supports us in understanding what might be helpful or unhelpful to a client's process. In general, humans can be poor communicators; we may have had poor communication role models, be unaware of our reactions and how others perceive us, or understand the world through our subjective reality and act from this as if it were objective 'truth'. Once somebody perceives themselves in a certain 'reality' they will often then fit the messages they receive to support this understanding of who they are – even when there is little evidence to underpin it (Bohart, 1999, p. 294). This is true for therapist and client alike, and therefore evidences the importance of reflexivity and open communication with the client in order to aid the therapist in understanding the client's internal process, as well as the therapist's own processes within the room-the wounds that are triggered, their beliefs, values, culture, and motives, all of which might leak out through their non-verbal communication. An example of this can be found in Chapter 28 – the case of Rachel.

11 Why do pluralistic therapists focus so much on collaboration?

Many who enter counselling have experienced, or felt a sense of, oppression and powerlessness. From external adversities, such as abuse and poverty, to internal struggles, including low self-esteem or feeling 'stuck', people can think that they do not have much to contribute to getting better, or 'life', and bring this perspective with them when they seek expert help. Many Western models, particularly within the public service systems, operate with a power disparity, with the 'experts' instructing the help-seeker, for example, education, medicine, justice, politics – even traditional forms of psychotherapy. This model can perpetuate the help-seeker's position as a 'less-than' individual and further disempower them (see Chapter 31). However, help-seekers are not empty vessels waiting to be 'healed' or 'educated', they come equipped with thoughts, beliefs, values, strengths, and resources. Therefore, when they are 'instructed' to do something that they do not like or do not believe in, they might resist (Glasser, 2003) or be seen to appease by half-heartedly following directions without investment or motivation, and are quick to let go of the instructions once they are 'unsupervised'. Children are a fitting example of this, I may ask (or instruct!) my children to tidy their room because *I* would like it clean, and they may offer half-heartened attempts whilst I am present but are quick to resume their normal 'state' when I leave, because they do not particularly mind if their room is a mess or not! If I didn't know better, I might label their behaviour as 'lazy', disrespectful, or rebellious.

Yet the example of my children equally applies to our relationships with adults, including our client work, and client contributions to therapy can similarly be defined with deficit language: problematic transference, resistance, cognitive distortions, etc. (Sparks and Duncan, 2016a), but realistically, if the client thinks that their behaviour is ruining their marriage, and the therapist continuously tries to explore their *childhood relationships*, the client is likely to become 'resistant'. Whilst

DOI: 10.4324/9781003305736-12

there may be merit in working with childhood wounds, if we work from the 'expert' position – doing therapy 'to' a client – then we have neglected the client's agency, goals, and preference for therapy. This will likely rupture the relationship (Glasser, 2003) risking the client becoming frustrated with the therapist's efforts and the therapist frustrated with the client's lack of engagement and progress. However, when a client is involved in a collaborative approach then they feel more satisfied with their care and have a greater sense of motivation (Bachelor et al., 2007). Although this is a crude example, it highlights the client as an agent for change and the damage that can arise from missing opportunities to collaborate on important components of therapy.

It is important that, as a pluralistic therapist, we collaborate with clients on their goals and tease out obstacles to achieving these, whether client related or therapist related, before identifying the tasks and methods. Many people have been coping with their problems in living for months, if not years, and already have some idea of what they believe the problem is, or at least what it is not, which can help shape what they would like to be different. Furthermore, clients are resourceful self-healers (Bohart, 2000), and prior to commencing therapy, they will have typically engaged in self-help techniques ranging from activities such as yoga and going for a walk, to reaching out to others including friends and their doctor, depending on the level of distress they are experiencing (Marley, 2011). Regardless of whether this is their first time utilising counselling, clients will have preferences about their therapy and therapist (see Chapter 22), collaborating on these will serve to strengthen the relationship, allowing the therapist and client to align on expectations of therapy. Whilst not every client will find collaboration helpful, and some would like their therapist to take the lead, research also indicates that clients still like to be offered a choice in their care (Vollmer et al., 2009), and we contend that it is through the process of collaboration that even these preferences can be understood. It is important that pluralistic therapists recognise that clients want different things at different points in time and so this act of collaboration is an ongoing process of aligning and re-aligning. If we neglect to offer, and involve the client in, a collaborative approach, then we repeat the age-old power story of the therapist as the expert and diminish how capable the client is.

Perhaps most importantly, pluralistic therapists recognise that ignoring clients as agents for change can potentially harm many aspects of the therapeutic process including the relationship, motivation, and future growth. Thus, collaborating with the client is rooted in the ethical commitment to non-maleficence, to do no harm, and the pluralistic commitment to valuing otherness. Pluralism acknowledges that there is no single truth and there are many ways of knowing; whilst the therapist may have some 'expertise' so does the client and, with increasing access to information, clients often present to therapy better informed about the problems they face, what they think might help them, and are more able to verbalise this. Therefore, including client expertise in their care, along with the therapist sharing their knowledge, aims to redress the power imbalance, understanding that both the client and the therapist have something to offer.

Whilst we understand that clients, within therapy and the health-care model, value therapist active engagement, perceiving it to have a positive impact on their sense of motivation and confidence (Ahmad et al., 2014) they also recognise that their own active engagement can aid change (Cooper et al., 2015). This is particularly important for the termination of therapy (see Chapter 27); models that place the therapist as the 'expert' and the client as the 'inexpert' help-seeker may mean that the client needs to re-enlist the help of an 'expert' to solve future problems. Instead, collaborative care means that clients have an increased sense of agency and ability to solve problems themselves. Furthermore, through the sharing of therapist knowledge they may also have theory and language to understand their problems in living, further supporting them in identifying areas to continue their growth.

We recognise that collaboration is not the destination or the sole source of healing and growth; it does not seem to influence psychological functioning or the quality of a client's interpersonal relationships (Bachelor et al., 2007), yet it is the vehicle that enables a therapist and client to build a relationship that we know has the power to heal. Without this solid foundation, other components will not be possible, and so collaboration is a method of engagement from which other discussions and processes can ensue.

12 What knowledge is appropriate to use in the therapy room?

Knowledge can be categorised into three sources: client, therapist, and common (McLeod, 2018a; Smith and de la Prida, 2021). Therapists have substantial knowledge and experience that they use to structure the therapy, aid the client to engage in, and with, therapy, and offer ways of undertaking the process of therapy. Furthermore, a therapist's knowledge grounds their relational skills, which provide support, safety, and understanding, and can involve the rich and sometimes transformative 'I – thou' stance (Buber, 1947). This knowledge enables the practitioner to determine the range of approaches and skills to offer clients, and which benchmarks could be used to measure the process in order to understand if change is occurring. Clients also hold a wealth of knowledge and experience that enables them to engage with therapy and understand what might help them meet their desired changes, and whilst other chapters will focus on how to elucidate this knowledge (see Chapters 14–17, 20 and 22) and how cultural resources fit with common knowledge (see Chapter 23), this chapter is concerned with what we mean by 'knowledge'. As mentioned in Chapter 8, John McLeod (2018a) details six domains of knowledge; Scientific, Theoretical, Practical, Personal, Ethical, Cultural, which is different from how we often understand knowledge, as a thinking or conceptual aspect. Others might argue for additional forms of knowing such as having a spiritual knowing, or 'intuition', which is discussed further in Chapter 25.

Through training we are introduced to one or more *theoretical* underpinnings of counselling, these different schools of therapy guide how a therapist's knowledge and experience are used by the therapist. Through a model of integration, such as Cheston's (2000) Ways Paradigm (see example in Appendix I), therapists are supported in beginning to order their knowledge, particularly theory knowledge, into

DOI: 10.4324/9781003305736-13

three distinct principles which can be developed over a career and include their:

- Way of Being – in the adoption of an 'accepting' stance on what the client is experiencing a therapist may bracket assumptions around what might be going on (such as that seen in person centred therapies), whilst other approaches empower therapists to provide a more directive approach, helping the client structure change (such as that seen in cognitive behavioural therapies).
- Way of Understanding – some schools of thought will understand a client's presenting issue resulting from the lack of a secure base (drawing on attachment theory), whereas other approaches will contend that the 'issues' are in relation to facing one (or more) of the four givens, namely freedom and responsibility, existential isolation, meaninglessness, death (such as that seen in existential therapies).
- Way of Intervening – different schools of thought also indicate appropriate levels of disclosure about how the therapist is feeling or thinking about the process, the level of interpretation or guidance provided by the therapist to the client, and the therapeutic activities proposed and facilitated.

There is also an aspect of 'evidence-based knowing' which reflects the increasing tendency for 'arts'-based counselling degrees, grounded in philosophical and creative knowledge, to incorporate more *scientific* evidence within their programmes in a bid to utilise the best practice and research available. This endows the advantage of being valued within a 'hard science' culture that values quantifiable results and evidenced-based practice. Research and scientific evidence are an important part of a pluralistic therapist's knowledge base and can provide an understanding into the aetiology (cause) of presenting problems, prevalence (how many people), comorbidity (co-occurring conditions), symptoms (common traits or features of the problem or illness) and the best practice guidelines (what works and for who) (see Chapter 6). In addition, scientific knowledge can offer us an understanding regarding *cultural* factors that may impact our clients and their problems in living.

Cultural factors are also intertwined with *personal* and *practical* knowledge, as the therapist draws from what they have done before with clients, what has worked and not worked in therapy, and their own first-hand experiences of adversity, therapy, power and oppression (see Chapter 31), strengths and resources (see Chapter 23). Alongside this is the process of 'intuition' which can be connected to a felt-sense at the gut-level, not always attributable to conscious decisions or thought, but that can help the process – a kind of 'I think this is what is going on' (see Chapter 25 for more on this). However, a therapist is required to always underpin their work with an *ethical* framework of knowledge, regardless of the other ways of knowing, these ethical principles are typically grounded within the therapists initial training and later assumed by accrediting bodies and supervisors as an external moderator of ethical practice.

Whilst these six domains are stand-alone, it is also evident that there is a high degree of interplay between the domains which can complement and conflict with each other. A therapist may have had practical experience of interrupting a client, for example, intervening when the client drifts from what they wanted to work on, with beneficial effect, yet this may conflict with ethical, cultural, or theoretical knowledge. Additionally, a client's knowledge will also exist in these six domains in greater-or-lesser degrees (see Chapters 14–17, 20, 22, 23 for practical details on including client's knowledge). The cornerstone of a pluralistic practice therefore centres around the therapist sharing their knowledge with clients, offering interpretations and options based on the therapist's own skills and knowledge whilst being sensitive to, and inclusive of, the client's own understanding. The use of therapist knowledge and expertise relates to the interplay between the need to be useful to the client and the desire to empower the client, enabling them to internalise their sense of control. As such, pluralistic therapists strive to be conscious in their consideration of knowledge, creating case conceptualisations (see Chapter 14) (pluralistic stance) and sharing these with a client (pluralistic practice), in order to allow for a sharing of knowledge, creating meaning-bridges, and co-constructing a shared understanding.

Regardless of our conscious consideration and care in inviting the client to share their knowledge, a dimension of influence exists which must be carefully navigated by the therapist. Although the client may initially defer to the therapist, over time, we typically see a shift occur whereby the client becomes more active in the work and takes an increased share of the responsibility. It is also important to consider what value the therapist's knowledge can add to the therapy, knowing and managing the structure (length, timing, and location) of the therapy is probably always going to be the remit of the therapist, and the understanding of what therapy is, what the therapist has to offer and what might happen in therapy initially lies within the therapists knowledge, although it is important to discuss these at the start of therapy and throughout. On the other hand, what the client knows and has experienced is vital in understanding their expectations and early preferences (Swift and Callahan, 2009) on their perceived outcomes and process of therapy (Glass et al., 2001) as it is closely related to their actual experience (Watsford and Rickwood, 2015) with poorer expectations being a barrier to engagement and vice versa (Gulliver et al., 2010).

How the knowledge of the client resonates with the knowledge of the therapist can influence the therapy, but not always in predictable ways. Shared experiences have shown to impact on the early formation of relationships fostering feelings of closeness (Min et al., 2018), the key here being a sense that the therapist will understand the client experience, which in turn engenders hope and a willingness to be understood. In contrast, research indicates that clients appreciate 'difference' in the therapy room, and that therapists may use this as a catalyst for exploration and overt 'bridging' (Williams and Levitt, 2008; Levitt et al., 2016). Furthermore, therapist preference and personal experience can differ from that of the clients (Cooper et al., 2019) and so there is a danger that the therapist can unwittingly override and dilute client knowledge effectively giving the client the therapy that they (the therapist) would like. The possession and development of knowledge is a complex process involving the individual's quest for a personal 'truth' (Oeberst et al., 2016), it is fluid because meaning is continuously being constructed, updated, and revised (Piaget, 1980) by both the client and therapist, and potentially other stakeholders including parents, psychiatrists, or social workers. It is also not possible to share everything with the client, and, whilst there may be several ways of knowing, multiple potentials within each domain, it is important not to burden our clients or exert our 'cleverness' or 'expertise' by merely parroting a textbook or offering a definitive 'I know you' perspective. Therefore, therapists carefully weed out and select explanations that best fit the client's understanding, and, whilst sometimes this can be attributed to skill and being attuned to the client, at other times (and I may strike the fear in the hearts of my colleagues) it is intuition.

Section 2

Pluralistic counselling and psychotherapy in practice

13. So where does a trainee start, and what skills and knowledge do they need?
14. How do pluralistic therapists create a formulation or treatment plan for clients, and why do they need one?
15. How do I create an effective timeline formulation with my client?
16. Why do pluralistic therapists work with client goals?
17. What is the difference between goals, tasks, and methods in practice?
18. What are task-lists and how do they work in practice?
19. What methods are used in pluralistic therapy and why?
20. How do pluralistic therapists monitor the process of therapy and whether the client's goals are being met?
21. I know I have a block to using feedback measures, want to help me?
22. How do I work with client's preferences if they don't know what they are?
23. Why, and how, do pluralistic therapists use extra-therapeutic and cultural resources?
24. Can you tell me more about creative and artistic activities in pluralistic therapy?
25. What is the role of intuition and 'felt-sense' for practitioners in pluralistic therapy?
26. How can I be pluralistic and offer short-term counselling?
27. I've started pluralistically, how do I end pluralistically?
28. Can you give some examples of pluralistic work?

DOI: 10.4324/9781003305736-14

13 So where does a trainee start, and what skills and knowledge do they need?

The starting point for pluralistic counselling is that the therapy is based on core counselling skills, which can be identified in every formal and embedded counselling approach. These include the ability to experience and express empathy, congruence, and unconditional positive regard to the client. These core conditions are supported by other skills, including the capacity to listen and use silence, to accurately reflect meaning and emotional experience, and to guide and monitor in order to prompt and support exploration of ideas and experiences.

Counselling skills (McLeod and McLeod, 2011) are developed through training and experiential learning, focusing on deploying skills, peer-learning and feedback. Individuals will arrive in training with different strengths and growth-edges in terms of interpersonal skills, on which counselling skills are based. Additionally, everyone has a 'usual' way of helping that impacts on this, for example, some students, and at times practicing therapists, revert to habitual behaviours such as the 'rescuer', whilst others may struggle to challenge clients or offer interpretations, therefore the use of deliberate practice (Rousmaniere, 2016) throughout training and beyond is encouraged to support development (see Chapter 37).

Within the portfolio of skills a person brings to the role of the therapist, and beyond the basic counselling skills, are interpersonal sensitives which make the relationship more attuned, for example, the ability to communicate effectively, through having an adaptability and flexibility of pace, pitch, tone, manner, and language to suit the client; an ability to detect and respond to implicit feedback as indicated by non-verbal behaviour, verbal comments, or significant shifts in responsiveness; recognising when a client might have difficulty speaking or giving feedback; to be sensitive and respond to emotional expression in all its forms, and a sensitivity to emotional shifts in the client process.

DOI: 10.4324/9781003305736-15

Skills which might be seen in all therapies but are considered essential to a therapist working within the pluralistic framework include:

Client empowerment – Which requires the therapist to recognise and communicate the active role for the client, the skills, knowledge, and resources they bring to therapy and actively promote client strengths (particularly in the early stages of therapy).

- *I hear you saying that in your relationship with Simon you were able to talk about your anxiety, it sounds like that was a brave move, and it tells us that you have the ability to do this.*

Open clarification of the process – Being able to discuss with a client, in a meaningful way, the process of therapy prior to it starting, and as the process evolves. This enables a discussion as to what is happening and support the client in giving their perspective so that it is mutually understood.

- *So, I see these first few sessions as maybe giving us the opportunity to talk through what's going on for you just now, it will help us get a sense of what you need from therapy. We can talk about how you would like us to work together and what we might be able to do in the eight sessions we have. How does that sound?*

Collaborative case formulation – As part of the shared understanding of therapy it is important to be able to conceptualise, in an accessible way, the issues that are coming up for the client, their interpretation of these, and the way they may be addressed in therapy (see Chapter 14). This process can be supported using a collaborative time-line formulation to allow an external reference point to both client and therapist, this aspect of practice is covered in Chapter 15.

- *How I understand what you have told me is that you think a lot of the problems you are facing now are because of what you have been through in the past. I have also heard that you notice you have unwanted and intrusive thoughts. Would you consider these to be the biggest challenges you are facing at the moment?*

Shared decision-making – This is key to how therapy is arranged and adjusted to suit the client, drawing on the knowledge and experience of both therapist and client through offering 'choice-points'. As far as possible, a therapist will work with the client to share relevant information about the choices on offer, and possible implications, then make space for the client to reflect and respond:

- *If we think about the options available to work through the stress, sometimes it can be helpful to learn stress-reduction techniques whereas we could also work together by first exploring where the stress comes from. You might also have your own ideas, what do you think would be most helpful to you?*

Preference accommodation (and underlying responsiveness) – This is linked to shared decision-making and is a holistic process threading through the therapy. In pluralism, it is an active process relating to a range of preferences. For many clients preference accommodation is reliant on knowing what is on offer and the ability of the therapist to know how flexible they, or the therapy, can be (see Chapter 22 and Swift et al., 2018).

- *Last week when we worked through the concern you had about disassociation, we talked about how it feels to do this in the room with me. It would be helpful for me to know how you want me to respond, so should I try and intervene if you start to feel it coming on, should I check out with you, or are you wanting to kind of self-manage?*

Working with representation and metaphor – Because the pluralistic perspective brings with it an assumption that there is no hidden nor objective truth, and that the collaborative therapeutic process is about a constructed and shared understanding, it is often useful to be able to work creatively with non-literal representation and metaphor (Freedman and Combs, 1996; McLeod, 1998), which enables new meanings to be created in shared ways. Using the client's imagery makes it more accessible to both the therapist and client, and moving beyond words can allow clients to find meaning in music, art, dance, nature, and many other experiences which can be shared to help explore their lives (see Chapter 24).

- *You said there that it was 'like a tsunami', that gives me a sense that it felt like it was an overwhelming and almost destructive force . . . Will the tsunami return if you leave?*

All these activities are carried out within the frame of a collaborative relationship (see Chapter 11) and the development of this involves the combining of three areas of skill: (i) the ability to meta-communicate, (ii) to accommodate preferences, and (iii) recognise and monitor the role of relational dynamics between therapist and client and subsequently the impact of this on the process. The art of meta-communication is to understand enough of what is happening in the therapy to be able to overlay the activities with a conversation about the process, including the ability to discuss the expectations, formulation, and experience of the therapy. This is key to ensuring a shared space: resisting pressure for the therapist to feel the need to direct (explicitly or implicitly) what goes on, on one hand, or handing over sole responsibility for the space to the client on the other. As the therapy progresses this meta-communication and preference accommodation is aimed at the client being empowered to make their own choices and direct the process, therefore the therapist must be consistently aware of the dynamic of power sharing and navigation.

Often of major concern to the therapist, but less so to the client, is the role of theoretical knowledge (see Chapters 12 and 30). This can be in terms of understanding the pluralistic model alongside a variety of theories about the cause of problems and the potential for change (ideas about *what* changes in therapy and *how* is a broad church!). It is also quite daunting for those coming to pluralism to envisage how wide their range of methods and activities on offer are, and it is important to remember that, if done well, core counselling skills are often enough to bring about change for the client. Many pluralistic therapists are interested in developing the methods they can offer, often termed a *therapeutic toolkit* which itself leads to the ability to offer a '*therapeutic menu*', and this palate is something that continues to be developed over many years. New ways of working can be learnt from training, clients, peers, personal experience, and in supervision, and at times the key judgement is *when* to offer a method and *how* to judge the helpfulness for *this particular client* at *this point in time*. Consideration of competence and capacity to offer different ways of working and respond to client preferences is ongoing, and may relate to therapist experience, sense of self-assurance, and personality (alongside their own worldview and preferences). The use of particular methods is further discussed in Chapter 19.

Tied to the idea of collaboration are ethical judgements of what is undertaken and how. The ability to establish and maintain a sense of safety for the client is essential, as it is the ability to make judgements on boundaries and understand the context of the conversation and the therapy as a whole, for example, the need for confidentiality and responsibility when client risk needs to be managed (this is explored further in Chapter 29). Confidence and hope are also shown to be important in engaging clients in the process of therapy, such as having early faith that their needs can be met (Cooper, 2008; O'Hara, 2013), and being able to instil this through clear preparation, for example, talking through what therapy might look and feel like, or having a dialogue about what outcomes could be achieved for a particular client from an informed position, this not only manages expectations but also helps progress.

Finally, it is important to recognise that underneath these skills and abilities is the person of the therapist (see Chapter 10), their principles and openness to difference, and their humility in accepting the potential value in all understandings, stories, and ways of being and acting. Being able to tune in to these with the client and accept that the journey towards creating a unique pathway of change for them is unlikely to be pre-decided, or necessarily clear, takes reflective awareness and constant striving for learning and development.

14 How do pluralistic therapists create a formulation or treatment plan for clients, and why do they need one?

When we meet with our clients our first conversations often centre around uncovering their current problems in living, 'what bought you here today?' and 'how can I help?', in addition to asking routine questions about their history including their family, health, social life, and education. Some pluralistic therapists will also use methods such as a timeline (see Chapter 15), family genogram, or sculpting stones to help the client tell the therapist about who they are, their perceived problems, strengths and resources. This might form what is termed as the 'assessment' period of getting to know the client and is necessary in order to create a treatment plan – how we might be able to work together, '*the suitability of the client for therapy, the focus or goals of therapy, and the type or length of treatment that would be most appropriate*' (McLeod and McLeod, 2016, p. 15). The notion and language of an 'assessment', 'to judge' (Cambridge, n.d.), can jar with that of being pluralistic, and those rooted in humanistic models, as it holds both negative and authoritative connotations conjuring an expert-led practice and diagnostic images. However, at our human core is a judgement system driven to make sense of the world around us, and form opinions based on the information we receive, *Our visual and auditory systems automatically make sense of sensory input; we cannot decide whether or not to understand what people are saying, or . . . to appreciate the significance of what we are told, and so on* (Chater and Loewenstein, 2016, p. 139). This is initially an internal process, and we make sense of the client's information by filtering through our various ways of knowing (see Chapter 12) and in doing so, we are formulating, or conceptualising, how we understand their problem(s) and how they cope. Individual case formulations and treatment plans are considered to be the *heart of evidence-based practice* (Bieling and Kuyken, 2003, p. 53) and are not unique to pluralistic therapy, many therapeutic traditions use case formulations or conceptualisations,

DOI: 10.4324/9781003305736-16

particularly within the CBT school of thought. However, there is a risk that if we keep this process as internal then we dilute or misshape the essence of how the client describes their world and therapy can become a 'smoke-and-mirror's intervention whereby it is undertaken with seemingly little rationale.

To ensure we can collaboratively work together, it is important to first understand the client *with* the client; as we formulate our ideas and theories, it is paramount that we tentatively offer these back to the client, forming a collaborative dialogue to verify that our formulation of the problem aligns with their understanding. Moreover, we might comment on this process by introducing why we have come to this idea (Inoue et al., 2020), for example, based on research and practice knowledge, '*Others who have bipolar disorder often commented that they struggle with anxiety and over-thinking, and I am wondering if this is how you understand your "bottom-less pit of worries"?*'. The client then has the opportunity to reject your formulation, '*No, I don't think so – I don't suffer with my bipolar anymore*', support the formulation, '*I have always said this to my doctor*' or clarify the formulation, '*Maybe, but I also think I get it from my father, he was a constant worrier*'. Of course, the client might equally reply with a non-verbal signal such as a shrug, head nod, or turning away, and we may need to clarify further what this means to the client through a process of meta-therapeutic communication. This sharing of information provides practice-based evidence for our conceptualisation and offers a stronger basis a shared therapy plan, as we seek to understand the client's reactions and thoughts about what has caused their initial problems, what keeps this active, what/who has supported them, what they would like for the future (goals) and what they think might help them achieve this.

Collaborative formulations can be a complex and somewhat 'messy' process as there is a shared responsibility to create meaning; you will note this chapter speaks from the therapist's position, but it is also important to consider that the client is also simultaneously active in this process, making their own meaning. Many a client has sat in front of me seeking to understand 'why' they are struggling and, as we talk and they hear themselves, they start to connect their story, sometimes with very little intervention from me. It is recognised that through talking there is a cathartic experience whereby we engage in metaphors, symbols and narrative, ordering and re-ordering events, to enable us to make sense of them (Marx et al., 2017). There is also a power in feeling heard, understood and validated by the therapist which can support feelings of self-acceptance and care, and help clients to persevere through more challenging stages of therapy (Geller et al., 2021). And so, the formulation is at best an estimation for that moment, a fluid concept open to revision, as we, the client and therapist, absorb information and simultaneously try to make sense of it together.

Creating a collaborative formulation is essential in understanding the type and duration of therapy. We know that different clients want different things at different points in time and whilst many clients might not have the language to ask for a particular theoretical approach, they may describe their lives in ways that naturally align with existing theories. For example, if a client expresses that their problems in living are entrenched in their upbringing and they want to understand their past then offering a solution focused, CBT, type of intervention can conflict with the client's understanding, and they may prefer a more psychodynamic or humanistic based therapy which typically occurs over a longer-period of time. This is not to say that CBT would not be a useful, indeed powerful, intervention but in the initial stages they may reject a formulation that they can change their thoughts and behaviour to feel better. Yet the client may also be time limited and so longer-term therapies would not be practical and would potentially set the client up to 'fail' and not achieve their goals. Through collaborating on both what they want (goals) and their understanding of the presenting issue we can ensure that the therapy fits the client, lowering internal 'silent' expectations, acknowledging preferences, and creating a shared understanding. We know that collaboration aids motivation and is valued by clients (Bachelor et al., 2007), has the effect of strengthening the working alliance, and ensures that both the client and therapist are more engaged in the process and possess a shared belief in the outcome and understanding of the problem.

In essence, creating a formulation and treatment plan helps the therapist to map the client's world to frameworks of knowledge, predominately theoretical, which will offer indications such as suitability for therapy/therapies, duration, and potential methods. However, without collaboration we are leaving clients in the dark and are more likely to be incorrect in our formulations and meet resistance from clients. Understanding the importance of collaboration (see Chapter 11) and meta-therapeutic communication will aid therapists in moving from being 'expert-led' to collaborative practitioners.

15 How do I create an effective timeline formulation with my client?

As indicated in Chapter 14, people often think of formulations as a hypothesis about the causes, events, or influences, of a person's problems in living (Eells et al., 1998). It is an imagined straight line drawn between client presentations to intervention planning to interventions undertaken, and the outcomes of these in terms of client progress. This kind of application relies on some theoretical construct that decides which bits of the client experience are important to note and, in recognising these, makes decisions about what to do in therapy. But in the flexible, preference-driven, and creative process of pluralistic therapy, many will ask how this can happen in a coherent way, as it is less often a straight line and more often spiralised, going back and forth. In a broad sense, formulation in pluralistic practice is the creation and evolution of a representation about what the client is experiencing, how it came about, and what might be done about it.

Whilst in some schools of therapy the formulation is closely associated with assessment, theoretical interpretation and pre-assumptions, and treatment planning, pluralistic therapy tends towards an open, more evolving, system of representation which builds on ideas from the field of individual case formulation approaches. These aim to differentiate between information seeking, which is often in the form of assessment on entry and early in therapy, and interpretation, what the information means when it is related to a theoretical framework, in order to promote the inclusion of a client's self-interpretation in the process (e.g. Hallam, 2013). In pluralistic therapy, the process is carried out in a co-creative and less-linier manner and is embedded in collaboration throughout the therapy. Therapists and clients will use the formulation to check their understanding, explore opportunities for insight and change, and

DOI: 10.4324/9781003305736-17

also to create a check point which can be referred to and developed as therapy progresses.

One creative way to capture the complexity and emergent nature of client experience is through a timeline (McLeod, 2018a; Smith and de la Prida, 2021). This is a drawn line running from early life (or for some clients the things that occurred in their familial or social context pre-birth), through to the current day and on into the future. Other timelines might choose to focus on a particular moment in time or presenting problem in order to help a client articulate and draw inferences from their visual representation. Usually instigated by the therapist, a timeline is often 'externalised' by being sketched out, either in real-time with the client on a shared piece of paper or by the therapist between sessions, and brought to the client for comment. The client is invited to reflect, amend, and develop the drawing, and in doing so is able to decentre from their life experience and take an overview alongside the therapist. Often this conversation results in the client being able to gain insight and start thinking about prioritising some aspects of their experience to work on in therapy. The timeline is not simply a depiction of what has been shared, it includes some thought on the meaning of experiences and themes drawn from both therapist and client knowledge and ideas.

Step 1 – Depicting what has been shared

In order to respect and capture the lived experience of the client, whilst allowing insight to develop and dialogue to occur around how therapy is undertaken, pluralistic therapists conceptualise the formulation of a client case from within the relationship – not before or separately alongside it. Whilst some information may be provided to the therapist through the referral process and any organisational assessment, the formulation really starts by first allowing the client to begin telling the story of what is going on for them. The timeline is then used to create a representation of events, experiences, and themes (such as relational patterns, focal points of distress, and strengths and resources) as they have emerged in the first two or three sessions of therapy (although this timescale may vary depending on the number of sessions available and the client and therapist styles). In practice, the discussion is a meta-communicative process touching on and recognising, but not necessarily exploring, the different aspects of the

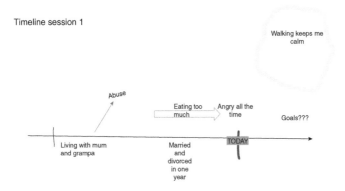

Timeline session 1

Walking keeps me calm

Abuse

Eating too much

Angry all the time

Goals???

Living with mum and grampa

Married and divorced in one year

TODAY

Figure 15.1 Depicting what has been shared in an initial timeline

timeline. The co-construction of the timeline also serves to anchor the therapy, and a sense of direction and goals, however nascent, can be recognised.

Step 2 – Reflecting on the first draft

Once the first draft is created, either in the session, or initiated by the therapist between sessions, a pause is taken in the process of dialogue to check in on what they have shared. Clients often appreciate this as it offers a chance to widen their lens from within their experience to see a preliminary overview of their situation. The therapist or client may make some initial interpretations of the links between what is going on for the client and the relative importance of some areas, as well as reflect with the client on the ways that the story is unfolding and how they are interacting with one another in the therapy space. These reflections may be understood using ideas from a theoretical standpoint, for example, '*you are talking a lot about how you wish you could accept yourself, and maybe there's a disjoint here between what you are trying to be for others and who you are in yourself*', or be simply resonant links, for example, '*you've talked quite a lot about anger, in your work, in your family, and in your loss of your husband*'. The therapist will also be pro-active in highlighting any client strengths and cultural resources which the client has mentioned, for example, '*so despite it all you are*

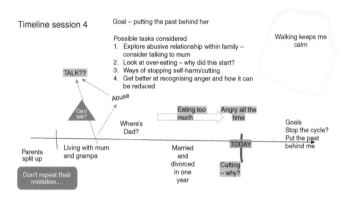

Figure 15.2 Revising the first draft timeline

still fighting for your children – you've been seeking to engage with the school to try and resolve this'. The early intention of the formulation is therefore to:

- Build and strengthen the collaborative relationship.
- Check in on the therapist and client's shared understanding.
- Create an opportunity to externalise the case and a forum for decision-making and preference accommodation.
- Gain feedback on how the activities are received in the sessions so far and the impact on the client upon seeing the formulation.

Step 3 – Deciding how the timeline might work in therapy

The next step involves giving the client some options of how best to work together from the formulation, so tentatively agreeing a focus of the sessions, and the direction the client would like to go in, allowing identification of emergent goals and related tasks. In some cases, the client may wish to be less structured and approach the formulation in terms of *'this is what we know – let's see it grow'*. Within this conversation the therapist can develop an early sense of how the client would like to work and what they would like to focus on. Whilst other clients can pinpoint exactly what they would like to focus on, which can then progress to a discussion around the goals of therapy and how they are undertaken, '*What's jumping out for me here is the death of my sister and how I really never got the chance to say goodbye to her, it feels like everything that has happened since has been under a cloud*'.

Step 4 – Process and outcome

The next steps for formulation will depend on the client, progressing from this initial dialogue can involve:

- Options about how therapy can progress and what that might look like for the client (goals, tasks, and methods; see Chapter 17).
- Preferences around where to focus the conversation, and within that the role of the therapist on keeping the topic 'on track' (see Chapter 22).
- Preferences on the integration of the formulation into the therapeutic conversation and use of feedback (see Chapter 20) and checkpoints – should the formulation be used throughout or at set intervals?
- Recognition and 'marking' of important insights, events, and changes for the client.
- Conversations about risk and safety for the client if this is coming up (see Chapter 29).

Once agreed, the use of the formulation is flexible, however many clients like to see the work they do in therapy evolve on the timeline and, even if they don't, pluralistic therapists will retain a record of this and ensure that whatever is being understood and undertaken is available to the client as part of the therapy. The formulation serves as an anchor for the activities undertaken and reviewing the work which helps to manage the process of therapy, and create a place to recognise progress.

Step 5 – Ending

Whilst the timeline may be used regularly in therapy, or viewed during review sessions, it can also be used to look at how therapy has impacted on the client and as a tool for capturing representations of change. Nearing the end of therapy, the timeline might be used to discuss achievements, strengths, and areas for future development, and there is always a space on the timeline for the future of the client. It is useful at this stage to add in pictures or words which help capture this change for the client. The final timeline belongs to the client, existing

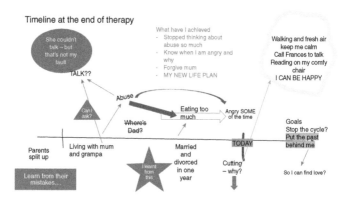

Figure 15.3 The final timeline

as a testament to their strengths, courage, and achievements in therapy. Many clients will take the timeline, or a copy of it, with them when they finish therapy and so it is important, where possible, to maintain a co-created version paying particular attention to the language the client uses and how they want events to be depicted.

Other uses

Whilst the timeline can aid the therapist and client to create a formulation, the opportunity for representations and expression in the form of a visual timeline is found by many to be a cathartic and meaningful experience and an important part of the therapeutic process, although this does not appeal to all clients. It is important to remember that clients have a choice as to whether they engage with this form of meaning making or not, and to be mindful of the impact of transferring thoughts to the permanence of pen and paper, which can be a powerful and emotional task. Even if timelines are not constructed with the client, they can be a useful way for the therapist to think about their work with the client and a tool to aid supervision. Additionally, therapists may wish to create their own timeline as a personal development tool and in order to understand the clients' experience of this intervention a little better.

16 Why do pluralistic therapists work with client goals?

Imagine you are going on holidays, maybe you have no idea where you want to go, from looking at past holidays you know that you do not want a city break – where are you going? How will you get there? Who is coming with you? What need or want does the holiday meet for you? It is very difficult to plan a journey if you have not selected a destination. We often use the metaphor of a journey to illustrate therapy and life. If you do not understand what you want to achieve then it is difficult to decipher how to get there, how long it might take, who/what might be needed along the journey.

The concept of therapeutic goals is considered essential to pluralistic therapy because they are so closely related to the strength of the therapeutic alliance (Bordin, 1979) and client outcomes (Norcross and Lambert, 2019). Additionally, within pluralistic work, therapists use goals to create case formulations, focus the tasks and methods, and understand expectations and preferences for the process (Cooper and Xu, 2022). However, the key to working with goals lies in how they are co-conceptualised and understood by therapists and clients; the negotiation and use of goals, how they can re-enforce the effectiveness of therapy, and that they may be considered an ethical imperative.

How can we conceptualise goals?

Pluralistic therapy seeks to establish a shared, pan-theoretical language working from a stance which is de-centred from theoretical assumptions about outcomes. The term 'goal' allows the inclusion of different process and outcome ambitions whilst avoiding an 'anything goes' perspective. Because goals mean what the client wants them to mean, they provide a primary point for collaboration, meta-communication, case formulation, and understanding as to why therapy is being undertaken.

DOI: 10.4324/9781003305736-18

Whilst goals can be transient and evolve as the client gains insight and self-knowledge, particularly within the earlier stages on therapy, ongoing goal collaboration provides a sense of awareness and purpose and can be used to both deepen understanding, empower clients, and to monitor striving.

In order to understand goals, we need to know what they can look like, and Cooper (2018) suggests eight dimensions which should be considered when therapy goals are explored:

1. Importance – which relates to motivation and goal transience.
2. Challenging – difficult but realistic goals support greater gains in therapy.
3. Avoidant (away from) versus approach (moving towards) – with approach goals being more beneficial and easier to measure (Elliot and Church, 2002).
4. Intrinsic (changes to self) versus extrinsic (externally referenced) – with intrinsic goals being more closely associated with well-being and positive outcomes (Sheldon and Kasser, 1998).
5. Specificity – a goal which is more specific and defined (and as a result recognisable if not clearly measurable) tends to be better.
6. Temporal extension – spanning 'therapy goals', 'immediate outcomes' and 'session goals' and may relate to bigger 'life' or 'longer-term' goals.
7. Consciousness – the impact, and importance, of unconscious or implicit goals.
8. Meta-level goals – which are more process orientated, for example, the client goal of 'getting better at meeting my needs'.

Before we talk about the use of goals in therapy, the concept of meta-goals in pluralistic practice is worth further consideration, as Cooper (2018) suggests, defining a goal which is too overarching and references the achievement of a goal as the goal can result in a cycle of unmet ambitions. A practitioner in these circumstances might engage the client in a dialogue, helping them to define something tangible as an example of goal achievement, in addition to exploring the relationship between the client and the goal. A meta-goal might indicate a life-position or pattern of thinking which could become the focus of therapy, for example, initially shifting 'getting better at meeting my needs' to 'understanding why my needs are not met'.

How to negotiate goals

When clients discuss what they want, both from therapy and in life, they often start by saying what they don't want. Perhaps because anything seems better than the current situation, or perhaps because their vision has become fixed on the perceived 'threat', which they want to avoid. Some clients may already be forming vague goals, such as to be 'happier', or have clear goals which compete with each other. Many therapists state that their clients do not know what they want, this perspective can be unhelpful to the therapeutic process. Instead, we should perhaps consider that, understandably, some clients might find it difficult to articulate goals at a conscious or dialogic level, but subconsciously, as humans, we have needs and desires some of which are unmet, and at the very least knowing what we do not want can begin to shape what we do want. Additionally, it is worth recognising that it might have been physically or psychologically unsafe for our clients to consider what it is that they want, or they may have had repeated setbacks in achieving their goals which has caused them to abandon their wants and needs. In an apparent absence of goals, Mackrill (2011) notes that clients will provide us with clues through their likes, dislikes, and symptoms. Whilst these might not always be explicitly named and may appear 'abnormal' (Rogers, 1961, p. 18 and p. 26) to us, they are, nevertheless, our client's efforts towards fulfilling unconscious or unacknowledged wishes and needs. Helping the client discuss this is a *'means of helping clients articulate something at the very essence of their existence'* (Cooper, 2018, p. 201), and, when empathically accepted by another person, tentative articulation of needs and wants can be the first steps to realisation for the client.

The benefits of conceptualising goals

When forming and articulating goals, clients can understand and re-understand their problems in living and where they want to go, which helps to create a shared understanding of how therapy might work, what successful therapy would entail, and development of realistic expectations (Di Malta et al., 2019). Even if the goals challenge the therapist's, or societies, values and are perceived to be unattainable or 'unacceptable', we can facilitate co-operation and build a stronger collaboration (Cairns et al., 2019) through the process of viewing clients as capable and needs driven, discussing the goals and what they mean to them. Many clients have felt dismissed due to their 'unattainable' 'counterproductive' or 'unacceptable' hopes and goals, for example, those with eating disorders who wish to lose more weight – an attuned and sensitive therapist will try to understand what it is that drives this want or need (such as safety, love, self-control, or confidence). This can create a 'back and forth process' whereby the therapist and client take time to understand the complex circumstances the client survives in, thematically linking their problems in living whilst exploring ambivalence to change, which strengthens the collaboration and potential to achieve goals (Oddli et al., 2014; Rose and Smith, 2018).

Therapy clients [across age, gender, mental health diagnosis, substance use, or vocational functioning] find goal setting helpful (Cairns et al., 2019) and setting goals is closely related to an increase in motivation, engagement, working alliance, and empowerment (Clarke et al., 2009). Additionally, a client's initial confidence in completing a goal has been found to link with their actual achievement (Rose and Smith, 2018), however many clients lack faith in their potential, perhaps because of past failures, poor self-esteem, a mood-related disorder or because the goal has yet to be clearly defined (Dickson et al., 2016). Part of the justification of goal setting therefore, particularly when goals are specific, is to instil hope, '*defined as the perceived capability to derive pathways to desired goals*' (Snyder, 2002, p. 249). Even if the client's confidence is initially low, progress towards their smaller goals results in a 'boost' in confidence (Rose and Smith, 2018) and encourages a motivation to continue (Biringer et al., 2016; Jensen et al., 2021), even when there are set backs. This provides an argument for setting realistic and achievable sub-goals, or tasks (Di Malta et al., 2019), discussed in Chapter 17.

The ethical dimension of purpose in therapy

Understanding and aligning with our client's goals is a distinctive principle of pluralistic practice, but moreover, it is considered to be an ethical component of any therapy comprising informed consent (McLeod and MacKrill, 2018). Whilst we have many available options to gather information about the client's wishes for therapy, such as outcome and process monitoring (see Chapter 20), preference matching (see Chapter 22), and meta-therapeutic communication, the best indicator of therapy effectiveness is moving closer towards their goals and the client identifying improvements in their problem (Biringer et al., 2016; Law and Jacob, 2015; Rose and Smith, 2018; Sales et al., 2022), which is a more reliable indication of satisfaction than measured improvements in symptom and function (Biringer et al., 2016). This is further illustrated in Chapter 48.

The problem with goals

Despite the evidence of the value and utility of goals, the concept can be anathema in therapy, this is because the term suggests insight and knowledge exist when goals are initially articulated, whereas for some clients, particularly those who come to therapy to find meaning and purpose in life, goals are better articulated at the end of this process, when therapy has served to get in touch with their 'true-selves'. Goal-direction can be seen as too restrictive, with an emphasis on change and 'doing' rather than accepting and 'being', indeed some clients feel 'put on the spot' believing it interfered with identifying unconscious goals (Di Malta et al., 2019). Additionally, sometimes the goal of therapy *is* to have a space to 'off-load' or to 'talk' and being flexible and collaborative in understanding the client's needs for therapy is essential (Di Malta et al., 2019). A pluralistic position on this is to focus on the nature of therapeutic purpose, for example, if someone is seeking a space simply to feel heard and understood, then a goal might be 'to feel understood' or 'to understand' something. Whilst this might be viewed as unnecessary semantics, it avoids the risk of the therapist undertaking therapeutic activities which they assume to be helpful without the knowledge, or permission, of the client, and will additionally aid the client in understanding their own needs.

In practice, therapists may also struggle with the dialogue around goals, from supervisory experience some challenges include:

- They don't like the sense of prescriptive targets.
- They fear that not reaching goals is associated with negative affect (as a contrast to evidence that suggests goal achievement is a positive experience).
- They don't really like talking about goals before they feel confident that they and their clients know what the therapy will entail.
- They worry about getting the goals wrong because the client is being asked to articulate them (sometimes hopes for outcomes of therapy are not easy to put into words).
- They worry that not doing goal related work in therapy is not helpful.

These concerns are usually resolved with a more nuanced understanding of goals in therapy. Most pluralistic therapists gain confidence with experience once they engage in the dialogic nature of goals, and find their discomfort is often not matched in their clients. When closely associated with the client's lived experience, goals can become conduits for making therapy effective and for defining the process of therapy in meaningful ways.

17 What is the difference between goals, tasks, and methods in practice?

This chapter provides some definitions of the various ways of identifying goals, tasks, and methods, and the differences that exist between each concept. It will also begin to offer some examples of how the goals, tasks, methods approach can be utilised across other disciplines.

Goals: 'What do you want?'

Working to goals is not a concept unique to pluralistic therapy and is shared across other disciplines including health care, social work, education, marketing, and many theoretical orientations. Goals provide a structure for the therapist, particularly at times of complexity or when working with several problems in living. Whilst more information can be found on why pluralistic therapists use goals in Chapter 16, broadly speaking, goals help to anchor the client (or student, team, etc.) in the destination that they would like to reach. In settings, such as education or business, the goal may be set from the top down, such as the state, principal, or manager, but achieving buy-in from all stake holders is essential in successfully moving the whole team towards the intended destination (Kotter and Whitehead, 2010). In pluralistic counselling, it is the client who sets the goal in collaboration with their therapist (Di Malta et al., 2019). Whether using formal measures or goal-directed communication, this process can take time and should be unhurried as the therapist aids the client in identifying and teasing out the complexities of these goals, such as whether they are attainable, if they compete or contradict other goals, are fuelled by unconscious desires or societal expectations, and the client's initial confidence in achieving

DOI: 10.4324/9781003305736-19

these (Oddli et al., 2014). Whilst formal goals- or idiographic outcomes forms- can be a powerful tool in reviewing client outcomes, not all clients, or therapists, like to use the language of goals (Murphie and Smith, in preparation) as it can serve to be 'business-like' and therefore many therapists sensitively weave in the discussion of preferred outcomes through gentle questioning. It is perhaps useful to note that the language is a mere reference point for the therapist and alternative questions to discuss goals might include:

- What would you like to get from coming to see me?
- What made you pick up the phone to me at that time?
- What is it that you are struggling with/what is the problem?
- If this is the problem,

    - What would you like to be different?
    - What would help you?
    - What would you like to get from coming to counselling?
    - How will you know when it is no longer a problem, or we have finished our work?

Similar to business, where all stakeholders need to believe in the value of the goal, the therapist must also share the goal, orientating themselves to what the client wants in order to be collaborative (Cooper and McLeod, 2011); the belief that this goal is achievable and in the best interest of the client. This is where we see pluralism slightly shift in its seat away from client-led work towards a collaborative approach, even at times when the goal seems 'unacceptable' or 'unachievable'. Through collaborative dialogue and viewing the client as an agent for change, we can understand what the goals mean to our clients, honouring the importance, as well as discussing our concerns. In doing so, we create meaning bridges and work towards shared goals (McLeod, 2018a).

Counsellors can become engaged in the language of goals and the idea that there is a desired outcome and so change must ensue, yet some clients voice that they are unsure of their goals or are happy to 'see where it goes'. It is through discussion that we can begin to identify these as goals for therapy such as having a safe space to talk, to process bereavement, 'or simply to be heard'. A further barrier to setting goals can be that the client has little confidence in achieving these and might disengage or find them overwhelming. It is thus helpful to breakdown goals into important sub-goals or tasks (Jensen et al., 2021).

Tasks: 'What steps are needed to achieve this?'

At times, tasks emerge quite organically when discussing the problem or goals and the therapist can help the client theme, or map, the link between what they want and what needs to happen for them to achieve it. At other times, clients can feel lost, they know where they want to be, but all the rungs of the ladder appear to be missing, and the therapist is required to help the client find the pieces. At this point relevant questions might be:

- What would help you meet that goal?
- If you want to do 'x' what needs to happen so that you can?
- Are there any barriers that would stop you achieving this?

    - If so, would it be useful to do some work on that?

- If you did this, what difference would that make to your goal?
- You named 'x' as a separate goal, I am wondering now if this is something you need to do (task) that helps you meet this goal?
- When you had achieved this goal before, what helped you?
- How do other people achieve goals like this?

Although questions here are posed as 'you', there may be an element of 'we' or 'us' depending on the setting.

Additional to the client's goal-related tasks for therapy, the therapist will also have a set of tasks required for successful therapy such as the therapeutic tasks of creating a safe space, a culture of feedback, and inquiry into preferences (Smith and de la Prida, 2021). Alongside this, counselling tasks including generic therapy activities such as meaning making, problem solving, behaviour change, engagement of social resources, expression and release of emotion, and negotiating transitions/crises (Cooper and McLeod, 2011) more of which can be found in Chapter 18.

Methods: 'How do you want to achieve this?'

Once goals and tasks are established it is important to understand which methods can be used to reach these. Pluralistic therapists do not direct clients by proposing a single method to address their tasks but instead engage the client in a dialogue about a number of options, a so-called 'menu'. The menu available will be relevant to the therapist's knowledge (see Chapter 12 for example of theoretical, scientific, practical, personal, ethical knowledge) and the client's own values, preferences, and knowledge. As a helper, we need a keen ear to be able to detect and create space to dialogue about these important topics which starts with placing the client as an 'expert' of their own life (McLeod and McLeod, 2011). Delivering a 'menu' of options, through language that is appropriate and 'real' to the client, takes care and consideration on behalf of the therapist and an ability to help the client direct the therapy based on their preferences about the methods on offer. It may involve questions such as:

- What did you do with your last therapist that you did/did not like?
- I hear you say 'x', there are a few things I am thinking of that might help us . . . Do any of those sound useful?
- Are there any things you used to do that would be helpful now?
- Are there any things you would like to do that might help, but that you have never tried before?
- A lot of people I have worked with have found 'x' helpful, is that something you would consider?

When training in pluralism, students often feel that they need to 'do' something as a method – employing worksheets and creativity to evidence a discrete activity – yet when we strip it back, the common factors approach has been evidenced to be '*important for producing the benefits of psychotherapy*' (Wampold, 2015, p. 270) and can be delivered through the core skills of counselling – reflection, listening, immediacy, self-disclosure, and humour – which are powerful methods in promoting client change. Additional examples of methods might include providing information, engaging cultural resources, using metaphors and images, and finding different ways of understanding (conceptualising) the problem (McLeod, 2018b), we further explore pluralistic methods in Chapter 19.

Worth noting is that some research (Papayianni and Cooper, 2018) demonstrates that tasks and methods often overlap, with therapists referring to them as one, 'tasks and methods'. Whilst this could potentially be attributed to a lack of clear distinction between task and method, it is likely that the task and method are the same. For example, a client in addiction who wishes to be sober (goal) and wants to attend AA, which is both a task towards sobriety and a method of delivery. It is important that the process of mapping (method to achieve task, task to achieve goal) is an ongoing dialogue with clients, which can be used as a tool to instil hope (Snyder, 2002), provide a benchmark for assessing client outcomes (Biringer et al., 2016), in addition to supporting client outcomes and strengthening the working alliance (Bordin, 1979; Oddli et al., 2014).

18   What are task-lists and how do they work in practice?

The therapeutic alliance (Bordin, 1979) is the basis for the collaborative relationship in pluralistic therapy, and is composed of three aspects (i) the quality of the relational bond, (ii) an agreement on the goals of therapy, and (iii) agreement on the tasks undertaken in therapy to address the client's problems in living. This tells us that therapeutic tasks need to be aligned between therapist and client for the therapeutic alliance and collaborative relationship to work. Originally, the idea of 'tasks' was used in the development of pluralism to give a cross-theoretical understanding of what it is that is 'going on' in therapy. A conceptual challenge to this terminology has been that, in practice, the differentiation between a task and a method can be problematic, and it can be helpful to think about this in terms of what is being done (task) and how (method) (see Chapter 17). Additionally, sometimes the term 'task-list' can sound rather impersonal and in pluralistic practice therapists work so closely with the client meaning and preferences that the sense of prescribing activities can feel counter-intuitive. As a result of practice and experience in using the concept, it is fair to say that as the approach has evolved, so too has the meaning of 'task'. The term 'tasks' is now used to denote slightly different categories of understanding and activities in pluralistic therapy, sometimes they are used to aid therapists in understanding their role and the aspects of therapy that they have the potential to facilitate. Alongside this are the client-defined goal-related tasks, created during and following formulation (see Chapter 14), and used when therapists describe their practice in terms of what they were doing, why, and how. Finally, there are also task-lists which provide activity 'menus' for certain client groups.

As a result of these different uses of the term 'task', the term has been used to describe a range of different 'task-lists', one which gives an overview of the kinds of things that can happen in therapy also known as the *task-taxonomy* (Cooper and McLeod, 2011), one that defines activities

DOI: 10.4324/9781003305736-20

which therapists strive to achieve in order to establish and maintain the therapy – *maintenance tasks*, and *therapeutic task-lists* described for different presentations or client groups. Alongside this there are *goal-related tasks* linked to individual client formulations. Task-lists are a useful way of thinking about what we do and why, and help to develop shared ideas about things that might be useful to address in therapy, in addition to the development of specialist training. A standard task-list might contain generic counselling activities, some which are more directed towards a particular client group experience, with the aim of both facilitating the therapeutic environment and focusing client work. This chapter is going to give an overview of these.

The *task taxonomy* provides all therapists with a guide to typical therapy activities (Cooper and McLeod, 2011), it is not overly detailed, but categorises a variety of things that clients have found useful in therapy. It is written in an action-directed form which reflects the ways that these activities are about '*doing something to change something*' which can relate to a range of client goals and be brought about by different methods, these are:

- Meaning-making, developing insight and understanding.
- Making sense of a particular problematic experience.
- Problem-solving, planning and decision-making.
- Changing behaviour.
- Navigating a particular transition or developmental process.
- Dealing with difficult feelings and emotions.
- Finding, analysing, and acting on information.
- Undoing self-criticism and enhancing self-care.
- Dealing with difficult or painful relationships.

Given this useful summary of 'things that might be covered' a therapist can reflect on what they offer clients, how they bring these into the case formulation, and how they negotiate tasks with clients to fit their needs. So, when thinking about tasks during case formulation it is wise to focus on tasks which, whilst sitting within the task taxonomy (although not necessarily), link to the client's goals and preferences for ways of working. Remembering that not all tasks are defined in the early stages of therapy, and some can be emergent qualities of the work the therapist and client are doing together. This task-list can also be a useful starting point for considering the methods you have to offer a client (see 'Way of Intervening' in Appendix I).

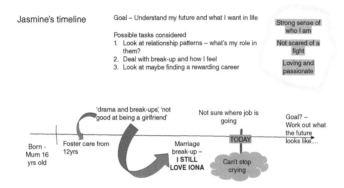

Figure 18.1 Emergent tasks from a case formulation

   The therapeutic tasks emerging from this formulation were discussed with the client and included looking at her relationship patterns (meaning-making), thinking of ways that her distress at the break-up of her marriage might be processed (dealing with difficult feelings and emotions), and looking at how she might like to move on in the future (planning and decision-making). These tasks could be undertaken through a variety of different methods according to therapist ways of working and client preferences, for example, Jasmine initially chose to look at relationship patterns, focusing on early life experiences and applying the idea that she had developed a relationship schema around how relationships function to her current responses and behaviour in relationships. As therapy proceeded, Jasmine's work environment changed and the decision to leave her job became the focus of the work, the task here was around decision-making for her future ambitions. Over time, Jasmine recognised that the influence of her cultural background had caused conflict in her internal understanding of her choices, the task focus then became her sense of identity which sat in disjoint with her career ambitions (making sense of a particular problematic experience). At this point the therapist turned to a task-list, looking at aspects of counselling that might be helpful for people working on developing, or challenging, their identity. Bringing this knowledge into the work helped the client and therapist discuss the possibilities available and recognise the potential depth and breadth of the therapeutic experience.
   Using tasks as a conceptual and practical device in pluralistic therapy, to help define and prioritise what clients find most useful in particular

circumstances, or with specific presenting issues, can catalyse conversations and also help the therapist to prepare when working with a particular client group. In a landscape of almost infinite ways of responding to client problems in living, task-lists are useful to understand the breadth of work that can be carried out and gives therapists some signposts as to how to help, aiding the meta-communication processes, and offered to clients like a menu of choices or simply a resource for ideas.

Task-lists highlight particular therapeutic activities which commonly occur with some client groups, but can also reflect the kinds of things that should be taken into consideration when developing a collaborative relationship with them. The development of task-lists stems from research establishing the client voice in exploring experiences of therapy alongside helpful events and preferences. In her work with the sight-loss community, pluralistic practitioner Mhairi Thurston (Thurston et al., 2013) developed a therapeutic task-list for clients seeking emotional support. Her research aimed to demonstrate the lived experience for this group, and showed that the following key areas were of importance to clients:

- Feeling understood.
- Expressing emotions around the loss of sight.
- Finding a new identity.
- Finding ways to cope with fear, loss, dependency, and other people's perceptions.
- Exploring the possibility of a positive future without sight.
- Making sense of things.
- Finding ways to become more socially connected.

In collaboration with medical services, and based on published research on the experiences of people living with the condition, Smith (unpublished) developed a task list to guide therapists working with people living with diabetes, using it to train point of contact NHS practitioners and therapists working with this group:

- Coming to terms with 'being diabetic'.
- Examining the impact of diabetes on relationships.
- Dealing with the emotional impact of diabetes.
- Looking at existential issues arising from living with diabetes.
- Managing the physical aspects of diabetes (including adjusting to the complications).

- Changing behaviour (including adherence to medication and physical activity).
- Dealing with loss and regret.
- Regulating eating and managing disordered eating.
- Addressing phobias, for example, needles.
- Navigating life transitions.

Similar work has been carried out by Weaks (2006) examining the therapeutic tasks that positively impact people with early-stage dementia and is included in Chapter 32. In his research and training for people working with bereavement, Wilson (2013, 2020) proposes tasks for clients experiencing loss.

- Making sense of events (surrounding the death).
- Making sense of thoughts, feelings, and behaviour.
- Coping day-to-day.
- Avoiding/overcoming rumination.
- Adapting to a world without the deceased in it.
- Forming a continuing bond with the deceased.

These kinds of task-lists, when used in practice, lead to useful ways of understanding or formulating problems and suggest methods and ways of working with the client. Task-lists engage conversations around therapist and client knowledge and understandings which, particularly for people dealing with health conditions, influence their interactions, for example, people with long-term medical conditions might tend to revert to the position of 'patient' and await guidance from the 'expert'. Task-lists also help guide aspects of relational working which might be offered up, for example, people with diabetes may benefit from coaching when working on adherence to medication, and may also need to have their anger about the enforcement of medical interventions recognised, accepted, and processed.

Ultimately, the evolving role and interpretation of the term 'tasks' has led to useful understandings and frameworks that support practice, which in turn allow conversations to be opened up about responsiveness and scope of practice.

19 What methods are used in pluralistic therapy and why?

Pluralistic therapy is not the wholesale application of particular schools or modalities of therapy, but a collaborative space where the therapeutic activities and methods are selected and used according to client needs and preferences. Rather than a client being introduced to the approaches *available and having their work focused, 'do you want us to do person-centered or CBT?' and limited to one modality over another because* it is the client's preference, pluralistic therapy operates through integration. To undertake this effectively, theories are dismantled into 'ideas and theoretical concepts', 'ways of working relationally' and 'methods'. In practice, the conceptual understanding of what is going on for the client is co-created and may bear little consistent relationship with any formal theories. As a result of this, the methods used in therapy are not directly linked to schools of thought but rather deployed in the context of what the client wants to address or change, and what method(s) might affect this change. The idea of methods and techniques being deployed is not a new one, and there are many useful resources available to aid a therapist in creating a portfolio of these (e.g. Rosenthal, 2011). It is important to note that core counselling skills are seen in all therapy interactions, but the emphasis on developing a shared understanding of the therapy process tends to lead to some methods being considered as discrete activities. Pluralistic therapists can sometimes feel the need to offer tangible methods, for example, worksheets, sculpting, value cards. However, it is helpful to think of counselling skills as 'methods we always use' such as listening, reflecting, immediacy, and challenging (as discussed in Chapter 13), and there are various other methods offered by therapists, depending on their competence and training, and the preferences of the client.

DOI: 10.4324/9781003305736-21

All pluralistic therapists will have a 'toolkit' of core skills and methods which they can draw from in practice, so it is helpful to have a guiding framework to think about the breadth of these. The pluralistic approach tends to rely on the concept of 'helpfulness' in terms of the activities and interventions offered, and therapist knowledge about these can help mitigate any overwhelming degree of optionality. By identifying nine categories of helpful aspects of therapy, Timulak's (2007) analysis of research regarding client experiences provides therapists with a possible guiding framework for method options, as well as for the overall character of the collaboration. In later work he revises this list to add two more factors (points 10 and 11 depicted in italics in the following list), which can be linked to a strengths-based attitude and the pluralistic concept of client empowerment (Timulak and McElvaney, 2013). Usually, any therapist would have some method(s) which allow them to undertake the following activities in therapy:

1. Increasing awareness, insight, and self-understanding.
2. Improving behavioural change and problem-solving skills.
3. Empowerment.
4. Relief/catharsis.
5. Exploring feelings and enhancing emotional awareness.
6. Feeling understood by the therapist.
7. Being involved in the therapy.
8. Feeling reassured, supported, and safe.
9. Experiencing personal contact with the therapist.
10. *Psychoeducation.*
11. *Sense of problem-mastery.*

The methods offered by different therapists tends to reflect their own skills, training, and preference for continued practice development. To illustrate this, some methods are outlined in the following text with details of when they might be offered in practice and an overview of how they are undertaken. It's important to recognise that these are just small examples from of a wealth of therapeutic methods that can be undertaken, and are written from the perspective of the author of this section (Kate). The main point of this is to try and help an understanding of how methods might be conceptualised in a framework of useful activities in response to the client.

Letter writing - In therapy, letter writing is part of a broader field involving 'expressive writing' which includes purposeful writing practices for a variety of mental health benefits (Pennebaker and Evans, 2014; Pert, 2013). The example here draws on the work of narrative therapists Micheal White and David Epston (1990). I tend to use letter writing to help crystalise ideas, sometimes thoughts and feelings get buried in the process of living, and it can be helpful for clients to retain an artifact which captures a particular moment in time. The way I introduce this approach is to reflect on the importance of recognising progress or a particular meaning-making process which has impacted on the client (usually in a positive way). I offer to the client that they might like to think about pausing to write a letter to themselves, or sometimes to a person who the client is close to or has had a loving role in their lives like a grandparent, to articulate what has happened and what it means to them. The letter can be drafted in the session – often I work in a free-style bullet-point way, asking the client *'what would you put in there?'*, and then the client can write the letter in their own time (to-date all clients have brought back what they have written to share it with me). This method aids insight, empowerment, and tends to bring emotional relief through catharsis.

Empty-chair - With its origins in Gestalt therapy, empty chair, and related activities such as two-chair work, involves the therapist facilitating and supporting an enactment using the language and behaviour of the client to better understand their 'in the moment' experience and the boundary between parts of self, self and other, or self and context (Kellog, 2015; Kolmanskog, 2018). Empty chair work is a method I use when a client is experiencing a sense of being silenced or frustration at inexpression. This can be for various reasons, but often the silencing is something that is imposed, for example, the person who needs to receive the communication is no longer in the client's life or the client wishes to avoid the potential impact of the disclosure. The method is also useful as a form of rehearsal for the 'real' conversation which might come later. I tend to plan the conversation in the session prior to trying it out, and I start by saying why it might be beneficial, for example, *it might be helpful to get the words out somehow, to take ourselves through the conversation and give you the opportunity to say what you want to say in this room so you can see how it feels*, and then talk about how we might go about it, how we set up the room, and how the client might imagine the person there (e.g. what are they wearing, what might their expression be, how they might respond), before making a plan for how the next session might be timed. I do this both to give a sense of structure and safety to the activity, but also so the client can reflect between sessions to consider if this will be helpful, I find this helps to balance my interventions with client preference as, for me, it can feel a bit bossy. Some clients return the next week fully invested, some change their minds, whilst on one occasion the client had completed the activity on their own and just told me how it went. The kinds of things people say can be wide ranging, but often they have something they need the person to know or have questions they would like to have answers for. The post-chair work reflections can pick up on these aspects, but the key insight is usually something about how it felt to be in the moment.

Window of tolerance - This is common in trauma-focused work and is a method used to help clients understand their experience and a way to ensure that what is explored in therapy is neither kept too safe, with aspects of experience unexplored and unaddressed, nor that the process is too emotionally challenging, potentially re-traumatising or triggering the client. Originally developed by Dan Siegel to recognise a space of optimal everyday arousal and emotional functioning for people who had experienced childhood trauma (Corrigan et al., 2011; Siegel, 1999), the concept is used to monitor the arousal of clients in therapy, to help them self-monitor and act as a framework for work which helps them maintain function within the window. I use this in practice when clients either report or present with what seems to be erratic or excessive distress and emotionality or that they experience anhedonia, a lack of response, or even dissociation associated with traumatic experiences. I try and give an accessible explanation (based on Siegel's theory), using examples from what the client has shared or how they have presented, and talk about steps we can take in therapy to observe this. Meta-communication is vital here as we shift from an observing perspective to being embedded in the client experience. Progressing from this, I work with the client on aspects which help them to learn how to be aware of the window of tolerance by themselves and act to manage it effectively. This involves conversations, practical steps, and psychoeducation in:

1. Aiding clients in recognising when they are outside their window of tolerance.
2. Supporting clients in shifting from hyper- or hypo-arousal.
3. Helping them to learn techniques to master their own ability to shift back into their window, for example, grounding or counting breaths.

4. Thinking of ways that might help the window get wider, for example, mindfulness-based activities or practicing tolerance of emotions.

It's important to remember that the use of these methods sits within the collaborative relationship, and the effectiveness of them is likely to rely heavily on this foundation. There are countless practice methods which might be helpful for clients, and practitioners often draw on their primary and secondary training experiences, for example, methods coming from acceptance and commitment therapy; self-compassion; emotional-focusing techniques; mindfulness; projective techniques; core themes and life-scripts, and rescripting activities. The important thing to remember is that what is done in practice is not reliant on sticking to a theory or approach in therapy, but rather draws on ideas from different theories to find things that work. More examples of a therapist's 'toolkit' can be found in Appendix I where Frankie has created her 'Ways Paradigm' based on the work by Cheston (2000), which can be a helpful tool to start thinking about your own available methods (Ways of Intervening).

20 How do pluralistic therapists monitor the process of therapy and whether the client's goals are being met?

Have you ever been told a joke where the punchline, instead of being 'clever', was staring you in the face? The reason these jokes might raise a smile, if not an eyeroll and groan, is because the punchline is obvious, yet the recipient of the joke will often overthink the question, ignoring the obvious. The same could be said for the question, 'How do you know when your client is getting "better"?', the answer, 'you ask them'. Whilst the 'punchline' might seem obvious, some therapists don't ask their client's how they are experiencing the process of therapy or if it is helping them to meet their goals. Instead, they might rely on observational changes in the client's behaviour, emotions, or thinking, noticing that the client has better relationships with others and in life, is beginning to reduce medication, or a professional alters their diagnosis. Whilst all of these, in part, are true and worth considering as evidence, therapists are not as good as they think they are at reading when clients are getting better (Lambert, 2013), the reasons for their changes, or why they wish to terminate therapy (Hunsley et al., 1999). As such, it is imperative that we look to the client for answers, and we can glean this information through an ongoing process of feedback.

There is a need in pluralistic therapy to understand a client's purpose and hopes for therapy, and to closely monitor how well the work is meeting these needs. This is conducted through direct meta-communication and feedback, along with the use of process and outcome reporting documents. Although clients are usually reticent about providing feedback to therapists, pluralistic practice infuses therapy with communicative opportunities aimed at ensuring that the client is empowered to get their needs and preferences met. These are discussed within this chapter in terms of outcome, process and preference measures (examples of which can be found in Appendix II), goals forms, and communication.

DOI: 10.4324/9781003305736-22

Outcome measures – These tend to be population specific and based on ratings of predetermined questions on factors such as mood, function, and risk. Outcome measures typically allow both an evaluation of the client's well-being and a comparison between them and 'average' client outcomes. This information can be used to examine the effectiveness, or impact of interventions, providing the client and therapist with 'off track' alerts which allows therapy to adjust to better meet the needs of the client. Outcome measures have a growing body of evidence finding that clients are less likely to deteriorate and more likely to improve when utilising them, and that even *'slight improvements can reassure skeptical clients that they are making recognizable progress in treatment and further improve the therapeutic alliance'* (Boswell et al., 2013, p. 3). Furthermore, outcome measures can help the therapist and client to identify strengths and interventions that aid the client, areas to improve, or experiences that are unhelpful to the client's well-being or therapy. Clients who are visually improving on the outcome measures are typically meeting their goals although there needs to be caution applied, that therapy does not become a number drive to get a better 'score' or 'result' – the measure needs to be meaningful for a client and, insofar as possible, be a true reflection of how the client is feeling (Evans, 2012).

Process measures – These move away from the clients' goals, and generic measures of well-being, towards the process of therapy in order to ascertain if the client is satisfied with the therapy, including factors of agreement on goals, methods, and the working relationship. Although research recognises the importance of client factors in the change process, characteristics of the working alliance have also been shown to be positively correlated with improved client outcomes (Duncan, 2015). In essence, it will be more difficult for a client to achieve their goals if they do not have a good working relationship with the therapist, in which they feel respected and heard, and can work on what they want, in the manner that they prefer. It is therefore essential that we understand how clients experience the process and adjust therapy to suit their needs. This is naturally not a perfect system and, on the rare occasions we cannot adjust, a discussion might ensue about whether the client wishes to be referred to a therapist who can better meet their needs (see Chapter 44) – for example, a client who wants CBT and yet the therapist has no training, or a therapist who struggles to hear their client's grief as they are recently bereaved themselves. It is important not to underestimate the strength of incorporating a measure of process, as much as we aim to create a collaborative 'shared-expertise' space, there is an unavoidable power imbalance created through the exchange of money, the location of therapy, perceptions of education and class, and the very fact that there is a 'helper' and 'help-seeker' (see Chapter 31). Whilst we can verbally ask about their experience of the process, providing a space that the client can silently reflect and answer can aid the client in expressing areas they might like to change through a 'low-risk' platform.

Preference measures – Further useful tools to understand if a client is meeting their goals, and having a positive experience of therapy, lie within the idea of 'preference accommodation' in pluralistic therapy, and preference measures help uncover and work constructively with these. Research states that clients appreciate being asked about their choices (Vollmer et al., 2009) and that those who receive their preferred therapy are more likely to meet their outcomes, state their have a stronger alliance with their therapist, and are less likely to drop out of therapy (Swift and Callahan, 2009; McLeod, 2012). However, the aspects of therapy that clients might have preferences on are complex, ranging from who the therapist is, how they behave, or their role, to treatment preferences [such as cost, interventions, belief about the problem]. Enquiring about these preferences empowers a client to express their desires and wishes for therapy, reducing their silent expectations and, even when preferences cannot be met, the exploration of these can be valuable. Like process measures, preferences can be difficult to articulate due to the power imbalance or simply because the client did not know their preference until they experienced something (Tompkins et al., 2013). Therefore incorporating tools can aid the therapist in meeting and addressing preferences, and discussing those that might be difficult to meet, which ultimately supports the client and therapist to develop a trusting relationship and facilitates collaboration (Bowen and Cooper, 2012). Further discussion of preferences can be found in Chapter 22.

Goals forms – The use of self-report goals forms can be regarded merely as a tool to record information (Cooper and Law, 2018), enabling the client (and therapist) to formalise and work towards the client's goals, and enable effective monitoring of whether the client is becoming closer to achieving these. However, recording goals aids the client and therapist to direct the focus and attention into the efforts (tasks) that will help the client achieve their goals (Cooper, 2018) and is thought, through the identification of such goals, to enhance outcome, hope, empowerment, and motivation (Lloyd et al., 2019; Tryon et al., 2018) and provide '*rituals or moments of social interaction*' (Cooper and Law, 2018, p. 24).

Communication – We understand that collaboration, through the use of meta-communication and shared decision making, is important for client satisfaction, motivation and confidence (Bachelor et al., 2007; Ahmad et al., 2014), and can aid change (Cooper et al., 2015). Therefore, not only should we collaboratively engage in utilising these tools, providing information, and seeking to understand their perspective, but we should also use these tools to explore the client's lived experience, supporting a conversation – '*The process of talking to clients about what they want from therapy, and how they think they may be most likely to achieve it*' (Cooper and McLeod, 2012, p. 7). Whether through the use of forms or not, keeping an open channel of dialogue supports the therapist in receiving moment-by-moment feedback about what the client wants (goal), how the client is feeling (outcome), their experience of the therapy (process), and what they would like therapy to be like (preference), which respects and values the client. Commenting on the impact or intention of what was, or is, said allows the speaker and client to be 'seen' allowing transparency which fosters collaboration and shared decision making. Meta-therapeutic communication serves to help the therapist align, and re-align, with the client on their goals, tasks, and methods, 'allowing' themselves to be 'corrected' by feedback. This initially minimises ruptures and aids any reparation work necessary, which reduces the potential for premature ending (McLeod, 2018a). Furthermore, whilst some therapists are required by their service to complete forms with their clients, and it is important that they try and understand the value of these tools, communication support the use of collaborative sharing of information rather than it being a 'bureaucratic' function.

Requesting feedback from clients, both verbally and non-verbally, asks a lot from the therapist and client, and therapists should utilise supervision, education, and reflexivity to overcome these barriers (more of which are discussed in Chapter 21), and to consider the impact on clients. It requires a client to have the ability to mentally conceptualise their perceptions and experiences, aggregate 'scores' across a week or session, translate experiences outside of therapy into therapy preferences, and have the courage in voicing what they do, and do not, like. Therapists can support clients in the use of these tools and communication styles through conveying warmth, acceptance, prizing the client's views, and openness to learning from the client. Additionally, providing the client with information and support as to how to use the tools, or prompting them to communicate in therapy, and why these might be important to their work together, is essential to gain informed consent, transparency, and buy-in from the client. It is also important to let clients know that these methods are optional, and the therapist should stop if they are interfering with the process of therapy or the client meeting their goals (Sundet, 2012). Having said that, the only way we can really know if it is hindering the client's therapy is to ask the client!

21 I know I have a block to using feedback measures, want to help me?

There are a number of ways that we undertake feedback in pluralistic therapy, including open dialogue and meta-communication, idiographic and nomothetic outcome scales (e.g. Outcome Rating Scales, Miller et al., 2003, and Goal forms, Jacob et al., 2018), well-being measures (e.g. CORE, Evans et al., 2003), and process monitoring forms (e.g. session-rating scales, Miller et al., 2003 and helpful and unhelpful aspects HAT, Llewelyn, 1988) (see Appendix II). We know that as therapists, we are not very good at understanding when our clients are getting better, but we also know that even those therapists who say they 'check in' and seek feedback regularly actually don't in practice (Miller et al., 2008). Feedback can provide us with important information about client preferences, their experience of the therapeutic process, and how they believe they are doing, and research into outcome and process measures shows that clients are more likely to improve when we explore these aspects of therapy (Miller et al., 2008). More evidence and exploration of the use of feedback can be found in Chapter 20. However, if you already know why we *should* be using feedback and are still struggling, then it might be important to explore some of the common barriers and how to overcome these.

Barriers to feedback

The first barrier to getting good feedback is often the therapist themselves. Research indicates that therapists generally believe they already know the information, whether intended or not this is an unhelpful barrier to engaging with systems that provide feedback, and comes from a position whereby the therapist is implicitly the expert. I am going to leave this to one side for the moment as this is not a characteristic of being a pluralistic practitioner, and there is lots of information through-out this book that can help practitioners to recognise the need to be flexible and collaborative with their clients.

However, therapists are also concerned that through engaging with feedback, they, or their clients, will be assessed on their work – a sense of fearing 'big brother' (Boswell et al., 2013). It is therefore under-standable that therapists might feel initially anxious and resistant to the concept of asking clients for feedback and may distance themselves from the use of formal feedback measures due to a concern about being judged (Unsworth et al., 2011). Standardised measures were not created to make individual judgements on therapist competence, and this is not how they should be implemented. In acknowledging that the majority of client change is from their own motivation and life factors (Duncan et al., 2004), one cannot simply say 'the client didn't change, you are a bad therapist'. Nonetheless, this shared fear of judgement can place the client in a position of deference to the 'expert' therapist telling them therapy is great! We explore power in Chapter 31, but it can be helpful to reassure the client that there is no right or wrong answer, it is merely aiding the therapist in knowing how to best help.

Sundet (2012) also discusses cultural and linguistic differences that can interfere with how a client interprets feedback invitations, for example, some cultures practice deference to 'authority' or doctor-like figures as a sign of respect. Conversely, others might 'put-down' their experience of therapy in order to create distance, as a way to discharge pain, or to keep the relationship from becoming emotionally close. None of this is 'bad' or the client 'lying'; this is the client's tool to express what is happening for them and if we can meet them there then we can explore ways out of it together. It is also important to use feed-back that meets the client's cultural and language needs.

Accepting and internalising feedback – 'is it me?'

Perhaps the feedback reflects a therapist factor, maybe the client doesn't feel heard and supported, or they had preferred someone different [age, gender, ethnicity, modality, experience], therapists can fear being per-sonally judged by the client, 'What if they don't like me?', and to put it bluntly, it might be true. Even as therapists we do not click with everyone;

some people's behaviour irks us and sometimes we know it is not about them, but something just gets under our skin (hello transference!). If this happens to us as trained professionals, why would it not be okay for it to be true for our clients? Whilst it might not necessarily be about you personally, it is a barrier that needs to be addressed and there are other counsellors who might be a better fit (see Chapter 44 for referrals).

But for a moment, let's say it is a 'you' thing; you speak when the client wants silence, you address the past when they want to work on the future, and you keep telling the client about yourself and they don't want to know . . . is it not worth finding this information out so we can change and be 'better' at therapy for this client? There are two considerations which might help you to do this, firstly, it is useful to recognise that a client will have preferences for how they want their therapy, and therapist, to be in the room and we know that if clients get what they want they are more likely to have successful therapy outcomes (Swift and Callahan, 2009). It is also important to separate your behaviour from the whole of you, so if you keep checking the clock and the client thinks they are boring you, that does not cancel out all the times you listen, empathise, and care – one part does not make the whole – but it is something to pay attention to. The client can provide us with some really useful insights (Boswell et al., 2013) about our behaviour and our internal processes which can further our personal and professional development, if we choose to use it.

Using feedback to improve client work

Honest feedback is likely to challenge us, and therapists can feel anxious that they might have to change the way they work in response to feedback (Unsworth et al., 2011). Whilst therapists may fear this situation, we would argue that changing, just enough to meet a client where they are at, can help us to 'do better therapy', sometimes clients just need to experience a therapist striving to help, even if the therapist is unable to meet their exact preferences. On the other hand, it is worth mentioning that there is also a risk of therapists 'over-molding' to try and meet client preferences (Bowen and Cooper, 2012), disrupting the relationship. So, whilst feedback measures can provide us with the best opportunity to spot clients who are not benefitting from therapy, offering us a chance to recognise and address these factors with the client, it is important that therapists and clients take due care to honour and consider the feedback in light of all other available information, in order to make decisions about what actions to take, or not.

In cases where the therapist might not be able, or willing, to meet preferences (such as increasing self-disclosure), or in situations where the feedback seems to reflect the client's internal or cultural processes, this raises an opportunity for communicating with the client and to tentatively introduce what might be playing out.

- *I notice you mark me very positively every week on all areas, thank you for this. However, I also know we cannot be perfect ALL of the time, for instance last week I interrupted you a bit, and I am wondering if we could discuss what the feedback means to you, and our relationship?*
- *I really appreciated your feedback last week, you were really open in saying you did not feel I respected you when I had to end the session at our agreed time but you were talking. I am wondering if this feeling is familiar in other parts of your life or therapy?*

These examples demonstrate how feedback can be used to strengthen the relationship, and perhaps lead to insight around the client's experience outside therapy, indeed client's themselves state that discussions with the therapist about feedback were 'therapeutic' (Unsworth et al., 2011). This is contrary to what many counsellors believe, fearing measures will disrupt the work, with clients either refusing or disliking the use of forms, and the risk they can therefore harm the therapeutic alliance (Miller et al., 2003; Boswell et al., 2013). In fact, clients value the chance to be heard and particularly like the use of visual methods to see their progress (Unsworth et al., 2011). But the ability to use these tools, in a therapeutic way, requires time to learn the craft with an ability to engage in research and reflexivity in choosing the right tool (Boswell et al., 2013).

Developing skills in working with feedback

Training can develop the skill in, and comfort with, seeking feedback. It was found that, as therapists became more at ease with feedback measures, they began to creatively adapt to using the forms to meet the client, and relational, needs, further finding that measures were a helpful and supportive tool in safeguarding their clients (Unsworth et al., 2011). Feedback can form a natural part of therapy, through conversation or by taking a few minutes to complete measures, providing clients with the best chance of successful therapy, which naturally has a knock-on effect on our professional (and personal) sense of efficacy and esteem. We would contend that the barriers therapists face, although normal, can be worked through with reflexivity, supervision, training, and speaking with the client. However, therapists must be willing to seek the client's perspective, be open and non-defensive to what they have to say – even if (especially if) it is 'negative' – and be able to respond appropriately. It is these core therapist attributes that will create stronger therapeutic relationships with increased collaboration, and thus successful therapeutic outcomes (Timulak and Keogh, 2017).

22 How do I work with clients preferences if they don't know what they are?

Through a growing body of research, we have come to understand that attending to client preferences supports a collaborative relationship, satisfaction with treatment (Lindhiem et al., 2014; Vollmer et al., 2009), client engagement, and outcomes (Swift and Callahan, 2009). Furthermore, it is considered to be part of an evidence based (Swift et al., 2010) ethical practice (O'Neill, 1998). With the advancement in technology, cultural discussion of mental health, and increased uptake in those who utilise mental health supports, there is also a greater awareness of what is on offer in terms of therapy and a therapist's role. Ultimately this means clients are often well-informed when entering counselling, with understandings about why they are struggling and what their therapy might look like, and these expectations, beliefs, and hopes can build into therapy preferences. Whilst we might think of preferences as simply being a 'greater liking for one thing over another', therapy preferences are far from simple and can often be quite complex, not easily mapping onto theoretical models (McLeod, 2015). Additionally, preferences can be *implicit*, just out of conscious awareness only surfacing through experience, *competing*, whereby two or more preferences jostle to be met such as wanting to work on the past and the present, and our preferences can *contradict* each other – perhaps a desire for CBT alongside a preference not to do homework.

Expectations or beliefs about therapy can also clash with preferences, for example, from television shows a client might come to expect a therapist to be neutral, a blank canvas, and this might be perceived to be the way therapists work, but the client themselves might prefer the therapist to engage and disclose a bit about themselves, but how would they know this unless they can expand their imagined therapist from the stock-image provided by the media. It will be difficult to name this as a preference if this approach has not been previously experienced, and

DOI: 10.4324/9781003305736-24

the therapist has not offered this style as an option. For this reason, some clients, and therapists, sometimes believe that clients *don't always know what they want*. Whilst there are aspects of this statement which could be agreed with, we would contend that through experience and making the implicit explicit, clients can know what they want. It is important to consider that clients have had many years to understand themselves, and multiple interactions with many people of varying characteristics, engaging in diverse activities [friendships, parenting, education, healthcare, reflection] in which to build up a knowledge of what they like and what they don't like. If therapists can tap into this pool of knowledge, then they have a base to start exploring preferences. Exploring and punctuating pivotal moments of a clients life can help to discover vital preference clues, through asking direct questions (Q) as well as reflections (R) which could include the following examples:

- Q: Have you had counselling/mental health support before? What was helpful/unhelpful? R: It sounds as if you found it helpful, when you were really ill, and they took the decision out of your hands.
- Q: What was your experience of school/education? What did you like/dislike? R: I see you shifting uncomfortably when we mention being tested.
- Q: What was your experience of learning [visual, auditory, kinaesthetic, reading, writing]? R: I notice you talk more enthusiastically about practical subjects where you tried things for yourself.
- Q: What are your interests and hobbies? Would any of these be useful to use now? R: If you enjoy reading, I could recommend some books that might be helpful.
- [When a client names an experience] Q: What did you like/dislike about that? R: That sounded scary.
- [When a client names a relational style] Q: Would you say that was helpful/unhelpful? R: It seems you liked it when people challenged you in the past.

Furthermore, we can begin to verbalise how we typically work and interact. A pluralistic therapist might discuss with the client that they look for the clients thoughts and feelings about different activities (feedback), and this means that they are likely to comment more on what is happening in the room to understand the clients meaning and what is helpful or unhelpful (meta-communication). Pluralistic therapists also explain the importance of knowing where they are heading together (goals), finding different ways to get there, partly through offering a menu of options (tasks and methods) and usually the therapist likes to explore these with the client (collaboration). Upon discussing the pluralistic process, the therapist will seek to understand the clients thoughts and feelings about these aspects, all of which begins to build a list of preferences.

It is also important to recognise that before clients even begin therapy, they may have already identified some of their therapy, therapist, and practical preferences including gender, expertise, age, ethnicity, language, location, time, and cost. However, it is also acknowledged that we cannot have it all and some preferences clash – for example, a client may want drama therapy, but this type of therapy is not offered in their local area – and so clients compromise on one preference for a greater need/preference. For others, preference consideration is limited as they access mental health supports through low-cost or community-based programmes who are under increased restrictions to deliver services in a timely cost-efficient manner. Discussing what the client had hoped for, even when it is not possible to meet the clients preference, can help a client to feel valued and may also start to build a knowledge bridge. A further example may be that the client had hoped for an older counsellor because they equate age with experience and wisdom, through discussing their expectations and hopes in more detail, and offering relevant self-disclosure, the counsellor can demonstrate the life experience and knowledge they do have, which might meet their more nuanced preferences. Yet there will always be unmet preferences (Tompkins et al., 2013), such as a different gender, on these occasions a client can discuss with the therapist what that preference meant to them and how they might work together without this preference being met.

Some pluralistic therapists also incorporate preference measures in their work (see Chapter 20), as a tool to aid the client in thinking about their therapy preferences and to facilitate a conversation between the therapist and client as to what can, and cannot, be met and how they might work together. Commonly used tools include the Cooper-Norcross Inventory of Preferences (C-NIP (Cooper and Norcross, 2016), the Therapy Personalisation Form (TPF (Bowen and Cooper, 2012)) or a Treatment Preference Interview (Vollmer et al., 2009), which can help to understand a clients pre-therapy preferences or, at review, to ascertain if the therapy is suiting them, for example, do they feel sufficiently challenged? Do they wish to know more about what the therapist is thinking? And, importantly, are they working on the goals they wish to in an effective way? As well as therapist traits and practical arrangements, important preferences involve the purpose of therapy [e.g. whether the client wishes to discuss the past, present, or future, or if the client prefers more emotional or cognitive based work], relational style [e.g. support, humour, challenging, structured] and therapy activities [e.g. teaching, goal setting, homework, expression of emotion, self-help, silence]. Whilst these provide the client useful and important clues about how therapy can be done, it is important to note that no preference is static, many are context and relationship specific, and it would be irresponsible to blindly adhere to every preference. It is important to honour and respect client preferences and consider these in light of the client-therapist relationship and the expressed goals and open these up for discussion.

> *Lucas, originally from the Netherlands, was 57 when he entered therapy and wanted help with his depression which featured a high degree of negative thinking. He reported that he grew up in a verbally abusive home where he was called names and silenced when he tried to argue back. He then entered a relationship with an alcoholic partner who, when under the influence, would also verbally abuse him and at times give him 'the silent treatment'. Lucas and his therapist had already discussed the need to check-in when silence was used, and this was working well. However, at a review session Lucas reported that he wanted the counsellor to challenge him more, the counsellor, being experienced in challenging, considered that she challenged Lucas frequently but in an empathic and supportive manner. In clarifying what Lucas was looking for (a blunt, interruptive style), the counsellor agreed she could try, although there were two points for them to consider, one was that the therapist's own style was gentler and she was not sure she would be true to herself if she was blunt, and secondly the therapist also noted that all of Lucas's life he had been challenged and interrupted, so the therapist wondered if that had almost become what he expected of relationships. Through this discussion, Lucas verbalised that he worried about what the counsellor really thought of him when she was being nice, and they agreed it might be important to continue with a gentler challenging style but with Lucas voicing his worries more frequently.*

In identifying preferences with clients, it is also recognised that many of these preferences become apparent after the fact, and some clients can find it difficult to name their preferences (Tompkins et al., 2013), it is therefore important that we attend to verbal and non-verbal cues during therapy. Cues from a client might include comments, '*that was a good session*', or, '*it's not really me*', whereas non-verbal information might occur in the form of sitting back, folding their arms, moving from an emotional to cognitive position or resistant to engage with agreed techniques or activities. Encouraging the client to provide more details as to their experiences begins to help the client to understand and share their preferences.

- What challenges did you have in completing the homework?
- When you say it was a good session, what did you find useful?
- Do you see any benefit/obstacles in doing this [exercise/activity/ intervention]?
- What was is like doing that [exercise/activity/intervention]?
- What do you think would need to change to make this [exercise/ activity/intervention] more helpful?

Session evaluation tools, which measure the process of therapy as well as the relationship, such as the Helpful Aspects of Therapy (HAT Llewelyn, 1988), Working Alliance Inventory (WAI Horvath and Greenberg, 1989), and the Session Rating Scale (SRS Duncan et al., 2003) (see Chapter 20) can also support the therapist and client in timely discussions and an honest appraisal of their experience (see Appendix II for more information). Whilst many therapists are competent and comfortable in discussing these preferences verbally, some clients are not, and may be fearful about providing this level of feedback, fearing judgment or offending the therapist. Therapists can also fear feedback with a feeling of 'getting it wrong' and may experience a time pressure within a session (see Chapter 21). From the outset of therapy, it is important to place feedback and preferences within a collaborative culture – it is not a 'right' or 'wrong' scenario, we all like and dislike different things at different times, and the more information a therapist has about the clients preference, the more they will be able to give the client what they need/want.

23 Why, and how, do pluralistic therapists use extra-therapeutic and cultural resources?

The focus on cultural resources in pluralistic therapy stems from the historic professionalisation of responses to 'disorders' and distress. Psychotherapists, along with other mental health professionals, have become designated wardens for the psychological aspects of health – be that the distress which ensues from diabetes or depression. Whilst doctors attended to the biological needs and religious figures and government attended to social aspects of living, psychotherapists' primary aim was, and is, to reduce problems in living and aid clients to be able to function. Many models have neglected to recognise the rich lived experience of clients within society and failed to incorporate resources of support, the enjoyment necessary for satisfaction in living, and actualisation of potential, even whilst the problems in living might exist. Disregarding this aspect of a client's world is particularly concerning when we consider that up to 86% of client change is because of client factors or life factors – not therapist effect (Duncan, 2015). Current models of wellbeing, both within psychology and health, look toward a more holistic view of what it is to be human, taking a bio-psycho-social view of problems in living. Whilst Shukla (2022) argues that humanistic-existential theories can serve to support therapist's understanding of a strengths-based perspective, pluralism helps both the therapist and client conceptualise problem resolution in this context and contends that cultural or extra-therapeutic resources are part of the 'Commons' – '*the great variety of natural, physical, social, intellectual and cultural resources that make our everyday survival possible*' (Nonini, 2006 p. 164). The Commons movement criticises the traditional 'Psy' practices for privileging 'expert' understandings of distress, which they state has professionalised resources such as empathy and positive regard and eroded 'lay' healing of self and others (Walker et al., 2017).

DOI: 10.4324/9781003305736-25

It is important to consider that our clients, have survived many adversities, 'life battles', and traumas, either currently or in the past, without intervention or treatment, and typically this is due to a combination of strength based psychological factors and cultural resources. Cultures and communities are steeped in traditions and strategies utilising stories, places, objects, art, music, work, sport, and people (McLeod, 2005) to aid healing. These resources range from grieving rituals to pain and fever relief and, with the advent of technology, support and remedies are at the click of a button. Jorm and colleagues (2004) discuss that the types of self-help and cultural resources vary depending on experiences of distress; they reported an intensification of daily activities such as exercise and seeing friends and family when the distress is mild, to seeing changes in dietary habits (alcohol, caffeine, vitamins) and activities such as massage and music when there is mild-moderate distress, before engaging professional help (doctors, medication and counselling) once the distress is severe. This research indicates that counselling is not the first option for emotional well-being, but that there are a range of other activities which are preferred in the first instance, and before distress gets too bad. For pluralistic therapists, these cultural resources are vital to the therapy process. The work of Jorm and colleagues also indicated that although 'every-day' self-help strategies, such as exercise and enjoyable activities, initially increase with mild distress they then decrease once the depressive symptoms become severe. However, Marley (2011) found that self-help did not decrease with the severity of distress and could be employed throughout all stages. What both of these studies highlight is the importance of 'things that people do' in response to challenges to their mental well-being. Furthermore, cultural resources can also be a protective factor (Wang et al., 2020). It is therefore important to consider that therapists who ignore these factors are attempting to start from 'ground zero' rather than exploring how their clients keep well, what they do if problems in living occur, and how successful their attempts are.

Pluralistic therapists consider that for clients to achieve their goals, a space should be cultivated that not only honours existing or prior cultural resources but also actively seeks to employ these to enhance therapeutic outcomes. This striving can be influential at different stages and in different ways during the therapy process, and involves the therapist's ability to recognise, acknowledge and harness client cultural resources and strengths (Sparks and Duncan, 2016b), which also promotes hope.

This requires the therapist's ear to be attuned to accomplishments, moments when the problem didn't exist, people who support the client, and may include asking informal questions or punctuating strengths and resources, particularly at the assessment stage, and during moments of opportunity:

- How did you get through that?

    - Did anybody else help?
    - What is it about you personally that kept going?
    - Were there any activities or belongings that helped?

- What do you enjoy doing?
- Given 'x' is your goal/I hear you want 'x', is there anything/anyone that would be important in helping you achieve this?
- Are there times now, or in the past, that you don't feel as anxious/ sad/angry?

    - Is there anything that you are doing differently at these times?

- Is there anything that you think would help but you haven't tried yet?[1]

Pluralistic therapists will often map the client's resources and strengths whilst formulating a timeline, or case conceptualisation (see Chapter 15). This can be a powerful technique that allows the client to visually see the impact that resources and personal strengths have had on their ability to cope with their problems in living, as well as to identify barriers which they have experienced in their ability to engage with these. Often this process can effectively reframe their view of their current striving and potential without diminishing their current sense of 'stuckness' and distress. Over time, monitoring the growth and potential of the actions stemming from the client can provide a powerful sense of achievement – a 'hero' story. Outcome measures can also provide a useful opportunity to explore extra-therapeutic resources and strengths asking, *'what helped?'* and *'can you do more of it?'* when things are going well, listening to *'what changed?'*, and the potential absence of resources that were being utilised, when things get worse. In effect the therapist and client build a 'bank' of resources that the client can tap

---

1 Marley (2011) notes people in her study were slow to engage in new self-help strategies.

into outside of a 50-minute therapy session, and dependent on their needs at a given time. Other useful interventions include conducting a strengths-based inquiry, verbally or with worksheets or value cards, or exploring how they think others cope with similar problems in living. The therapist might offer any number of interventions to review strengths however, with the client's permission, it is important to be able to regularly and seamlessly reflect and punctuate strengths in order to create a new strengths-based narrative about their life, that the client has potentially not explored.

Once a bank of resources is established, the client and therapist can collaboratively draw from it to support and empower the client, both in and out of therapy. Using resources inside therapy might also include the therapist inviting the client to utilise self-healing activities as part of therapy to aid skills in regulation, exploration, and reflection, to name a few (see Chapter 24 for more). In considering the power of this technique for yourself, have you ever had a song, painting, or poem that 'spoke' about your own private pain or joy in ways that you could not articulate? Imagine being able to share this with your therapist whereby it can become a metaphor or symbol, sometimes words alone do not do justice to the human experience. However, some clients think that using their passion and resources to aid therapy can mar them, and it can become 'work' rather than 'fun' and so they prefer to keep them separate. Ultimately though, supporting clients in making use of their extra-therapeutic resources enables them to self-heal for the 10,030 minutes they are not in counselling each week, which can continue for a lifetime.

24 Can you tell me more about creative and artistic activities in pluralistic therapy?

There is a rich tradition of the use of arts-based therapies including work using visual and physical arts, movement and bodywork, puppetry and drama, dance, music, writing, and poetry (De Witte et al., 2021). Recently, a specifically pluralistic approach to group-based arts work for people with depression has been developed (Karkou et al., 2022; Omylinska-Thurston et al., 2021; Parsons et al., 2020), and how to work pluralistically using sand-trays has been explored (Fleet, 2022). The benefits that creative expression, art therapies and activities bring to clients and practitioners should not be underestimated and, whilst a review of the possibilities is beyond the scope of our book (see Vaculik and Nash, 2022a, for a contemporary integrative approach to this), this chapter aims to bridge the gap between these and offer a broad understanding to support a practitioner in infusing art-based techniques or methods into their work.

One of the achievements of pluralistic therapy is that it presents an opportunity for creative working because a fundamental aspect to the approach is that, once something is mutually agreed, understood, and embedded within ethical practice for the good of the client, then nothing is off limits. The process of co-creation of unique experiences and meaning can occur throughout therapy, but arts-based therapies are shown to be particularly effective for processes of change through the creation of metaphors, representations, and activities that can be used to understand the client experience and their story through embodied experience (De Witte et al., 2021). This can lead to therapeutic change by way of emotional processing, insight and meaning making, as well as catharsis. It can both concretise ideas and stories (representational elements), and uncover subconscious or 'warded off' experiences (projection and objectification) (Enright, 1972; Rastogi et al., 2022). The interpretation of how creative and arts therapies function, and how they

DOI: 10.4324/9781003305736-26

render change, tends to be theoretically positioned and it is valuable to have insight into the rationales given for their use and effectiveness (Hogan, 2016; Vaculik and Nash, 2022a), as whilst clients may not need detailed theoretical explanations (see Chapter 30), they can help a practitioner in knowing when to offer them up as potential therapeutic methods. Alongside this, arts-based work can aid clients in creating the story of their therapy and it is therefore welcomed as another way to open opportunities for deepening experience, enhancing communication, and finding alternative ways for change to occur.

Evidence for the use of creative and arts-based therapies is strong, with a recent review evaluating the effectiveness of art therapy with adult clients in seven clinical categories (cancer patients, clients coping with a variety of medical conditions, mental health clients, clients coping with trauma, prison inmates, the elderly, and clients who have not been diagnosed with specific issues but face ongoing daily challenges) revealing some positive outcomes, mainly on standardised measures of well-being symptom alleviation, but also indicating that many interventions were based on work carried out by untrained arts therapists (Regev and Cohen-Yatziv, 2018). This general sense of effectiveness of arts therapies is a good sign but a deeper consideration of how creative work can be helpful to each specific client is important.

When considering the words of Winnicot who said that therapy is really '*two people playing together*' (1968, p. 591), it seems like an open invitation to allow unplanned and spontaneous activities to be undertaken often resulting in mind-body integration, creativity, and role rehearsal (Ward-Wimmer, 2003). This offers a satisfying experience, with insight and learning, and we can recognise that playful activities represent a form of meaning-making and processing that pre-dates our ability to articulate our experiences. Ward-Wimmer (2003) also notes that play can be beneficial to our self-esteem and sense of calm, as well as joy, empathy and intimacy, and can be an affirming part of therapy. Yet creative activities can also be purposeful and focused on specific tasks, for example, mind-mapping in order to seek strengths and resources in the client's life, sand-tray or sculpting work to deepen insight in to how a person responds relationally in their lives, and abstract artistic expression to overcome the need to articulate experience through words. Creative and arts-based activities are anything that sits to one side of the 'conversation' which occurs between therapist and client, creating a new space for meaning, experiencing, and representation. The experience itself can provide a conceptual space, a symbolic space, and experiential space, but also a tangible space for the production of physical artefacts (Vaculik and Nash, 2022b). In pluralism, particular care is taken by the therapist to support the undertaking and sequential nature of the creative process, for example, setting the space, timing, agreeing the scope and purpose of the undertaking. It is important that the therapist discusses with the client significant features of the process such as whether the activity is co-created and dialogic, or if they are simply providing a space for the client to experience something, and the therapist is there to serve as a witness. The therapist must understand their role at all times and respond to the activity empathically and skilfully. Much of the arts-based therapies are explorative and open the space for imagination and emergence of experience, the unexpected is expected and a therapist needs to be both prepared and accepting of this and, where possible, be able to prepare the client.

In creative therapies, there can be a tension between the role of art as a communication tool, and its role as a personal resource. As always, in pluralism, we would acknowledge the 'both/and' rather than 'either/or' and the therapist and client work together to ensure there is a shared understanding and consideration of the purpose of any therapeutic activity. Usually, methods are introduced and facilitated by the therapist (see Chapter 19), who may suggest creative activities as part of their therapeutic toolkit, or in response to a client task. But this need not be the case, as a client may like to bring creative activities, as part of their cultural resources, into the room and a therapist might do well to be sensitive to the opportunities for this and be guided by the client as they describe their life. A musician may wish to play a piece they have written which helps them express their situation, a visual artist may like to bring a depiction of a dream for interpretation. So, it is worth having a beginners view on what sorts of things creative methods can achieve to help guide this.

In this introduction to the use of arts-based therapy methods, and in simple terms, there are three purposes to consider which will influence whether a creative method is proposed:

Insight – Whatever the theoretical school in which it is based, the action of creating a representation in an open and free hand way can lead to insight, understanding, and acceptance. This can be in response to tasks which ask, *how can we understand this better?* and, *how can I come to terms with this?*. Creative artistic exploration can also facilitate deepening of emotional awareness, *why did I not paint a face on this person?* and promote acceptance of uncomfortable and warded off experiences, *if I cannot talk about it, can I make sense of it through drawing?*. It can be helpful to support the client to undertake the creative process and then aid them to interpret their representations and motivations during or after the creation.

Change-focus – Creative methods can allow a client to depict desired scenarios, moods, and situations which can evoke ideas on goals and how this might be brought about. This kind of work is drawn largely from the cognitive behavioural school of thought in that people are aided by creative representation to walk through alternative states and outcomes before evaluating whether or not they are desired (or even realistic). An example might be that the client depicts the current situation and the desired situation and the therapists prompts them to reflect on the difference, what feels important, and how might the change be undertaken

Emotional exploration and embodiment – Alongside the role of arts-based therapy to develop insight and meaning for the client, arts therapies can also be a useful way to aid the client in integrating and processing emotion. Gestural work can allow greater connectivity between the mind and body, using the body to enact or depict movements and meaning, for example, a bereaved mother might unknowingly enact the physical movements of holding her child to connect with her sense of loss. Expressivity can shift the focus from dialogical 'cognitive work' to the body, allowing freedom of experience. The process of physical and artistic creation can also support clients in managing emotions, for example, introducing activities as resources for calming anxiety, and for some clients, who don't like the face-to-face aspect of therapy and find things are hard to say, this can reduce the impact of exploring issues in a direct conversational way.

In their excellent review of creative arts therapies, De Witte and colleagues (2021) identified 19 aspects of client experience that aided the therapeutic process. Those unique to art-therapy activities included the processes of symbolism and metaphor, embodiment, and concretisation. Whilst we do not 'prescribe' how therapists should use their tools, these are certainly some activities which lend themselves to current pluralistic skills and concepts, and offer practitioners, and the wider pluralistic therapeutic field, food for thought around how practice can be enhanced and advanced through creative arts work.

25 What is the role of intuition and 'felt-sense' for practitioners in pluralistic therapy?

In the therapy room, pluralism conceptualises three sources of knowledge: client, therapist, and common knowledge and these reflect a huge resource which can, and should, influence the therapeutic process (see Chapter 12). Within all this is the process of 'intuition' which can be thought of as knowledge connected to a felt sense and insight, linked to empathy (Rogers, 1986) and not always attributable to conscious decisions or thought. Defined by Pacini and Epstein (1999) as a, '*precon-scious, rapid, automatic, holistic, primarily non-verbal, [and] intimately associated with affect*' (p. 972), the use of intuition in practice is common and, whilst highly valued across therapeutic schools, it has been linked to a reduced engagement with evidence-based practices (Gaudiano et al., 2011). Evidence for the effectiveness of the use of intuition in practice is hampered by the range of definitions and experiences of its use, but most practitioners believe intuition, and their felt sense, can help the therapy process sometimes 'hitting the nail on the head' (Fox et al., 2016). Through understanding and trusting their sense of what is right, therapists can act in ways which facilitate and even transform the therapeutic experience for the client – a kind of '*I think this is what is going on*' and the reason for this is at a '*gut level*'.

Whilst it is common for therapists to 'tune in' to this process and use this knowledge and experience to make gut-level decisions in the moment (not everything can be subject to a meta-communicative process), they may also choose to retain a non-committed felt sense about the client, deciding perhaps to 'wait and see' if the sense re-occurs or plays out. Usually, therapists will make this judgement according to the power dynamics and potential impact on the client. Therapists doubtless have an internal process which is not revealed to the client and sharing this will depend on their school of thought, the relationship they have with the client, and whether it is likely to be in service, or benefit,

DOI: 10.4324/9781003305736-27

of the client. Often the judgements of sharing may be thrashed out in supervision '*does this client need to know what I am seeing or feeling?*'.

Even if risks are taken, intuition is something that can successfully guide a therapist to behave in certain ways or support the client in a particular direction, which may be well received by them – '*it's like my therapist just knew what I needed*'. Despite this, pluralistic therapists are wise to the fact that a lot of what is assumed by therapists is not aligned to what the client experiences. For example, research has shown that only around 30–40% of clients agree with their therapist ratings of the quality of the therapeutic relationship (Cooper, 2008), whilst Rennie (1994) undertook a large-scale study of things not shared by clients (and not shared by therapists in supervision) and found a troubling disjoint (this subject of client deference is explored further in Chapter 31).

If we work on the principle that pluralistic therapy is about sharing what is in the therapist's head with the client, this must involve checking out intuition. So, what are the things a therapist must be aware of? First, that we often don't know how our clients are experiencing the therapy because they are not telling us, are unsure, or are not thinking about it. Therapists themselves might not ask because they are concerned it will impact on the power differential, the process of the therapy, the value of the therapist positive regard of the client, and the capacity of the therapist to 'get it right' and be sure that they are 'getting it right'. In essence, being intuitive comes with a health warning.

The role of power within a therapeutic relationship is of vital interest to therapists (see Chapter 31), and intuition, however well-meant can resonate with the power differential between therapist and client. Intuition is closely associated with 'assumptions', the validity of which might reflect whose lens takes precedence in the interpretation of what is going on in the therapy. An over-reliance on unchecked beliefs is problematic. Different theories around the implicit and explicit role of power in the therapy room have been proposed; however, it is clear that power relations cannot be denied (Proctors, 2017) and can cause problems when intuition is relied upon. Consider this statement, 'I could *feel* that this experience had a profound impact on the client and moved to focus them on the meaning of this', in some respects this could be seen as deeply empathic and, in responding to this felt-sense of impact, the client might feel more understood and the focus of the therapy could be deepened, this could lead to something useful or important as a result the connection between client and therapist. However, if the intuited response is inaccurate, or misinterprets the cause and effect of the experience, the client may feel that the therapist is not hearing and understanding what is going on, might feel a sense of isolation in their experience, or an obligation to explain or correct the therapist – particularly if the intuitive response leads to the therapist pursuing an unhelpful dialogue or building a belief around the assumption which strays from the experience of the client. Furthermore, it can be extremely painful for a client to articulate this, naming the correct impact, and 'risk' humiliating the counsellor, feeling they are 'disrupting' the flow of the conversation. So, there are some important aspects that a pluralistic therapist needs to understand and be conscious of when using intuition.

Knowing what you know as a therapist

Where does the intuition come from? Throughout our lives we have developed a knowledge base, and this exists as both unconscious and conscious knowledge – what you *know you know* and what you *don't know you know*, knowledge which is so deeply set that you are not aware of it (or don't usually notice it). Essentially, therapists hold epistemological and ontological assumptions about the world (Willig, 2019), a reflexive awareness of their assumptions about what there is to know (ontology) and how they came to know about it (epistemology). These are likely to impact on what they think and how they behave, therefore active exploration into these aspects of understanding and knowledge is important. A self-aware and reflective practitioner will be able to recognise the beliefs, assumptions, and biases which might guide their practice – there is no neutral position-and everyone has these! In pluralistic training one of the most important developmental stages is to articulate a 'philosophy of counselling', which begins with the process of being aware of the origins of thought around practice – a person might find their philosophy touches upon their upbringing, socio-cultural origins and context, their theoretical understanding of problems in living, and their beliefs on what helps in therapy. This is a good starting point for recognising the lens through which we see clients. A process of challenging assumptions through, for example, deliberate practice (Rousmaniere, 2016) and personal development groups, will create a growth edge around the accuracy and helpfulness of the therapist's lens – 'what do I know?', 'what assumptions am I making?', and 'how do these resonate with the experience of others?'. In practice, it is fair to say that clients are unlikely to directly challenge our assumptions, so space needs to be created to open up therapist ability to test these.

Knowing how and when to use what you know

How can I deploy accurate intuitive responses in the most helpful way? No therapy can be entirely negotiated, and there is not scope for each step to be checked in on when taken, so a pluralistic therapist must learn, through practice, to align with each client in turn – is there resonance and can it be checked out? Alongside this, supervision can be utilised to check out and test any emergent patterns around how and when assumptions are made, for example, a pattern emerging in practice that each client case formulation is constructed with the same themes (e.g. 'early childhood trauma' or 'poor self-image') or that the therapist regularly perceives the same patterns of emotion (e.g. 'misplaced anger', or 'fear of relationships'), or even that unevidenced statements are made by the therapist (e.g. 'I could tell the client needed to just let off steam', 'I knew they would not want too much challenge' or 'I knew at that moment all they needed was a hug'). Ultimately, a space is needed to check patterns of intuition to find out if the assumptions stem from the client, or from the therapist.

Knowing how the intuitive response might be received

As therapists, it is important to consider the impact of our intuitive response, will our client welcome the sense of being known and will the response impact on the their confidence in the therapy process? What seems to be key to using intuition as a pluralistic therapist is the ability to support the client in hearing what is being communicated and encourage them to amend or correct the intuitive response. In practice, welcoming insight on experience can give an opportunity for the client to examine their perspective on what is, and is not, the case for them. Framed as a source of relational growth, empowering clients to take the reins when an intuitive response is made, whether accurate or not, can be a step towards greater insight and growth. When offered with humility and framed as a source of relational growth, empowering clients to take the reins when an intuitive response is made, whether accurate or not, can be a step towards greater insight and growth. However, often, and perhaps unfortunately, the client will simply forgive the therapist for their assumptions and allow the therapy to progress. In pluralistic practice, meta-communication, feedback (see Chapter 20) and collaborative discussions (see Chapter 11) are ways to mitigate inaccurate intuition, being able to check your sense of things rather than use it as an unquestioned skill. This can be supported by utilising 'I' statements, being tentative in the language, tone and pace, and seeking clarification such as, '*I have a sense here that you are needing to look at this, but I am not sure if I'm picking it up wrong*', or '*I've noticed that there seems to be something going on in your relationship that you need to share, am I reading this right?*'.

As you can see, the use of therapist knowledge and intuition relates to the interplay between the need to be useful to the client and the desire to empower the client through encouraging them to internalise their sense of control. A dimension of influence exists that must be carefully navigated, and this dimension shifts as a result of active work towards the client becoming the choice-maker in how therapy takes place. Whilst what the client knows and has experienced is vital in understanding their expectations and early preferences for the process of therapy, how the knowledge of the client resonates with the knowledge of the therapist can influence how it unfolds, but not always in predictable ways. It is hard to predict how well you will get along with another, shared experiences such as cultural origins (Cabral and Smith, 2011) and emotional response matching have been shown to impact on the formation and maintenance of the therapy relationship (Elliott et al., 2011), with the key factor being a sense that the therapist will understand the client experience, in turn engendering a sense of safety, hope, and a willingness to be understood.

26 How can I be pluralistic and offer short-term counselling?

It is fair to say that, despite the development of short-term versions of traditional therapies (Feltham and Dryden, 2006), many models are based on an assumption that therapy takes time. Unfortunately, the financial costs involved in the provision of longer-term therapy are outside those which are available, and the arguments for this investment are weakened by the evidence that points to the gains for clients peaking at around six-to-eight sessions, the drive for cost-effectiveness in all areas of therapy provision (Castelnuovo et al., 2016), and many clients not being willing and/or able to commit in the longer-term. Increasingly, therapy service provision is being restricted to six sessions, in some cases as few as four, and the single-session therapy approach (Dryden, 2020) is increasing in popularity. However, many therapists feel unprepared and unskilled in being able to meet client's needs effectively and pragmatically within these timeframes with some relying on the 'safety-net' of '*we'll see how far we get and ask for longer from the service if needed*'.

Pluralism is based on the establishment of effective collaboration (see Chapter 11), feedback (see Chapter 20), and preference accommodation (see Chapter 22), and the development of this relationship can take time. It is therefore necessary, within a pluralistic therapy, that steps are taken to draw on its distinct features of client empowerment and open dialogue in order to aid clients working in a short timeframe, be this service or client led. These incorporate the co-creation of shared expectations about therapy including the transparency on what can be done, how the pace might be set, and how therapy can aid in uncovering change preferences, processes, and concerns. Key to this is acknowledging that whilst some of these change processes and concerns may not be addressed at the time, they can be taken forward by the client through various alternative means which the therapist can 'guide' them

DOI: 10.4324/9781003305736-28

towards. It is a sense of supporting the client, during this short period, with what is available and encouraging them to work out ways to thrive.

Being pluralistic in a short time-frame can help focus the attention on what is important for the client and aid open dialogue (because how else will the client know what they are choosing to do, and therefore choosing not to do, when you can't cover everything?). It is, however, fair to say that many clients enter therapy without knowing much about it. When told they are being offered six sessions, they might use this information to guide their expectations of meeting outcomes, but equally they may have no idea if this is an appropriate amount of time to address whatever it is they are facing. The starting point for pluralistic therapy is to ensure that the client knows something about what is going to happen and gets a sense of what might be undertaken and achieved in relation to the problems in living. Pre-therapy information can be really useful for this but often it starts with an early conversation which would draw on the therapist's own experience and ways of working.

The concept of directionality and pace in therapy is often used in pluralism to denote a preference, or to consider different ways forward, it is a characteristic of therapy, which is not constrained by time limits, to be an emergent quality of the relationship – and hopefully fit to the client's way of being and preferences for working. Shifts in pace can sometimes occur depending on the focus of therapy, and the tasks and methods used, so an exploratory dialogue around a difficult subject can take time and patience, whereas setting behaviour change activities can be relatively fast paced. In short-term therapy, the pluralistic therapist will be aware of the nature of the work, sensitive to the client pace preference and, from this, use meta-communication to ensure the client is aware of the constraints (particularly when thinking about their goals). The question that a pluralistic therapist might pose to their client is:

> *Is it better to direct therapy to something that is important, and can be the focus of the work, with the desire that one area of change can instigate an other, or can the time be better spent just opening up and exploring what is going on with the hope that a plan can be set for how you might take things forward?*

Underlying these questions are the ethical judgements around how best to help the client with what they are facing given the limitations on time, and many therapists find the idea of short-term therapy frustrating because they feel 'deep' shifts for the client are not possible. Some therapists will talk of it 'papering the cracks' or loading the client with resources and activities to undertake between sessions or once therapy is over, but this attitude is perhaps not helpful to the client. A more useful consideration, for the therapist and client, might simply be a conversation around 'what can we achieve in this time, and how might that have a positive impact for you?', as well as for the therapist to understand the kinds of methods which might be helpful in the time available and open the discussion with their client.

During short-term therapy it is also wise to aid the client in locating and evaluating cultural resources (see Chapter 23) which can be incorporated into their lives once therapy has ended. This kind of future planning is strengths-based and not aimed at sending the message that the therapy will not be enough, but rather that the client can be an active seeker of their own well-being and therapy is just a part of this.

An overview of the focus and content of sessions in short-term therapy is shown in Table 26.1; it is important to note that this is not prescriptive, but should encourage the conceptualisation of how to balance the work across six sessions of therapy.

Table 26.1 Example of short-term therapy session plan

Pre-therapy	• Information on the therapy offered, the number of sessions available, and the kinds of methods which may be offered.
Session 1	• Getting to know one another, outlining the process.
Session 2	• Early formulation of ideas and discussion on what might be prioritised.
	• Agreeing 'in therapy activities' and what might be undertaken and how.
	• Discussions around goals can include 'this therapy' goal and other goals.
Session 3	• Undertake priority tasks.
Session 4	• Undertake priority tasks.
Session 5	• Undertake priority tasks.
	• Develop conversation around cultural resources in context of other desired outcomes.
	• Plan ending.
Session 6	• Ending.
	• Celebrate engagement and relationship – valuing progress for client.
	• Review process of therapy – articulate helpful aspects of this – what have they learnt, what are they thinking or doing differently, and what do they need?
	• Plan forward for client including available cultural resources.

27 I've started pluralistically, how do I end pluralistically?

As relational beings, the end of therapy can be complex and confusing. Many clients have not had positive experiences with endings in their personal lives, the same could be said for therapists. At the very least, the ending of therapy is an artificial dialogue that rarely happens in 'normal life', for example, in how many of your relationships have you said, '*I had a really positive experience, I got what I needed, and now I don't want to see you anymore*' and the other person replied, '*super, I am so pleased!*'. In effect, our job as therapists is to do ourselves out of a job – we are continuously moving towards helping our clients achieve a place in their lives where they no longer need us. When things go well, and there is a shared understanding of the work undertaken, then we can communicate with our client around a *mutually agreed* ending, that is, we both think the goals have been met wholly or partially and you (the client) would be better served by closing the work, or we consider that the client would benefit from a referral to a different therapist/type of resource. It may even be that the work is *time-limited*, either because of the service requirements or client preference, or the client and therapist agree to a *gradual* ending, whereby the frequency of the sessions decreases until eventually the client stops reaching out for an appointment.

However, not all endings are as collaborative, some could be termed *unwanted* whereby either the therapist thinks there's more work to be done but the client chooses not to continue, or when the client would like to continue but the therapist closes the therapy. Generally, the therapist should only set the pace for the closure if they believe therapy is no longer needed or beneficial, or indeed if it has the potential to do more harm than good. There are also therapist factors such as risk, if they feel personally threatened in their work either by the client or by someone in the client's life, or if they are experiencing personal problems that may impact the work they do (Davis and Younggren, 2009).

DOI: 10.4324/9781003305736-29

There is also the phenomenon of 'drop-out' or *sudden* endings, which largely covers failure to show, leaving prematurely, and/or having no contact. Generally speaking, 35–55% of cases are considered drop-out but research indicates that therapists do not typically know the reason for termination with many citing client dysfunctions (low motivation, not ready) and external problems (finance, time, etc.) as possible explanations. However, therapists were quicker to identify that 'therapist factors' may be responsible for other therapist's premature termination rates, indicating that there is perhaps a self-serving bias (Hunsley et al., 1999; Murdoch et al., 2010) and strengthens the argument for therapists to have a high degree of self-reflection (Davis and Younggren, 2009) (see Chapters 10 and 37). Interestingly, therapists have a better understanding of termination for 'positive' reasons (the client met their goals) but not how often this occurs.

Low concordance on reasons for terminating therapy may be due to differences in expectations between therapists and clients about the goals for psychotherapy. In separate studies, less than half (44%) of clients viewed accomplishing goals (Hunsley et al., 1999) and experiencing improvement (13.3% of participants) as the key reasons for termination (Bados et al., 2007). Essentially, many clients didn't end therapy because they had achieved their desired outcomes, but rather because of low motivation, dissatisfaction, and/or lack of confidence with the treatment or the therapist (46.7% (Bados et al., 2007); 33% (Hunsley et al., 1999)). Hunsley et al. (1999) note that instead of doubting client motivation, therapists would do well to consider problems in the therapy, and review both the client's experience and expectations of therapy, when they hear 'flags'. These may even be overt bids for help which need a clear response such as:

- 'I am feeling worse'.
- 'I don't feel I am going anywhere/getting better'.
- 'You don't understand'.

Clients may not always give direct indications that they will withdraw from therapy, but frequently there are covert signs, like missing sessions, a lack of engagement or commitment to tasks, and 'forgetting' payment, all of which are invitations which might be explored.

The key indicator of sustaining a client in therapy is the strength of the therapeutic relationship (Roos and Werbart, 2013) with clients who reported good working relationships taking care to plan and consider the ending, processing the loss (considered the 'ideal ending'), and leaving due to extra-therapy factors (such as finances or time commitment) (Knox et al., 2011). Whereas those who perceived that they were unheard or unhelped, and had less agreement and mutual understandings with the therapist, dropped out. Although the relationship was a factor in this decision, the clients also cited extra-therapy factors (Roos and Werbart, 2013; Knox et al., 2011), which should always be on the therapist 'radar'. Therapists can discuss these subtle (or not so subtle) signs through utilising outcome tools (see Chapter 20), case formulations (see Chapter 14), clearly defining goals (see Chapters 16 and 17) (Davis and Younggren, 2009), and discussing client preferences (see Chapter 22), all of which will promote therapeutic communication, better inform a client about the nature of therapy (even if they do not remain in therapy at the present time), and also better inform the therapist about the way that the client wants therapy to be (even if they cannot meet their preferences at this present time). This will support and aid re-engagement with services in the future, if required.

In fact, working pluralistically means discussing endings from the beginning! Understanding time frames for work undertaken, conducting assessments and a case formulation, which includes what the client wants to accomplish and how (see Chapter 16), will all begin to set markers for the length of time therapy may take and enable therapist and client to identify when the work is complete (Davis and Younggren, 2009). The work will require a high degree of open dialogue around expectations and experiences, and may also involve offering time to talk about what it is like to be ending the work, and referrals if the client wishes to pursue other avenues of therapy or interventions. Even in instances that this is not possible, therapists should have skills in risk assessment (Davis and Younggren, 2009) and take due care to follow-up with clients who are deemed to be at risk and require additional support, or who have 'dropped-out' and may wish to seek help elsewhere – *'I might not be right for you, but it does not necessarily mean that therapy is not right for you'* (Davis and Younggren, 2009; Hunsley et al., 1999).

Whilst some clients welcome the opportunity to discuss finishing therapy, and view this as an indication of their achievements and gains, both authors have had difficult experiences in discussing endings with clients (see Chapter 28). In a bid to be pluralistic and open about the client's expectations and experiences of therapy, including the possibility of terminating, the client can experience a sense of abandonment or rejection, as if their goal or achievement became more important than the relationship, and we know from research that clients value the relationship (Norcross and Lambert, 2019). In a bid to balance walking between therapy being beneficial, 'I can do this because of, or with the help of, my therapist' and the client becoming reliant, 'I can only do this because of my therapist' or unhelpful, 'my therapist does not help me', there is a need to understand the client's perspective regarding their goals and experiences, their view of the relationship, and their reactions to ending therapy. In doing so, therapists need to have skills in managing the therapeutic relationship and working with abandonment (Davis and Younggren, 2009), being able to identify ruptures and bringing these out into a shared space with an ability to effectively repair. Of note is that some of our most rewarding and satisfying work which has produced change has been through the reparation of ruptures.

Further competence in closing safely with clients requires counsellors to have a grounding in ethics, knowledge of how to apply these in a variety of settings utilising scientific knowledge (methods), an understanding of diversity and individuality, and be able to work within interdisciplinary systems (Davis and Younggren, 2009). Whilst some therapies will build in discussions of satisfaction with therapy, the relationship and loss (such as psychodynamic, collaborative, and experiential), others will place focus on gains, future growth, and potential obstacles, and there may be a structured ceremony in others (Norcross et al., 2017; Goode et al., 2017). Norcross and colleagues (2017) identify some common termination 'behaviours' that practitioner and client move through including the need to, (i) process the feelings of the client and therapist and (ii) discuss the client's future functioning and coping strategies including (iv) how they might use their new skills beyond therapy and framing personal development as ongoing, occasionally using metaphors such the journey. It was identified that, when working towards closing therapy, therapists help clients to (v) anticipate post therapy growth and generalisations, which may include taking scheduled breaks so clients can experience what it will be like, before they begin to (vi) explicitly prepare to terminate through discussing practical arrangements such as the date/session, post-therapy contact, reviewing the work, (vii) reflecting on client gains and consolidating skills and knowledge, and (viii) expressing pride in the mutual relationship and bonds that have been formed, as well as the client's progress. Consideration of all of these factors in pluralistic therapy optimises the potential for a 'good' ending and the chances that the client will progress and thrive.

28 Can you give some examples of pluralistic work?

There are challenges to providing examples of pluralistic therapy, as whilst it is helpful to try and draw out some of the key features, there is a huge variability in ways of working and the types of activities that can be undertaken. So, whilst a 'typical case' might be constructed, there is a fear that some of the complexity and nuance of the client process will be lost. The four examples here are presented to highlight the nature of pluralism in order to emphasise that working pluralistically is not like putting together a step-by-step set of tasks towards a client goal, but takes active collaborative engagement and decision-making, for both therapist and client, and is not without challenge. Each client case is an amalgamation of case-examples, and none are a 'real client', the key themes, however, are used to illustrate real-life practice and will be described in terms of their core case-elements, the particular challenges that occurred, and the resolutions of these. This is partly to acknowledge the complexity of application, but also the degree to which therapists must at times 'dig deep' to work effectively in awareness of their own limitations and anxieties without the security of a manualised approach.

Rachel

Rachel initially presented to counselling with low mood and wanted to process the broken relationship with her parents and the loss she felt, which she believed was the key factor in her low mood. Rachel engaged enthusiastically with therapy, practicing new skills between sessions which consisted of validating and engaging with strengths and resources, as well as exploring and challenging her worldview. At week 13, Rachel noted that she had reached somewhat of a resolution

DOI: 10.4324/9781003305736-30

in herself, regarding the broken relationship with her parents, and was feeling much better. The therapist punctuated this achievement and identified that the client had met her initial goal and explored with Rachel the idea that sometimes, when people have completed a piece of work, they take a break whilst others choose to continue, the therapist asked Rachel what she would like to do. Rachel said she would think about it and let the therapist know before the next session, but later sent a text to say she wanted to end therapy.

Towards the end of this 13th session with Rachel, the therapist had an uneasy 'sense' something happened in the session, that there was a rupture, but felt vulnerable and lacked time to name this and explore it with Rachel and so 'took it home'. Upon reflecting on the work, the therapist realised they were concerned about how useful Rachel was finding the sessions and afraid of 'keeping' her over the piece of work that she initially wanted to do.

Due to this reflection and 'gut' sense, when Rachel sent the text to end therapy, the therapist asked if they could talk about closing face-to-face which Rachel agreed to. When they met and discussed her decision to end, Rachel expressed that, when the therapist offered a break, she heard that there was *no more they could do for her*, because she was a *hopeless case*, which echoed everything she had been through with her parents. Whilst she said she initially felt hurt, she later noted that she became angry that the therapist was *just like them* and had sent the text to end their work. They explored both of their reactions, and the therapist acknowledged that Rachel had accurately detected that they (the therapist) were worried they could not help anymore and that was not because of Rachel being hopeless but because of what the therapist themselves might be able to offer. This aided the processes of beginning to repair the rupture in the relationship, build meaning bridges, and further the depth and congruence of communication.

This example demonstrates that when a therapist is closed to their own vulnerability, they may not be able to purposefully communicate with the client, which in this case ruptured the relationship. However, even in the 'mistakes' made, it was through reflection, drawing on personal knowledge and communication, that it was possible to help repair the relationship. It is also a testament to the client's willingness to be vulnerable, open to their own experiences, and a trust in the relationship being different, that they returned and helped to repair.

Eleanor

Eleanor came to therapy after her GP suggested it might be helpful in dealing with her depression. She presented with a range of medical problems, and in the early stage of therapy would relate details of the medication regime she was taking, including her anti-depressants prescribed around six years previously, and conversations she had with her GP, who she appeared to hold in high regard. Eleanor's goal was to reduce her feelings of depression, and the tasks undertaken involved understanding the stressors in her life, tapping into cultural resources, understanding her relationship with her husband, and coming to terms with her 'life-position'. The work tended towards talking and to some extent 're-storying' her experiences, alongside trying to create space for her to find pleasure in life, and in later work looking at challenging some of the 'life-positions' she held around her own sense of being a good person.

In the interactions with the therapist, Eleanor tended to be deferential and seek approval through affirmations about her behaviour towards her husband and other people in her life, who she largely appeared to dislike. She would recount events in her life where she appeared to direct blame outwards and be quite dismissive of other's experiences. These patterns could be interpreted as defence, but when it was suggested by the therapist that she criticised others because she feared criticism herself, she did not agree, giving examples of when she herself had been criticised and accepted it.

The pattern of therapy rolled on with a number of focus areas, but the key challenge was that, despite Eleanor being aware that the therapy was open-ended, she would rate herself on the outcome measures (CORE-34; GAD-7, PHQ-9 (see Appendix II), and Goal form) as being significantly worse when the conversation strayed towards the possibility of an ending (a kind of implicit feedback noted by the therapist). As therapy progressed, the space became increasingly used by Eleanor to list the events of the previous week, her frustrations at a variety of people including her husband, family, and neighbours, and her stated preference was for a 'space to reflect'. However, the therapist was concerned that what they had created was a space for her to rehearse a strong narrative about how unjust the world was towards her, and how virtuous she was. Her use of the scales seemed to indicate that on some level she needed to keep attending, yet the therapist felt a sense of anxiety that they were not really helping and, should they flag Eleanor's behaviour patterns, they would become another 'bad person' in her life.

What had been missed in terms of the pluralistic approach was the establishment of the therapist – not as an adjunct to the client, but as a whole person who was seeing patterns of behaviour, and experiencing the impact of counter-transference which was imposing a sense of being in a pseudo-powerful but actually deferential position – and they missed, for a long-time, the opportunity for the client to feel fully safe because the therapist was only partially there. In supervision, the therapist worked on ways to bring themselves into the relationship by reflecting on the validity of their experience, and by doing this moving more in to the room, in a trusted way, in order to bring a counterpoint to the narratives she was constructing for example, rather than challenge Eleanor directly the therapist reminded her that they weren't going anywhere, and asked her to bring some photographs in, mainly pictures of herself in different times, and together they tried out a few different imperfect stories together.

This example speaks to the need in pluralism to recognise the relational dynamics that can impact on therapy, and how to best manage this in a congruent supportive way, ultimately using therapist experience as a source of information for the client.

Leonard

Leonard was an international student studying for his PhD, he entered therapy as a result of a concern about his homosexuality. He came from what he called a '*patriarchal and anti-gay culture in eastern Europe*' and whilst finding acceptance in the United Kingdom, was concerned about how he might return home, initially during a trip to visit his family, but more broadly in consideration of his return to live there permanently. Leonard's goal was to understand and manage his anxieties, and the work mainly focused on deepening his understanding and insight into his own experience and patterns of behaviour – he wanted to have an explanation for what was going on which made sense to him.

In the initial exploration of his history, the therapist 'toyed with' some psychodynamic interpretations, and as this somewhat intellectualising stance continued it became clear that Leonard was a person who was spending time reading and thinking about complex interpretations of his experience and leaving the therapist behind! This triggered an anxiety in the therapist around their ability to help him, the pace of his thinking was fast, he batted away many of their observations, and seemed to be creating meaning which the therapist played no part.

Notwithstanding their sense of intellectual inferiority, the therapist decided that the most pluralistic route for the therapy was simply to review with him what he felt might be helpful for them to do. In conversation he pinpointed some minor things that the therapist had done which had helped, but overall, what he wanted was someone to keep him company whilst he spoke. He wasn't quite sure exactly what would come of the therapy but wanted to have space to develop an understanding of his experience on a deep level and tying it to Jungian theory was his choice. The therapist asked for Leonard's preference on how he wanted them to behave whilst he did this and was given the response, '*broadly speaking chip in but mainly listen*'. The therapist learned a lot about trusting the client process, and at the end of therapy they genuinely felt thankful to him for allowing them to join him in his journey as a witness to his meaning construction.

This example speaks to the need for accommodation of client preferences and the idea that 'two experts in the room' is a metaphor for owning your own knowledge, and empowering the client to use theirs in the way that is most helpful for them.

Sarah

Sarah was a solicitor who presented with very high levels of work-related stress, and she identified some suicide ideation and talked in one session of throwing herself from a high tower in the local town. She had both stressors and resources in her life, her husband seemed kind, her kids were happy, and she had a close relationship with her father. She cycled to work and at the weekends spent time walking and wild swimming. Sarah's goals were clearly stated from the outset, she wanted to manage her stress, and the therapist helped her to articulate the areas of her life which imposed most stress, alongside exploring methods for relieving this, for example, managing her out of hours working.

The therapist and Sarah had an apparently functional and collaborative relationship, and she reported that they were doing some good stress-relief work together which helped her to understand why she found particular circumstances in work hard. Around seven sessions in she was recounting an experience of finding herself so stressed by their eight year old's behaviour that she struck her in anger. When she said this, it appeared to the therapist that it was given as an example of how stressed she was, and that she felt that beyond that it was nothing untoward. The therapist on the other hand, had a strong sense of anger and concern for the child, immediately she was no longer collaborating with Sarah but risk assessing the situation, re-evaluating their beliefs about her, and trying to hide their emotional response.

Taking the case to supervision the therapist was supported in thinking about this risk, the judgements and fears they had, and the potential impact of their reaction and any further actions they might take. What they decided to do was 'come clean', in the next session. Rather than trying to get her to explore her situation in order to find out if she presented a risk to her children, the therapist spoke of their surprise at her behaviour and that it didn't 'feel like her'. Sarah opened up about her behaviour in the context of her own stress but spoke more about the ways that she found her children difficult and frustrating. She mentioned that violence was common in her own childhood, and that compared to her father she was both level-headed and even-handed. The therapist struggled to keep their own perspective (that one should never hit children), balanced with Sarah's worldview (that it is a normal part of child-rearing), along with 'practical' tasks including her stress levels, the collaboration, and the need to prioritise the well-being of her and her children. They agreed to work on her anger-management and monitor her responses to her children, but for the therapist there was a sense that much deeper work was needed for this client to look at where the anger stemmed from, and how she could manage her children (and her relationship with them). In the later stages of therapy, they were able to reflect on balancing her role as a mother with her ideals for her career, but also to imagine her future relationship with her children.

This example speaks to the management of risk, taking a considered, intuitive, yet ethical stance on practice when an initial reaction is steering the therapist in a particular direction (in this case, to intervene and breach confidentiality). With the use of supervision, the therapist was able to evaluate a range of options, from reporting the risk and breaching confidentiality to working constructively and congruently with their client. It also illustrates the often 'incomplete' nature of the therapy process and learning to accept that outcomes are subject to the choices made in therapy with imperfect information and no crystal ball.

Section 3

Working with specific client factors in pluralistic counselling and psychotherapy

DOI: 10.4324/9781003305736-31

29 Can I really collaborate and manage risk of self-harm and suicide in pluralistic practice?

Risk in counselling and psychotherapy is determined through a range of situations. It can be considered as the presentation or significant indication from a client that they are likely to harm to themselves, either through suicidal behaviour or through 'non-suicidal self-injury'. This risk presentation contrasts to the risk that the therapy itself is harmful and the risk to the client from others, or that some clients may present to others. This chapter examines the first example of risk, as it is a common experience in therapy. Pluralistic therapist Andrew Reeves has provided the most contemporary model for a dialogic and collaborative approach to managing suicidality and self-harm in practice (Reeves, 2015, 2016), addressing the nub of this question, '*How can a therapist best broach the subject of suicidality and, once broached, develop an environment for exploration of risk, identifying spaces of safety and resources for the client (including the role of the therapist in this), whilst holding the professional duty to prevent harm?*'

The management of the boundary between the client experience and needs, the existential threat, and the context of practice is without doubt anxiety inducing for therapists (Moerman, 2012; Richards, 2000; Reeves, 2013), and when managed poorly can result in the client feeling isolated, unheard, and potentially at raised risk of harm. It is not within our gift to impose on our clients an environment of safety and so the best approach to take is to establish a collaborative relationship with the client which best enables them to keep themselves safe.

In an ideal world, a client who is presenting risk would come to therapy, the risk would be disclosed and the client willingly receptive to support available to manage that risk until it subsides. Even as I write I can hear the voice of a student in my head saying:

> *Is it ever that simple, If I cannot disengage from the therapeutic encounter and put interventions in place, but rather draw out and work with the perspective*

DOI: 10.4324/9781003305736-32

of the client in their state of 'riskiness', does that not make the whole thing unmanageable? Where does that leave me professionally and emotionally if they complete suicide?

In many mental health services, evaluating risk can be a uni-directional assessment of factors which increase the likelihood of suicidality and self-harm (e.g. age, gender, point of crisis, mental health diagnosis) and factors which serve to protect them (e.g. engagement in 'pro-social behaviours', problem solving skills, and socio-emotional skills) (Fonseca-Pedrero et al., 2022; Kleiman and Liu, 2013). Practitioners may be in a context where risk is cause to extend the confidentiality boundary and sometimes initiates the end to the relational processes of therapy. In this situation, clients may swiftly move from being perceived as active and engaged participants in a relationship of equals, to the position of being 'managed'. This experience is inherently disempowering, especially given that clients choose to divulge suicidality carefully and often avoid doing so, for example, Blanchard and Farber (2016) found that 31% of 547 adult clients recalled having lied to their therapist about suicidal thoughts at some time in the past. The reasons for this are likely to be varied but may include the client feeling embarrassment or shame, and also the client's evaluation on the potential impact of disclosure, such as fearing that it will lead to hospitalisation (Blanchard and Farber, 2020). Similarly, young people report that they did not disclose suicidal thoughts to their therapist as a result of concerns about how their confidentiality will be breached (McGillivray et al., 2022). In pluralistic therapy, there are three collaborative steps which can be taken to aid clients in disclosing and working through risk:

1. Establishing an open invitation for dialogue – In pluralistic therapy, culturally sensitive broaching and normalisation can be used to establish the possibility that the subject of suicide and harm may come up, for example, information may have been shared in the pre-therapy period, and a conversation about risk is likely to have taken place in the early stages of the process, where the client identifies the potential for risk or not. Depending on the practitioner and the client, this may have been done lightly – often in the context of when confidentiality may be breached – but it is however useful to have some statement or reference point which can be used should the subject come up. Most important is the establishment of a dialogic culture which allows the client to raise the discussion of risk and for

the therapist to be able to respond in a non-reactive way to what is disclosed. Additionally, this broaching provides informed consent about the nature of confidentiality and also enables the client to feel confident and empowered to talk about risk.

2. Responding in an empathic and collaborative way – A practitioner needs to have a sensitivity to the language used by the client at risk, often the subject of suicidality and self-harm is introduced metaphorically, *I'd be better off not here* and so exploring where 'here' is and the meaning of these statements can lead to clarity for both the therapist and client. Once a client has indicated that they are at risk, the therapist may be driven to keep the client safe and impose this need on the client, but as Reeves says, '*it is not us, as therapists, who will keep a client safe, but rather it will be the client*' (2016, p. 262). The therapist's role in these circumstances is to facilitate a discussion around the client's experience about the meaning of the situation, what might be helpful to them in reducing risk of harm, aiding the client in understanding, and potentially changing their position in terms of their relationship with risk, and finally to help establish resources that the client might use at times of raised risk.

3. Safety-planning – This task involves collaboratively shifting the client into a position of being able to view their potential for risk and acting to mitigate it, rather than being subject to it. Drawing on narrative therapy, externalisation of the risk can be a useful method, for example, changing the manner of speaking about the risk as something which is sitting *with* the client but not a fundamental *part* of them, and as something that may be sitting with them more at some times compared to others, even giving it a name and asking the client to talk about its characteristics, which can help both bring it in to focus and make it feel more manageable. For example, a client who self-harms discussed this in therapy using a metaphor and titled her self-harming as 'the drawer knives':

Client: 'I know when the knives are jumping out of the drawer at me'
Therapist: 'Can you tell me what helps keep the drawer shut?'
Client: 'If I can get out of the house then I am away from it, when I am busy and can focus on my work, and when I'm with my grandkids the drawer is shut because they could be hurt by them'
Therapist: 'So there are times when the knives don't push the drawer open and get out?'

The active role of the client parallels their role in the collaborative relationship. A therapist might ask how the client has managed up to this point, what might help in the future, and what role they wish the therapist to take in their management of risk. They may also clarify if there is an active wish to die, or whether they do not know any other way to cope right now. Understanding risk as an inherent part of everyone's life allows the maintenance of a 'barometer' of risk, agreeing to check in on this whilst therapy progresses but also asking what the client would like to happen if they do feel that they may harm themselves. This can lead to a deeper consideration of the client experience, not simply in relation to risk but the factors that have brought the risk about, and what might then be done about them.

There is important personal and professional development work which a pluralistic therapist might undertake in anticipation of managing client suicidality and self-harm, which might include those of conceptualising and reflecting on risk and asking themselves the following questions:

- What are my philosophical beliefs and responses to suicidality and risk, and where do they stem from?
- In what ways, and for what reasons, might I respond to risk if presented by a client, or this particular client, and why?
- What warning signs, and invitations to discuss suicidality and risk, would I see, and what opportunities might I miss, and why?
- What words might I use to broach the subject of risk, what would I need to put into my verbal or written contract to ensure the client understands my approach and feels empowered to speak?

Ultimately, whilst this chapter has focused on the risk of suicidality and associated harm, in order to offer concrete examples, many of the tasks and processes of working within a collaborative relationship are transferrable to any adult client at risk, be it from self-harm, abuse, or potential harm to others. The ability to engage with collaboration, and the boundary limitations, might differ depending on the client's capacity to comprehend information, provide a voluntary decision, and the information about the risk, more of which can be found in Chapter 29.

30 Do clients actually want to know about the theoretical explanation for their problems?

In short, no, it is unlikely any client will want you to throw a textbook of theory at them; however, being able to offer snippets of theoretical explanations and apply these to their lived experience can provide a useful framework of knowledge for the client and aid in the construction of meaning in terms of their experience. Theoretical explanations can be welcomed by some clients to help them make sense of their experiences, to aid them in communicating their understanding, and in some cases, to engender a sense of validation and explanation for their experiences. In the same way, a practitioner might work from a single theoretical stance and have at their disposal a 'formal' explanation for what is happening for the client, for example, a CBT therapist might propose that a client is subject to cognitive filtering.

A pluralistic therapist can offer up a range of 'ways of knowing' to the client, ideally settling on the one(s) they find most suited to their situation. The theoretical explanations often lead to tasks and methods that fit the explanations given. For example, a client who understands their experience as being subject to cognitive filters might feel that work exploring and amending these is appealing. Clients will also have preferences about whether they need external explanations for their experience or if they prefer more emergent and individualised meaning-making to occur. In this chapter, we discuss some of the things that a pluralistic therapist should be aware of.

Offering theoretical explanations for a client's problems in living is an important skill in pluralistic therapy and falls under the category of psychoeducation, teaching 'how' as well as 'what', which has been defined as a 'systematic, structured, and didactic knowledge transfer for an illness and its treatment, integrating emotional and motivational aspects' (Ekhtiari et al., 2017, p. 239), effectively providing a predetermined 'ready-made' explanation and guideline, psychoeducation is an evidence-based practice for

DOI: 10.4324/9781003305736-33

many mental and physical health conditions, offering clients improved functioning and problem solving, a decrease in symptoms and hospitalisations, increase in time between relapse, knowledge, self-esteem, and quality of life (Ellen et al., 2004). Ellen and colleagues (2004) also observed an improvement in overall satisfaction with medication and treatment – indicating that giving an explanation for things helps. Psychoeducation is found to offer a holistic strengths-based approach, a core feature for any therapist working with clients, and can enhance coping and empowerment (Ellen et al., 2004), with Motlova and colleagues (2017) further emphasising the importance of sharing information about the illness and its treatment with clients to aid building a collaborative relationship. With this in mind, pluralistic therapists would be wise to consider that if we are asking clients to become '*competent partners and to cooperate*' (Motlova et al., 2017, p. 407) then what we are striving towards is the notion of two experts in the room (see Chapter 31); if I, with my theories about the clients' problems in living, share this information, then we can do things together, that fit with the client's perspective of what is 'wrong' and what might help. Collaborating in this manner is thus a component of informed consent and ethical practice. However, if I have my theories about the clients' problems in living, and thus operate out of these in 'treating' the client then, I am doing things 'to' them, which we know they can find unhelpful (Bowie, 2016).

However, psychoeducation (teaching) and learning is strongly associated with meaning making; when information is imparted and the learner is, '*actively engaged in making sense of the situation – the frame, objects, relationship*' (Zittoun and Brinkmann, 2012, p. 1809). Through a process of reflecting on their prior experiences and cultural resources, a client can interpret the information and assimilate (or cast out) theoretical ideas which aid (or hinder) their understanding of their current lived experience. As humans, we can only handle so much new information and so clients, like us, tend to prefer information that is roughly consistent with prior determinations (Chibucos et al., 2004). This is useful to know because if a client tells me the problem is the relationship with their great aunt, and it is all her 'fault', and I offer my client explanations about their irrational beliefs, without clearly linking their words with my understanding, I might lose them. As Rogers once wrote,

> *it is the client who knows what hurts, what directions to go, what problems are crucial, what experiences have been deeply buried . . . unless I had a*

need to demonstrate my own cleverness and learning, I would do better to rely upon the client for the direction of movement in the process.

(Rogers, 2020, pp. 11–12)

It can be argued therefore, that it is important to frame explanations within the realms, or just outside, of what the client already knows, based on their lived experience. However, we also know that the majority of clients desire a directive and active therapy whereby they can be challenged, learn skills, and be encouraged to go into and express emotions (Cooper et al., 2019). Offering theoretical explanations can help to both challenge and support what clients already 'know' to be true. Additionally, it is important to consider knowledge within the context of society, Brown and Augusta-Scott (2007) contend that '*knowledge is never innocent and thus culture bound*' (p. xv) as it is socially constructed and subjectively interpreted, and through utilising a narrative process we can help clients to normalise some experiences and beliefs, whilst challenging others. In this way, theory offers us a link between the abstract world [e.g. client's concepts and ideas about their life] with the concrete world which is both empirical and observable (Chibucos et al., 2004).

Whilst there is little empirical evidence to argue whether, and when, clients want a theoretical explanation, nestling theoretical explanations within psychoeducation for individual clients provides us with early clues of its efficacy in promoting adherence and preventing relapse (Sarkhel et al., 2020). Additionally, humans require information to be able to explain their own understanding, and many clients enter therapy to do just this. Theory begins to offer a framework to test the reliability and validity of what they understand to be true and, through utilising empirically based theory to structure the client's understandings, we can offer three things they do not necessarily have access to in everyday life (adapted from Chibucos et al., 2004):

1. Ideas which are consciously public (tested, refuted and open to scrutiny).
2. A language that is clearly defined and articulated.
3. Explanations as free from bias as possible.[1]

---

1 Through development and empirically testing, bias has been controlled. However, it is important to note that the theorist may hold, or have held, biases and the therapist offering the information is also likely to have a therapy preference or bias for one theory over another.

(Cooper et al., 2019)

For example, a client struggling with anger might wish to understand concepts about things we can and cannot control and learn about their irrational beliefs regarding certain situations (CBT), which may help them to 'let go' of outdated beliefs which are no longer helping them. This in turn might produce a conversation about their childhood whereby psychoeducation offers information about coping strategies we use as children in order to stay safe and get our needs met (attachment) and at times these stop serving us. This offers clients a framework for understanding their experiences both from the past, the present and going forward and means that if they come across bumps in the road, they have the information necessary to put this into context and begin to problem-solve. This can be incredibly empowering and provides something 'tangible' that a client can take with them.

The problem with sharing theoretical or psychoeducational explanations is that, simply 'telling to' and not 'engaging with' the client can damage relationships and create a power position of expert and help seeker, teacher and learner. This can be detrimental to the client, especially if they already have unhealthy relationship patterns assigned to the teacher/expert role, and because power disparity is counterproductive to collaborative therapy and may not be what the client desires, which ignores their preferences. As such, Motlova et al. (2017) offer some principles that therapists should consider when engaging with psychoeducation.

- Information should build on existing client strengths and resilience; we can begin to frame unhelpful behaviour as coping or protective strategies and draw on human assumptions about human needs and drives to help explain their strengths and resilience.
- Education should encompass emotional aspects of the clients lived experience, not work purely from a cognitive aspect. Problems in living, or 'mental illness', often mean that clients goals, plans, and dreams have been altered or lost. Coupled with this, the client may have experienced trauma and there can be a catharsis in telling one's own story.
- Psychoeducation should offer interventions which provide alternative ways of thinking or activities, to support them in their recovery. This often goes hand-in-hand with meaning making, '*If I understand 'x' is the problem because of 'y' then I can do 'z' instead*' for example, '*If I understand I am unhappy and resentful because of rescuing my brother*

during arguments with our mum, then I can try and be caring by listening instead of rescuing by getting involved'.

- Clients should be offered guidance towards reliable and valid resources if they wish to know more about the explanations offered. This can assist clients in accessing material that is unbiased, in order for them to assimilate information for themselves.
- As therapists, it is also fundamental to the relationship that we communicate in a manner that the client understands, balancing empathy with knowledge, and considering our own motives,

  - Am I merely demonstrating my 'cleverness'?
  - Whose benefit is this for?
  - Are there any other theories that might help the client explain their lived experience?

Moreover, our theoretical explanations should be in line with client understandings and preferences, which should be sourced prior to offering psychoeducation where possible. In cases when it is not possible to check if the client would like psychoeducation, it is important to seek feedback as to how they experienced this method of intervening, paying close attention to verbal and non-verbal clues (Motlova et al., 2017). In summary, no, not everyone will want a theoretical explanation, but many seek to understand and answer the question 'why'.

31 Can you really ensure power is distributed between two experts?

As Bohart and Tallman (1999, p. 224) put it, 'a mutual, equal, active collaboration between two intelligences in which two streams of expertise enrich one another and blend'. This is not about 'empowering' clients, but respecting, recognizing and responding to the power they already have.

(Cooper and McLeod, 2011, p. 35)

Whilst the philosophical underpinnings of power are beyond the scope of this chapter, we consider it prudent to briefly examine the concept of power distribution in therapy within sociological and philosophical thought. Going back to Marx, power was considered to be a socially structured resource and therefore finite, often found amongst the ruling class who use it over proletariat, working class, populations. Ultimately, he believed this translated into false consciousness and subordination and, as such, was grounded within social relations which were reciprocal and dependent on each other, although typically there was an uneven (asymmetrical) share of power such as a master and slave – both of whom need the other to function within this power asymmetry (Jessop, 2012). Foucault had potentially opposing views, as he did not consider power to be a resource but a transactional or relational aspect of experience, moving from discussions of 'power' to 'power relations', highlighting the interactional element of power. Foucault understood that power emerges through everyday interactions, rather than a 'thing' in itself, and whilst Marx believed power to be a negative force, Foucault understood that power had the potential to generate discourse, knowledge, and subjectivities (Flaskas and Humphreys, 1993). Power can be recognised and harnessed through positions and interactions, and the position of the therapist and therapy in society is not immune to this. Brown and Augusta-Scott (2007) offer Foucault's view that therapy

DOI: 10.4324/9781003305736-34

is a mechanism of power, whereby the subjects (clients) can objectively view themselves through 'science' and strategies of power determine which people are normal/abnormal, good/bad, strong/weak, moral/ immoral. It is precisely at this point that pluralism strives to change the power dynamics of therapy and reach clients on a human-to-human level, offering a collaborative space to share decisions and consider themselves from a strengths-based perspective.

In further exploring power within therapy, feminist theory seeks to dismantle the 'male-bias' of therapy which stems from its origins in psychoanalysis (Maguire, 2004), the impact of this is seen as an embedded paternalism which means that female-gender and feminine characteristics are defined only in relation to masculinity, and that female ideals are embedded as signifiers of both therapeutic and client capacity to engage in a therapy process. Being a male 'expert' therapist is a more powerful position than being a more female 'empath' for example. The goals and functional reference points for our gender-defined clients are likely to emerge from this system of understanding. Feminist theories also align to the concept of 'power-within' and an awareness or drive to sustain control over our own lives, resist the power imposed on us, but also to revoke our own power on others (Arendt, 1963).

In combining these philosophical perspectives, taking Foucault's understanding that power is visible through everyday interactions and that therapy, and the therapist's help or knowledge is a resource, then therapy is perhaps a hothouse for power whereby the 'everyday' interactions become a basis for analysis and understanding. Whilst asymmetrical relationships can be complementary, the 'expert' with knowledge offers the 'help-seeker' this knowledge, often in return for monetary or experience gains, it is not considered a 'power relationship' unless one or both parties are conscious of the inequity of power (Serrano-Garcla, 1994). Serrano-Garcla (1994) determines that this consciousness falls under four states:

1. Submissive - whereby people accept the asymmetry as 'natural' and out of their control.
2. Pre-critical - when individuals start to feel resentment and consider that solutions to this unsatisfactory feeling may be within their means.
3. Critical-integrative - the consideration of inequity as unjust and analyse social and historical roots.
4. Liberating - when asymmetry is constructed as oppressive and demand transformation.

We can view these conscious states throughout history in social change movements (race, gender, sexuality, (dis)ability). This also raises moral and ethical dilemmas, are we, as therapists and practitioners, happy to keep clients in a submissive state or, could we consider a movement toward social change and a greater share of the resources through questioning the ideological underpinnings and totally, or partially, transferring control of the resource, in this case knowledge? This is what pluralism hopes to move toward.

Whilst power and oppression can enter the therapy room in many guises, including but not exclusively client marginalisation, choice of location typically being the therapists, concept of 'ill' and 'healthy', payment, etc. this section will focus of power and oppression in regard to the transference of knowledge and the willingness to engage in a relationship in return for gains, be that financial, experience, or personal satisfaction. A method for raising this inequity in the room is through 'broaching' whereby the therapist is aware of '*the workings of power in the therapy dyad and makes deliberate efforts to demonstrate this understanding to the client which includes explicit discussion in sessions*' (Lee et al., 2022, p. 322). Typically broaching is discussed in terms of race, ethnicity and culture and it is the latter which we consider power over knowledge. Whilst many might balk at the idea of using terminology such as power in the therapy room, we can discuss power in terms of expertness and knowledge, with the client as the expert on their life who has existing knowledge prior to commencing therapy, some examples might be:

- *"Whilst there are things that I might know about life and theory, there are also things that you know which are unique to you. It would be great if we could share what we both know with each other."*
- *"I am not trained in EMDR (Eye Movement Desensitization and Reprocessing), if it is something that is important to you, we could look at who else might be able to help? Other things, that I can offer are..."*
- *"You say you want me to 'fix' you, but I don't have that kind of magic power. What's that like to hear?"*
- *"Something I was thinking we could discuss today, that might be useful, is assertiveness. Do you know anything about that already?"*

Pluralism is concerned with the sharing of this knowledge with each other and building meaning bridges between each other's resources. However, it is important to note that even with this invitation to share knowledge there is a power imbalance and almost a 'giving of permission' to share, nevertheless we perceive it to be a more ethical vehicle toward distributing power.

In considering inviting the client to take some power, they also must want it. Various life experiences and associations with power can exist; fear of ridicule, fear of responsibility, and/or fear of failure/success. Additionally, cultural norms about help seeking create expected relational styles and these can manifest as preferences, we know that many clients (not all) want a choice but prefer the therapist to take the lead (Vollmer et al., 2009) and offer a more directive style (Cooper et al., 2021). In fact, what we might see in a collaborative relationship is that power changes hands gradually, initially the therapist might assume more power/responsibility for imparting knowledge and overtime this may shift to the client taking more of a lead (Bachelor et al., 2007) (see Chapters 11 and 47 for further information on collaborative relationships).

There are many in-session processes for distributing power, some of which fall under the 'human' aspect whereas others are more technical. Human aspects are considered core to humanistic fields and which many therapeutic modalities utilise – warmth, genuineness, acceptance – but there are layers that can facilitate this further. For example, appropriate self-disclosure and humour can evidence acceptance and genuineness in a way that reflecting, and summarising do not always effectively communicate. Similarly, seeking the permission to get it wrong occasionally, or even still to not necessarily be the 'right' therapist for them (and that this does not mean that counselling is not right for them), evidences a humanness and step away from power, which invites the client into a shared relationship whereby we are 'in it together'. More formal tools can include requesting feedback (see Chapter 20) and asking the client to name their preferences (see Chapter 22) and thoughts on the process of therapy, or through utilising meta-therapeutic communication in order to understand the client's inner world, all of which can create a more equitable relationship.

It is also important to note the social change that has occurred as a result of therapy providing language and legitimacy to claims of suffering. We can see the real-time effects of therapeutic discussion which point to a cultural shift *'especially in terms of changing relations of authority and power'* (Wright, 2011, p. 222) which is aided by developments in medicine, economics, education, professional practices, and the way that we disseminate information, particularly in the use of technology

(Wright, 2011). The internet has increased both the access to information and the promotion of lived experience groups, anti-psychiatry, and more broadly the links between society and mental well-being. Clients, quite rightly, are increasingly empowered in seeking the right help for their needs, and therapy is developing to progressively serve the needs of each individual. However, for now, it is difficult to imagine a shift so great whereby there is no asymmetry between client and therapist because therapists themselves are beholden to others in power, and the power is merely transferred from systems (health, education, social, etc.) to education providers, to therapists, to clients. This occurs not simply as a result of context but because therapists also need to charge to pay for their own professional development, insurance, and cost of living.

Yet, if we, clients and therapists, can liberate ourselves from the 'less than/more than' positions, then clients are empowered to make decisions based on choice, rather than necessity, and can identify themselves as resourceful during periods of crises.

32 Is a pluralistic approach really suitable for people living with severe and enduring mental health problems?

The answer to this question is 'maybe', if undertaken with wise judgements in terms of therapist competence, considered accommodation of the capacity of the client, and the purpose and goals in therapy. Many people seeking counselling and psychotherapy are living with mental health problems which have a profound effect on their well-being, their ability to engage with the world emotionally, socially, and economically, and this often serves to undermine their sense of independence and choice. Notwithstanding the difficulties perceived by many practitioners in the concept of diagnosis, and taking what is seen by many as an inappropriate stance on medicalisation or politicisation of psychological functioning (Kinderman, 2019; Smith, 2022), we need to dwell a little about what is meant by 'severe and enduring mental health problems'. Usually, the implications of these words are that the person experiences the world in ways which are fundamentally different in terms of perceptions (e.g. having auditory or visual hallucinations), that their emotional experience is debilitating over a long period of time (e.g. major depressive disorder), or that their cognitive function is impaired for biological reasons (e.g. dementia). The perceived challenge for these groups is that they may have a reduced capacity to orientate themselves towards well-being and are often considered unable to make rational decisions. It is clear that, given this challenge, it might be difficult for a person to actively engage in the collaborative process of pluralistic therapy, and they might benefit more from structured interventions targeting specific symptoms or experiences. If they are offered talking therapy the question arises, '*can consideration be given by a pluralistic practitioner to the principles of practice and accommodations made within the model to work with the client?*' Of course, this must be considered on a case-by-case basis, however, the inherent flexibility of pluralistic therapy can allow people who might otherwise been viewed as having 'too limited function' to

DOI: 10.4324/9781003305736-35

find ways forward. Tasks and methods can be usefully deployed by setting aside the notion of 'curing' mental health problems, but rather seeking to strengthen and enhance aspects of living.

The nature of client capacity and consent (and therefore who is holding responsibility) is an important consideration, as there will almost always be issues with empowerment and collaboration with the client when they are experiencing disturbances which are chaotic and sometimes disjointed. As an example, there might be someone whose function has been severely impacted by alcohol addiction in a way which renders them emotionally volatile, at times confused, and subject to periods of profound depression. When managing risk (see also Chapter 29), Reeves (2015) discusses capacities to consider for working with clients that are useful in this context.

- Understanding – does the client have sufficient understanding of the process at hand?
- Recall and memory – does the client retain sufficient information to orientate and track the process?
- Ability to weigh up options rationally – are they able to evaluate options and preferences?
- Communicate decisions – can they effectively communicate their perspective and preferences?

In these circumstances, a further consideration for a therapist would be their own capacity to understand and anticipate something from the clients' experience – what is it like to live with this problem and what might be expected in terms of behaviour and presentation? Resources available from lived experience groups are incredibly useful in these situations. The therapist may also need to consider how they provide and maintain a relationship within the context of service provision, often therapists are situated in multi-disciplinary teams which may maintain a paternalistic approach to service-user well-being. The therapist might usefully discuss the suitability of an approach with the client but may need to include a family member or other responsible person in the conversation on whether therapy is helpful. The therapist should also be aware of potential pitfalls and relational dynamics, particularly for those who have experience of institutionalisation or who have predetermined experiences of disempowerment and consider the impact of this on their work.

Given these considerations, it is worth remembering that a strengths-based approach is not uncommon in mental health care, with concepts such as the 'Tidal Model' of mental health (Barker, 2001), and the recovery movement (Slade, 2009) providing accounts of how individual experiences of people with profound mental health difficulties can be fluctuating and how therapy can be rewarding. Using a non-diagnostic approach can broaden the scope for creative work if the therapist meets the person where they are at in their journey, responds to this sensitively, and also understands that they may have experiences as a result of psychiatric interventions that create barriers to the work (Boyle and Johnstone, 2020).

Another question may be around how a particular diagnosis might be meaningful to the client, seeking to explore whether the client understands mental health problems as real and effective categories of experience, and how these are often culturally defined, for example, someone being diagnosed with autism may, in the current cultural context, find this to be empowering and validating of their experience, whilst someone who is labelled 'schizophrenic' might find the experience distressing and struggle to accept it (Boyle, 2022). Refocusing on personal experience and chosen direction may also help. A pluralistic therapist may have a position on the social justice impact and validity of diagnosis and this discussion with the client can form part of, or develop, the shared formulation alongside the knowledge of how diagnosis fits within the clients' cultural frame of reference.

> *Iain, 46, came to therapy stating he had Major Depressive Disorder (MDD) and had recently been resident in a mental health ward, having been unable to self-care and attempted suicide, and was on anti-depressant medication. He reported that he had been badly beaten by a stranger on a night out when he was at university, and a year later he was diagnosed with MDD. The therapist and Iain began to explore his symptoms, understanding his diagnosis and other factors present at the time of being diagnosed. They began to consider that his symptoms of insomnia, restlessness, severe low and persistent mood including suicide ideation, loss of interest in activities he enjoyed, and feelings of worthlessness (DSM-5;* American Psychiatric Association, 2013*) might also be understood as a product of his trauma. He noted that whilst the diagnosis of MDD was helpful to get support from healthcare services, he felt it has blocked him in dealing with the assault, which he never spoke about, and found it helpful to consider his symptoms in relation to his experience.*

With clients presenting with severe and enduring mental health concerns, some of the tasks that might be undertaken in practice to facilitate the work, include:

- Contracting and exploring possible ways of undertaking therapy – thinking about temporal stability of experience and responsiveness in the moment.
- Developing self-awareness using an environment of acceptance and positive regard.
- Working with traumatic events and experiences.
- Learning strategies for managing difficult experiences and emotions.
- Making sense of client life-story – for example, moving beyond the thin narrative of diagnosis.
- Understanding the relationship between the client and the diagnosis, exploring for example, looking at the meaning of the diagnosis to the client.
- Identifying strengths and opportunities for growth.
- Seeking cultural resources and evaluating them.
- Managing and coming to terms with limitations (imposed or otherwise).
- Managing and working constructively, ethically, and collaboratively with risk.

Finally, the distinction between organic and inorganic mental health problems can be important in planning work with clients. Whilst most clients with profound mental health problems will be on some medication, organic mental health problems are more likely to be addressed by medical interventions and the symptoms, presentation, and progression are more predictable (Bell et al., 2020). When a biological cause is recognised, this must be an important consideration about how therapy is undertaken, for example, if someone has been diagnosed with dementia it is reasonable to expect lapses of memory and some therapeutic tasks and methods may be more likely to be beneficial but, as the condition progresses function reduces, no matter what therapeutic interventions are used, and thus the potential for collaboration is reduced. A comparison of the task-list from early (Weaks, 2006) to mid stage (Clare and Woods, 2001; Smith, unpublished) can be considered below, whereas later stage dementia patients, experiencing cognitive challenges such as speech loss and confusion, may benefit from 'in the moment' relational work drawn from person-centred therapy (Lipinska, 2009).

Table 32.1 Comparison of early and mid-stage dementia tasks

Early-stage dementia (Weaks, 2006)	Mid-stage dementia (Woods, 2001; Smith, unpublished)
• Exploring a sense of 'self' with the diagnosis. • Renegotiating relationships. • Existential issues. • Coping with symptoms. • Dealing with health care and broader social attitudes.	• Preparing for the journey. • Finding personality strengths that will enable an individualistic overview of potential needs and resources (drawn from Kitwood, 1997). • Maintaining a sense of 'self'. • Helping a person find ways to deal with their emotional responses to their illness. • Maintaining independence. • Maintaining social contact. • Coping with behaviour problems.

What pluralistic therapists can do when working with people experiencing severe and enduring mental health problems, is align with the principles of practice in the best way they can for this particular client in this particular context. Holding fast to this idea allows choices to be made and a creativity in responding to the questions of what the client wants, needs, and is able to do. Notwithstanding this ambition, the principles of pluralistic therapy would also support a transition to other therapeutic approaches and can involve a reversion to decisions being made in the best interests of the person rather than by the person themselves.

33 How can pluralism be adapted to working with young people?

Counselling for children and young people is becoming increasingly common and sought after, and initiatives for counselling in schools are found across the United Kingdom and Ireland. Counselling for young people tends to be based on some core models (e.g. humanistic, systemic, and CBT), but many practitioners report being integrative in practice in order to prioritise the needs of the client (Norcross, 2005). Overall evidence points to young people appreciating a safe space to talk, being respected, and heard '*almost as an equal*', and in some cases feeling empowered '*almost like an adult*' (Griffiths, 2013; Källström and Thunberg, 2019, p. 556) in that they can express without imposed expectations for behaviour and topic. Therapist qualities are also reported as being very important (Lynass et al., 2012), and change processes include relief, increasing self-worth, developing insight, enhancing coping strategies and improving relational skills (McArthur et al., 2016).

The primary agent of change in pluralism is the client themselves, but this individuation process – to establish what the client wants and how they might go about it - is complicated for a young person used to being situated within a family, education, peers, and the influence of social media. It would be fair to say that young people are surrounded by external expectations (how to be a 'good' friend, student, son/daughter, member of society), and their parents or caregiver may also have expectations of therapy for them. Additionally, they may enter therapy with not only the weight of the problem but also the perceived stigma of needing therapy (Prior, 2012). It is important to also recognise that adolescents may have their own expectations around how they want therapy to 'be' (the process) and what they want to achieve (the outcomes). For therapists this reflects the porous boundary between the work in the room and the client's lifeworld, there are also questions of choice and capacity to choose, and usually a set of expectations about

DOI: 10.4324/9781003305736-36

who you are as a therapist and what you 'want' them to do as another adult in their lives, so how might we work pluralistically in this unique relationship?

Expectations of young people in therapy

Pluralistic therapy functions through the creation of collaborative spaces where knowledge and power are shared and opportunities for choice are generated. Limitations on choice-making and perceived control, means that young clients may not have imagined, or understood, what therapy, or life, might look like separate to that of other people in their lives. This can present a challenge for several reasons, first, we have to acknowledge that the client is not easily positioned as an equal, there is a responsibility to ensure their well-being and social and legal systems do not afford them much power, agency and control, which are dependent on the client's age, circumstances, social and ethnocultural environment (Clamp, 2022). Furthermore, the client themselves is likely to be sitting in a role of deference (and sometimes defence). How the client is referred to the service can be a barrier because it can be percieved as something the 'adults' want for the young person, with the risk that young client's do not feel included in the process, for example, one young client stated the referral had taken place 'behind her back' (Midgley et al., 2014 , p. 5). Subsequently, goals for therapy can be predetermined by other stakeholders such as parents or the referral source (GPs, schools, colleges, etc.), resulting in a hindrance to the therapeutic alliance and thus the therapeutic outcome (Everall and Paulson, 2002). Researcher Mark Clamp (2022) examined the nature of hopes and goals within these contextualised factors and proposed that initially exploring these can align therapy to *their* needs even in the context of other factors. Clamp (2022) further argues that, whilst therapy alone cannot give young people control over all aspects of their lives, adopting a pluralistic framework to therapy with children and young people can offer a positive space and an opportunity for young people to experience being in control – which, in itself, is therapeutically valuable.

Many young people who come to therapy have no prior experience of what it entails, which can cause anxiety, and so setting base expectations for what therapy might look like, and how it can help, will be useful. Midgley and colleagues (2014) explored adolescents' expectations of counselling and found a common phrase which many will recognise, 'I don't know', which can result from indifference or hostility about attending therapy or because it manages the anxiety of being asked what they think will happen, but it can also be a simple fact - they don't know! - and for some a precursor to imagining what they want (Midgley et al., 2014). For a pluralistic therapist, 'I don't know' can be a useful start and through a meta-communicative process we can acknowledge their resentment, distress, puzzlement or 'stuckness', but also that 'not knowing' is an invitation to finding out. In seeking feedback and clarification, we can understand if we should probe further or back off, either working on the relationship or offering information that might help them to create their own expectations.

Collaboratively finding hope with young people

It is always helpful to start therapy with a sense of purpose, and ideally some hopes for the outcome of the process. Children and young people can begin therapy with a good idea of what hopes they have for therapy and may even have agency in guiding the therapist towards what is helpful for them (Hoener et al., 2012; McLeod, 2012). Once past the initial 'I don't know', many young people in Midgley and colleagues (2014) study did articulate clear ideas on the purpose (catharsis, focusing on feelings and problems) and method (talk, free space, questions and answers) of therapy, along with an understanding of potential vulnerabilities including, that they might cry, feel exposed, or have to endure awkward silence. They also had visions of what the relationship would be like, with some hoping for someone who was 'nice', non-judgemental, and a real person, whereas others identified the therapist as a doctor-like figure, distant, and giving advice and solutions – albeit safe. Whilst it was argued that this might be because it would be hard for anyone to imagine a relationship with someone they have never met (Midgley et al., 2014), or because this doctor image soothes anxieties about developing an emotionally close relationship with an adult caregiver at a time when they are also seeking more autonomy (Midgley et al., 2014; Bauminger et al., 2008), the image of a responsible doctor, whilst seemingly appealing to a client, establishes a power imbalance and reinforces an interventionist 'medicalised' view of therapy which does not play out in pluralistic practice – nor that of many modern therapy approaches. This can be a barrier to therapy as young clients seek outcomes to 'eradicate' negative feelings, and expectations that the 'doctor' can fix them and that they have the answers. In reality, and conversely, this also goes against their wish to 'keep control' and have the therapist be like a 'friend' (Gibson et al., 2016). Supporting clients through human-to-human connection, and ensuring they are involved in the process as the expert on their own life, is something that pluralistic practitioners strive towards – a collaborative relationship.

So once any assumptions that the therapist will tell the young person what they need to do are dispelled, the focus can turn to the client's hopes for therapy. For young people, future-approach goals may be less common (in one study a large majority expressed avoidant goals, and even many of the approach goals were to regain their old self) (Midgley et al., 2014). Some young people cannot articulate goals, but when they can imagine what they could achieve there is often a focus on self confidence and self-esteem (Rupani et al., 2014), school (improving grades, doing well in university or work) and relationships (with family and friends) (Midgley et al., 2014).

If I work with young people, do I have to involve the parents and other stakeholders?

Young clients are surrounded by people who can impact on their therapy, and there may be little choice in practice whether to involve them or not. Without parental agreement, retention and adherence are hard to maintain (Kazdin, 1996). Parents and other stakeholders such as teachers or social workers, can support therapy by being involved as *consultants,* which can aid assessment and formulation, and the identification of goals and tasks, *collaborators,* joining through engagement strategies to understand their concerns, enquire about their own past, and validate and affirm their commitment to supporting their child (and treatment), and *clients,* such as providing support in helping their child with homework exercises (Pereira et al., 2015) and psychoeducation and skills (communication, problem solving and affect regulation). All of which can enhance parental care and engagement by removing barriers (Martinez et al., 2015; Diamond et al., 2010; Hall and Mufson, 2009). Conceptualising those around the client as cultural resources can help with understanding their role, and perhaps aid them in evaluating the value (or otherwise) of those involved in their lives.

On the other hand, young clients typically say they do not want their parents involved (Gibson et al., 2016), some will reach the age that parental consent is no longer a legal requirement, and it may also be deemed that involving the parent/caregiver is not in their best interest. Stakeholders can also sometimes complicate the therapy process as they have their own agendas and expectations for the process which raises the question of goal priority. In an ideal world, collaborative goal setting (see Chapter 16) will ensue however, in a practical world you are the young person's therapist and are there to meet their needs, therefore it is the young person's goals we work with, otherwise we can risk rupturing the relationship. This may need to be explained and explored with the other stakeholders.

What skills do I need to work with young people?

Coming into therapy can be an uncomfortable and challenging experience for a young person. So, whilst when working pluralistically with young people, the core practice principles and skills used (see Chapter 13) are the same, the balance of skills may differ. Young people may need more work on establishing a collaborative relationship, developing trust, and addressing the power difference (whilst retaining a sense of safety) (see Chapter 31). Furthermore, they are more inclined to do active work and will tend to be more interested in resolution than insight – they also report that some aspects of therapy are less helpful compared to adult-therapy, for example, use of silence. Young people may also find it less comfortable (and sometimes quite strange) to give feedback and meta-communicate about the process of therapy so utilising routine outcome monitoring (see Appendix II) may be preferred (Law, 2014), especially if the measure used reflects progress visually, such as through graphs. As with adults, positive engagement with therapy predicts more positive outcomes (Dobud, 2017), so, the better the process and outcome monitoring the better the tailoring to client experience, preference, and unique needs (Dobud, 2017).

Some aspects of who you are as a therapist are also likely to be important, so drawing from your unique toolkit to establish a connection and address common 'problems' that young people experience is vital. Some examples that Frankie uses are provided below but expanded upon in Appendix I.

Relational skills

- Humour and the 'light-hearted' aspects of me.
- Self-disclosure.
- Adaptation and emphasis of language and tone.
- Validation.

In addition, the kinds of things that are discussed and the attitude towards the client can make a difference.

Therapy and methods

- Recognising the power, strengths and resources they do have, even within constraints.
- Providing information from which they can make choice.
- Discussing their behaviour and the effect it has and exploring if it is getting them what they want.
- Celebrating and punctuating achievements.
- Creative methods (metaphors, art, their cultural resources).

In terms of empirical evidence for pluralistic practice, pilot work conducted by Joyce and colleagues to establish how to evaluate the effectiveness of pluralistic counselling for children and young people at an addictions service (Joyce et al., 2023) found no difference between pluralistic therapy and person-centred child therapy on outcome, measured by the YP-CORE (Twigg et al., 2009) and the Strengths and Difficulties Questionnaire (Goodman, 2001). The differentiation between the interventions was a confounding factor in this study, but it still represents early steps into establishing how a pluralistic approach might be developed for young people. Perhaps most importantly, young clients want adults to listen to what they want and what they have to say – even if they don't always make the 'right' decisions, they are the ones who know what they are going through (Law, 2014).

34 Does pluralism address questions of inclusivity and equality?

Equality, diversity, and inclusion cover all aspects of organisations and relationships where differences can lead to barriers to access, reduced representation, individual, systematic, or institutional bias, along with minimisation or silencing which leads to disadvantages relating to personal and social characteristics (which can include ethnicity and race, sexuality and gender, neurodiversity, and disabilities). In an equitable therapeutic world, all individuals, no matter what characteristics are held, should expect the experience and outcomes of therapy to meet their needs however, we recognise that inclusivity and equality are not at the standard they should be in the counselling and psychotherapy profession, and membership organisations are working on addressing these issues. The need for equality in pluralism goes beyond our moral, ethical, and legislative requirements because, at its heart, is the perspective and belief that difference and 'otherness', in all its forms, is enriching, with each different perspective, lived experience, and dialogue adding new opportunities for understanding and routes to living better lives. Because of this, pluralism is strongly aligned to movements within psychological therapies which work to more broadly address the levels of competence needed to work across diverse groups (e.g. APA, 2017).

Few would argue that we must strive to work effectively with all clients however, even when we endeavour to recognise difference our capacity to do so may be hindered by two things, the first is that we may not be very good at recognising difference and the impact of this on our clients, and also fail to acknowledge the embedded inequalities in our organisations because of what has been termed '*compromised conceptualisation*' (Bradby, 2010), a little like not being able to see the wood for the trees. The second is that we often don't know how to recognise and work constructively with difference (Singer and Tummala-Narra, 2013), and attempts to create frameworks for 'multi-cultural'

DOI: 10.4324/9781003305736-37

competencies have received mixed results in terms of impact on therapy process and outcome (Tao et al., 2015). In alignment with a social justice agenda, pluralistic therapy strives to recognise the able-ist white spaces in which much of therapy takes place, and to create a 'safe-space' (Palfrey, 2018) for the impact of inequality to be recognised and discussed with the client, which cannot be done without action. Pluralistic therapy goes beyond the assumption that we can '*meet the person in the room*' because we also need to consider who the client is meeting in the room, the therapist, and all they bring and represent, along with where the room is positioned in metaphoric, socio-cultural, as well as geographic terms! Pluralism highlights the need for therapists to be aware of the cultural imposition of their role and identity as much as possible, in order to facilitate and aid this awareness in the client including macro (e.g. power-positions and cultural frames) and micro (e.g. interpersonal responding and 'manners') factors. This emphasises the complexities of multiple aspects and changing sense of self-hood and difference, depending on the context and the dynamic between therapist and client, and so, using an approach stemming from cultural humility is important (Hook et al., 2013).

This starting point for recognising the impact of difference is perhaps to think about past notions of psychological and spiritual well-being as our historic (and often implicit) context, and whilst we have 'moved on' from this, there will be a future in which our beliefs and practices will also be considered archaic. For centuries, cultures have exercised a range of 'treatments', which drew on physical, biological, spiritual, social, or moral interventions, aimed at curing their understanding of psychological and physical distress, including some religious and tribal cultures believing in supernatural powers or demonic possession as a cause for mental ill health (Foerschner, 2010; McLeod, 2013a). We are also often unaware that our Western concept of psychological help has evolved from pre-1800s to the present day. Historically, members of society collectively 'tolerated' those with psychological disturbances within their rural communities, 'managing' them through social expectations, shame, and religion. With the advent of the industrial revolution the disruption of these stable communities is thought to have rendered people to being more 'inner-directed', with more responsibility for themselves and less so for others. Science began replacing religion, and in parallel those who were once cared for within their families and communities found themselves in asylums, where 'modern' morals and social care was institution-based. With the professionalisation of responding to psychological distress and mental health, and a concurrent reduction in the expectations and capacity of communities to care, there have been emerging narratives around 'interventions' by 'experts' and effectively a sense that distress is abnormal and must be 'cured' (Oswald, 2015; McLeod, 2013a). We see this social exclusion echo through our daily lives and our acts as therapists should be framed within our understanding of the culture in which we function and respond to others.

This historic context means that within the modern Western world there are culturally embedded understandings of what therapy is, what it does, and how it is undertaken. This limiting view is influential in training and practice, but also imposes restrictions on both therapists and clients in their views on what can be done 'in the room'. Philosophically, pluralism demands the ability to incorporate all potential perspectives and for practitioners this is an active process of inquiry and development of knowledge. Limitations on what is brought to therapy and pre-assumptions about the knowledge base, on which the therapist and client draw, may already be in place for us. Therapy which does not recognise and broach issues of difference is not only likely to be less effective, but it can also be harmful to the client (Lee et al., 2022), and so it is important that actions are taken to address the effect of power and silencing (see Chapter 31), before it is established in the room, in order for therapy to be effective.

Underlying equality and inclusion is the role of power in society, across a range of dimensions (Boyle, 2022; Proctor, 2017). This sits across therapy, not just in terms of the social justice agenda, as distress itself is often perceived as evidence of disempowerment (Rao et al., 2007), but includes perceptions of extreme emotions, particularly negatives ones which may be associated with poor judgement, even irrationality, leaving clients in a position of needing to 'normalise' before acting or responding. This dynamic intersects with existing socio-cultural systems embedding and perpetuating inequalities, for example, the interception between horizontal cultures (such as race and ethnicity) and vertical cultures (such as class) mean that being from a minority group subjects clients to the drive to assimilate in white European middle-class norms espoused by most Euro-centric therapeutic schools and Western care provision. This can erode and reduce an individual's capacity to celebrate and utilise their own strengths, rich cultural history and traditions. For many clients, the complex knowledge and communication systems originating from cultural backgrounds can also impact on both presentation of problems and help-seeking. For example, Pederson and colleagues (2022) found complex interlinks between spiritual beliefs and concerns about institutionalisation and stigmatisation of Nigerians. In Indian cultures there may be a greater tendency towards somatisation than psychological and emotional interpretations (Rao et al., 2007). Given the potential for belief systems which are significantly contrasting to the Euro-centric assumptions of many therapists, it is unlikely that all these factors can simply be unpicked in the room, and this drives pluralistic therapists to make attempts to understand them, not just through the client but before, and whilst, the client work is being undertaken.

Al-Roubaiy and colleagues (2017) in their work on counselling for Iraqi migrants proposed that pluralistic therapists focus on three multi-cultural competency domains (Sue et al., 1992, 1998) and they include that the counsellor (i) holds an awareness of their own cultural values and biases, (ii) holds an awareness of the client's worldview, and (iii) is able to offer culturally appropriate intervention strategies. In addition to this, there is the need for 'dynamic-sizing' (Sue, 1998), an ability to navigate generic knowledge of cultural contexts which impact on the client, and when and how to translate this to the individual client.

Drawing on these ideas, inclusivity and equality are addressed in pluralistic therapy in a number of ways because pluralistic therapists:

- Actively strive to be open to recognising and exploring understandings beyond their own. Actions are taken, to broach issues of power and inclusivity, which is threaded through a co-creation process drawing on lived experience.
- Focus therapy on positive identity work, recognising the client as being 'Heroic' (Duncan et al., 2004) and exploring and identifying cultural strengths and resources.
- Bridge meaning gaps and use language in therapy to closely map to the client more than the therapist.
- Offer a 'safe-space' to discuss issues experienced or arising, outside and inside the therapy room, and build bridges across 'differences'. Importantly, some clients are interested in focusing on difference (Williams and Levitt, 2008), and if so, therapists may disclose their own perceptions and experiences as an affirmative or counterpoint for discussion.
- Utilise meta-communication which can be undertaken to discuss practical and practice issues around inclusivity, valuing the

client perspective, for example, gaining feedback on attempts at 'dynamic-sizing'.

Given the expectation for a pluralistic therapist to actively strive towards inclusivity and acceptance of 'otherness', it is important to recognise that the perception of 'difference' can be something which is influential from the outset but can emerge as a factor during therapy. A client who comes to therapy to consider their experience, and as a result identifies 'autistic traits' for example, needs this to be acknowledged and the opportunity to purposefully explore the impact of this undiscovered 'difference' on their lives.

These ideas can be contextualised in a growing movement within psychology to focus on a social justice agenda. Whilst not limited to the pluralistic movement, Cooper (2023) has offered further points for consideration in his new book, *Psychology at the Heart of Social Change: Developing a Progressive Vision for Society*, which offers the reader a historic and contemporary view of how we can move forward and can increase our knowledge of the social justice and social change movements.

35 How does pluralism align with other therapy approaches that aim to impact societal issues?

Social justice has been developed as a concept to which pluralistic therapy is aligned and it is argued that, compared to other therapies, it has the capacity to best address societal inequalities (Winter et al., 2016). Social justice involves a raising of social consciousness to power differences in order to enact a moral responsibility to eradicate limits to individual freedom, injustice and inequality. The concept of social justice is an evolving one, over the last 100 years it has increasingly focused on individuation of need rather than socio-political resource redistribution (Thrift and Sugarman, 2019), and in parallel with therapy it supports the right for recognition and identity (Garland-Thomson, 2002; Young, 1990). The social justice agenda is now rooted in a philosophy of equity (fair access to justice and resources) over equality (fairness of distribution over equal distribution) underpinned by values of 'inclusion, collaboration, co-operation, equal access and opportunity' (Ayala et al., 2011, p. 2795). Ayala and colleagues (2011) discuss the link between social justice and health and well-being, the impact of which can be experienced by those who do not have access to justice resulting in poorer physical and emotional health and increased susceptibility to illness and mental health diagnosis. In therapy, the implications of this go beyond the therapist awareness of discrimination, socio-economic imbalance, environmental and sustainability issues, and identity politics. Pluralism, it could be argued, is in a prime position to support people whose experiences sit outside the frame of 'usual' therapies, and as it provides an open-system, responsive and not fixed in the conceptualisation of the cause and resolution of problems, it is to some extent 'future-proofed' (as social agendas change so does the pluralistic practice response) to develop responses to societies problems.

There are few simple answers to the question of how and whether therapists should speak out in the room around social justice, or even

DOI: 10.4324/9781003305736-38

across society about these issues, and this tends to revert to personal choice and preference. However, what the pluralistic social justice stance does speak to is that these issues cannot be ignored by locating client problems wholly within themselves and requiring them to be personally responsible for resolving them. Pluralistic therapists expand their thinking into the provision of resilient and healthy communities and societies, rather than just resilient individuals, by locating the possible origins of distress in both context and psychology, but also recognising the interactions between the two. After all, '*if a plant were wilting, we wouldn't diagnose it with "wilting plant-syndrome" – we would change its conditions*' (Ahsan, 2022).

Whilst feminist therapy has led the way in shifting the lens from the personal to the socio-political for clients subjected to oppression and embedded power dynamics (Butler, 1997), pluralistic therapy is seen by many to be an evolution of this in that it incorporates an understanding of the impact of societal, cultural, and political causes and solutions to client distress. Recognising the societal trend towards the individuation of the cause of problems (Read and Dillon, 2013), therapists can help the client acknowledge that the solutions to these are not necessarily an emergent quality of the client's thoughts, emotions, and behaviour.

Feminist therapy works at a foundational level to remove the power imposed on women, who are disadvantaged in society through their sex, gender, and the intersection of this with age, race, ethnicity, and religion (Brown, 2018). Their assumption is that the recognition and removal of the imposed oppression will result in the client being empowered and act towards their own interests. In practice, this aligns well to aspects of pluralism, given the acceptance of the current understanding of the world being embedded in a patriarchal state. Feminist therapy is also characterised by the overt recognition of strengths, where even extreme difficulty can be reframed as representing strengths and capacities. This movement has had a strong influence on the ways that collaboration and empowerment occur in pluralistic practice. Work done by pluralistic therapists to share information with the client on their roles, intentions, ways of working, and offer to collaborate and share responsibility for change, *rather than to help or rescue*, resonates with feminist therapy practice. Pluralistic therapists are also charged with maintaining a reflective awareness of the impact of context on the work they do, how they respond to this themselves, and how they can make judgements on sharing their perspectives with clients.

Latterly, the pluralistic therapy movement has explored its resonance with social-action and emancipatory praxis (Gupta, 2022). This is an

influential concept drawn from social work which encourages the recognition of minority or excluded groups of people or thought, and finds
means by which they can be used to influence, or challenge, established
ways of being and understanding the world. Specific points of resonance
for this within pluralistic practice include direct engagement with client
experience, and the provision of a space where therapeutic intention is
not to align with any particular model or understanding in order to render socially appropriate change. Rather, the focus is on allowing unique
voices to be respected, developed, and learned from.

The debates around the role of therapy in a broader social justice
agenda have led to practitioners considering their role in the world.
One example of this is the move towards addressing and responding to
concerns around global crises such as climate change. The anxiety and
distress caused by the recognition of the climate crisis and the implications, both social, economic, and emotional, are likely to impact on
all clients (Mapp and Gatenio Gabel, 2019; Watts et al., 2018). This
creates a tension for therapists – the existential question of the survival
of humanity can feel too big to address, whilst acting to alleviate the
distress caused by emotional responses to climate change might render
the client passive in terms of their need to respond to the difficulties,
and therapists need to find a position on this. Alongside this, there is
likely to be a drive from the therapists themselves to act on the climate
change agenda and balance how to bring this into the room. Pluralism
enables the therapist and client to collaborate on the best way to progress, validating the concerns by considering the knowledge they have
of the crisis and exploring how these impact on the client, with a view
to engaging in the management of these concerns whilst also supporting
preferred actions inside and outside the therapy room. The differentiation between what is done by the client, what is done by the therapist,
and what can be done by the profession, is not always obvious.

Social justice is also concerned with protecting those who have to
live within less-than-ideal models of justice. Whilst we do not want
to recreate the narrative of 'you just need to get better', expanding
the client's view of their problems in living within societal contexts
can root exploration of how they have protected themselves in spite of
their society (Ayala et al., 2011). This may include resilience building,
educational attainment, becoming involved with their community, and
enhancing communication and self-efficacy. Understanding, alongside
this, that systemic interventions within social settings offer an increased
level of protection for clients and their communities (Ayala et al., 2011).

How does this look in practice with an individual client?

As individuals and practitioners, we can feel disempowered, and sometimes it is 'easier' to leave it to someone else. However, we are then at best ignoring and at worst perpetuating cycles of social injustice and ultimately this is in contrast with the ethical and moral values of pluralism and the profession. Pluralism is not particularly interested in you donning a cape and saving the world; it recognises change often happens gradually, therefore understanding the actions that *can* be taken is a useful place to start. We have listed some useful interventions that practitioners could be reasonably expected to engage with, depending on client preference.

- Awareness and invitation – It is important as practitioners, that we have an awareness of social and political aspects of the client's life and invite clients to talk about these.
- Advocate – This is an area that we feel is underutilised within therapy, instead often working from a position of empowering the client to do their own work. Whilst this remains a vital piece of work, sometimes, no matter how empowered the client, some social systems disregard their power. As a profession which has, and is, gaining power and reputability, we are in a position to collaborate with the client in raising awareness of social issues, provide information, be present with the client in addressing their own need and, in some cases, speak on behalf of the client (or clients).
- Conceptualising – We are already familiar with the process of conceptualising the clients story (see Chapter 14), but it is also important for us to be able to conceptualise (form ideas) about the their social environment. Concept-maps and Eco-Webs are useful tools (Williams et al., 2015).
- Take an active stance and position – When working in an organisation we have the ability to move away from doing therapy on a case-by-case basis, and to begin to shape culture, policy and discourse.
- Multi-disciplinary work – It is important that practitioners are open to working in collaboration with those from other disciplines in order to best meet the needs of the individual and community.

Ultimately, therapists are required to be responsive to their clients' basic human needs, as well as emotional needs and wants. They need an ability to respond to acts of inequality, utilising the tasks and methods above as well as foundational pluralistic skills (see Chapters 5 and 13) and their own unique toolkit (see Chapter 19 and Appendix I), in order to help clients address their unmet needs, in addition to the emotional problems that have, partially or fully, resulted from these unmet needs.

This chapter has given some details of how social justice is addressed in pluralistic therapy, and whilst only a few issues are given, we recommend consideration of all aspects of socially imposed difficulties. For example, McLeod (2018b) pinpoints further specific examples such as disability, human trafficking, and poverty.

36 How does cross-cultural working enhance the pluralistic approach?

This chapter develops existing issues of equality and diversity (see Chapter 34), to outline how cross-cultural working has the potential to enhance the pluralistic approach. This is achieved through a recognition of the world-wide existence of cultural practices, knowledge, and ways of knowing, which offer opportunities for growth and well-being. In pluralism the context and impact of what is culturally 'given' is recognised, but an optimistic and open stance maintained as the practice evolves. The big question here is not, '*how do we accommodate otherness?*' but, 'what are we yet to learn?'.

It is fair to say that there is no neutral position when it comes to culture and ethnicity, no default position of being 'at home', and no ethical position that allows a unidirectional otherness. Cultural misunderstandings can disrupt or even damage the therapeutic process (e.g. Al-Roubaiy et al., 2017) and is enacted through language, assumptions, power-relations, recognition and focus on barriers (e.g. language/semantics), enactment of therapist goals for social justice through the client, and silencing. These aspects are addressed in pluralism through key skills in:

- Transparency.
- Openness to learning and curiosity.
- Checking out.
- Broaching.
- Respecting otherness and creativity.
- Instilling client confidence/hope.
- Responding to needs.
- Social justice values.
- Empowering.
- Advocating (where requested as a preference).

DOI: 10.4324/9781003305736-39

- Cultural competence (therapist responsibility).
- Recognising nuance within cultural contexts, for example, cultural identities, roles of gender.
- Therapist reflexivity and development.

We are currently experiencing an unprecedented growth of client diversity in terms of ethnicity, culture, class, ableness and disability, religion, gender, and sexual orientation (Wilk, 2014), but it is generally accepted that most models of psychotherapy in the Western culture are firmly embedded within its own understandings and value systems (Koç and Kafa, 2019). This draws into question the degree to which they are suitable for all those who might consider engaging with us, and the pluralistic thinkers (the authors included) are hopeful that combining interventions from across cultures can improve outcomes in therapy for all.

A useful metaphor here is the 'melting pot' of therapy; pluralism is a dynamic system allowing integration of ideas and practices from theoretically limitless sources, and the framework is designed to bring these together in ways which optimise the experience and outcomes for each client who comes to us. Ethically there should be no exclusion of potential opportunities to help, but the stumbling block tends to be the confidence and skills of the therapist and client in harnessing these. Integrating cross-culturally is not simply a process of developing understanding and focusing on difference, but rather closely monitoring opportunities for inclusion of ideas for things that help. This is undertaken in various ways, and so it is helpful to think about how cross-cultural practices have been drawn into mental health in the past, and how this might give some contrast to how they can be done in pluralism.

An example of this is the ways in which mindfulness has become mainstream in Western society. Meditation is embedded in Buddhist culture as a religious practice linked to enlightenment, introduced into populist Western cultures by Jon Kabat-Zinn, both a practitioner in meditation and a molecular biologist, through activities such as 'mindfulness practice' or 'mindfulness meditation' (Kabat-Zinn, 1990), which was translated into something that was culturally significant in the West when he proposed it as a route to 'de-stressing' for people living with health conditions. Increasingly, the practice of mindful meditation was researched by neurologists, psychologists, and mental health practitioners, and the process and impact of 'becoming mindful' embedded in existing cultural meaning frameworks, for example, the foundations of mindfulness in the changes to brain structures (e.g. Pernet et al., 2021), the impact of mindfulness on the workforce (e.g. Janssen et al., 2018), people with diagnosed mental health conditions when used alongside Westernised interventions such as cognitive behaviour therapy (e.g. Gu et al., 2015; Spijkerman et al., 2016). Alongside this integration into scientific and medicalised understandings, mindfulness as a concept has been adopted by mainstream Western culture in the form of activities as diverse as sports training and colouring books, all loosely linked to the core idea of changing your relationship to your thoughts. As with many psychological techniques, it has also more recently been scrutinised as potentially harmful if undertaken in the 'wrong way', or by vulnerable groups (Van Dam et al., 2018). This story of mindfulness is an example of cross-cultural adoption and adaptation, and one which can inform pluralistic thought. In the first instance, an openness to the positive benefits of a practice originating from a non-Western culture can be seen, but counter to this is the dissolution of the meaning of the practice, the rich history and difference which it represents. In some ways, an exploration of the meaning of Buddhism and the experience of relating to thoughts as a philosophical or conceptual proposition is an opportunity missed, as Westernisation has filtered mindfulness down to a palatable activity, aligned it to our existing evidence-based therapy practices, which in turn makes it easier to continue with our limited view on what it means to be human and how we live our lives. Mindfulness could have been used as a doorway into new ideas and meanings, but instead has been commodified and repackaged as an intervention for mental health, a helpful (or not so helpful) well-being activity.

The point of this story is not that Westernised mindfulness practices and resources are unhelpful, but that pluralism in practice may help aid an openness to the introduction of new ideas to, and from, a client, and we are missing a trick if we don't broaden our lens to ensure that we are seeing the whole cross-cultural 'picture'. If we don't, we risk attrition of meaning through decontextualising methods in practice. When working with clients we would do well to dwell on their philosophy of life, their assumptions and beliefs about the world, and consider how our understandings and suggestions for activities best align to these. We also need to allow our clients to teach us something of the wonders of the world outside our own field of vision, and working cross-culturally is an opportunity for this. Many cultures have their own forms of healing and therapy related to spiritual and religious practices, rituals and ceremonies, and alternative interventions (e.g. Kirmayer et al., 2003; Oulanova et al., 2009), and perhaps this is the pluralistic route to recognise our efforts which can counter the 'well-being hegemony' and the world-wide adoption of mental health narratives (Nadirshaw, 2009). This wonderful quote, cited by Wilk (2014), serves to reflect this richness which we might lose:

> *People bring with them not just their unique skills, and qualifications and experiences. They bring with them their hopes, their aspirations, their ambitions, and of course their fears (known and unknown) and their uncertainties. Their own cultural beliefs and values, their traditions, their religious practices, their customs, their rites, rituals and ceremonies, their dietary practices, their family structures and, equally importantly, their own language(s) are an integral part of their upbringing. No immigrant in that sense ever travels light. No immigrant ever sheds his or her cultural legacies and acquisitions easily.*

> (Palmer and Laungani, 1999, p. 2)

Whilst pluralism recognises that cross-cultural working is a source of strength and learning, the practice of this can be understood by thinking about three essential areas of working in therapy, (i) the co-creation of an understanding of the origin and perpetuation of problems in a way which is meaningful for the client, (ii) the recognition of cultural resources that fit with a person's lived experience, and (iii) the ability to draw on methods which stem from different culturally embedded practices. Active within this is the opportunity to increase and validate the power of the client's cultural voice. This may be done by following the kinds of work set out by White and Epston (1990) and Denborough (2014), de-centring from an explanatory frame and hearing the narratives and stories emerging from any culture with equal value. Other ways of locating opportunities from out of our own socio-cultural context might include:

- Intellectual travel – before we ask, '*how do we do what we do?*' in other cultures, ask first whether you, '*can do what they do?*'
- Conceptual bridges – recognise the process of understanding culturally embedded practices.
- Retain a curiosity – having an openness to, and with, clients and others around cultural practices.
- Self-practice – consider self-practice before client-practice and explore how your culture imposes structures on your experience and understanding of the world (see McLeod and McLeod, 2014).

Whilst we cannot present a solution to the 'problem' of multicultural-ism, we demonstrate how pluralistic practice has the potential to open the door to the many ways that people across the globe understand their existence, their experience, and suggest how it might be an opportunity to improve therapy for everyone.

Section 4

Pluralistic developments outside of individual counselling and psychotherapy

37. Right, I think I have this, but how do you maintain and develop what you can offer a client?
38. If I want to work pluralistically, do I need a pluralistic supervisor?
39. Is pluralism a concept relevant to other disciplines in mental health/ therapy?
40. As an agency, how can we work pluralistically if some of our therapists are not pluralistic?
41. How can pluralism influence approaches to research in psychotherapy?
42. Where is pluralism going?
43. Pluralism is still so new, what support is out there if I want to work pluralistically?

DOI: 10.4324/9781003305736-40

37 Right, I think I have this, but how do you maintain and develop what you can offer a client?

Research, technology, and cultural perspectives have vastly altered our understanding of mental health. Within a 50-year period, the cultural understanding of, and interventions for, mental health have changed considerably with an increased holistic bio-psycho-social consideration and new and changing diagnostic criteria (e.g. DSM-V American Psychiatric Association, 2013). These include the culturally informed shifts such as the de-categorisation of homosexuality, and spotlight on mental health care through government policies and celebrity culture. We have supports including the likes of 'Dr. Google', Apps, single session therapy, and guided self-help. Over this period in history, we have also faced several 'crises' with the potential to impact mental health on a collective and individual level – a pandemic, wars, economic downturns, global migration, climate crisis, alongside movements that require a re-evaluation of the power dynamics within society, for example, #MeToo and Black Lives Matter. Coupled with the diversity of the clients we meet, and their individual needs and preferences, it is hopefully evident that maintaining and developing a therapeutic practice that is responsive both to the collective needs of society, and the individual members within, is essential.

The psychological professions are rich with learning opportunities, and therapist development begins with the initial training provider selected, and the level of training undertaken, which will determine the developmental goals and trajectories based on the curriculum. Ultimately, what you want to achieve during each year and module is largely defined by the course structure. Many programmes of study are accredited by professional bodies and are themselves subject to strict criteria on curriculum development, delivery patterns, and modalities. As learning and practice progresses the therapist might develop an interest in a specialist area or identify under-represented and excluded

DOI: 10.4324/9781003305736-41

groups in society and lived experiences, for example, addiction, gender-based violence, child and adolescence, sexuality, disability – and begin to centre research and assignments on these topics. This may further lead to seeking additional training and qualifications to supplement their initial qualification. Once qualified, a practitioner can have both a sense of conscious competence, '*I now know how to do it*' and conscious incompetence, '*I now also know how much I still don't know*' whereby best-practice and research are continuously changing and developing the field. To evolve what they can offer clients, a practitioner requires dedication and commitment to ongoing learning, which is reflected in the Continued Professional Development (CPD) requirements of many professional bodies including the British Association for Counselling and Psychotherapy and Irish Association for Counselling and Psychotherapy (BACP, 2022; IACP, 2019). Yet understanding what to develop can be confusing. Duncan and Miller 'Cycle of Excellence' (2008) offers a useful model which passes through deliberate practice, feedback, and reflexivity and can aid therapists, and other professionals, in identifying areas of strength and development.

Methods to Develop Your Practice

Identify sources of development

- Learning opportunities; supervision and peer-mentoring; special interest groups; independent research/inquiry.
- Trying things out, practice learning.
- Observation and internalisation.

Therapy skills take practice, but experience alone does not demonstrate an improved skill (Goldberg et al., 2016), in fact some studies show that, over time, skills can plateau (Chow et al., 2015), and to counter this, practitioners in pluralism often use the 'deliberate practice model' (Rousmaniere, 2016) to develop and enhance new and existing skills. Deliberate practice is somewhat self-explanatory – you intentionally repeat an activity (Campitelli and Gobet, 2011) with one client, or peer, at a time (Bolton, 2018), with the goal of improving – but that activity will largely depend on the model you ascribe to (e.g. humanistic, psychodynamic, cognitive-behavioural, systemic, integrative) and the area identified for practice (e.g. attentive listening, offering choice, open questions, etc.). It is the art of taking a small task or activity and 'honing' it so that with time, and practice, these skills will become a natural part of the individual's repertoire. Ericsson et al. (1993) note that there are several components necessary for deliberate practice, which include the ability to be fully attentive during the activity and the motivation to engage in the repetition of effortful tasks which have been tailored to the individual. They also discuss the need for rest and recovery and to take breaks from practice.

However, deliberate practice alone is not enough to ensure effectiveness and the attainment of desired outcomes. To illustrate this, I (Frankie) am an awful singer and paradoxically I get worse when I deliberately practice singing – especially with a backing track! I try hard to keep a tune, and I can continue in this vein (and have done) without improving because what I am missing is feedback in order to understand the areas I am capable or excel in (hopefully there's one) and the areas I can improve in. Engaging in deliberate practice (Rousmaniere, 2016), harnessing feedback though supervision and, particularly, immediate feedback through our interactions with clients, can illuminate areas we are performing well in and areas that may need attention (Ericsson et al., 1993); '*if we get information about what seems to be working, and more importantly what is not working, our responsiveness to clients will improve*' (Lambert and Shimokawa, 2011, p. 72)

Identify your growth edges

- Direct and indirect feedback.
- Supervision.
- Process and outcome monitoring.
- Interests and ambitions.
- Awareness of cultural changes which may require a response, for example, trauma-informed care.

Feedback is not always offered through direct communication; we would be unlikely to hear, '*will you brush up on your knowledge of sexuality please?*', even if it were helpful! It will most likely be subtle moments, such as a change in communication, which are invitations to seek clarification through the process of meta-communication. Nevertheless, cli-ents might not always have direct access, or the courage, to share this feedback, and they are also less likely to have the insight into the therapist's professional and personal world in order to identify and offer areas that the therapist could develop. Therefore, even with the gift of feedback, there is a considerable amount of reflexivity required from the therapist. Reflexivity is the ability to examine our own and other's feelings, actions and reactions, and the impact that these have on our practice and thoughts which can be a key process in facilitating change (McLeod, 2018a), and '*deepen our understanding and our ability to respond with sensitivity and care*' (Hawkins and Shohet, 2006, p. 77). Caetano (2019) argues that reflexivity is not a new concept, and that we often reflect on our daily lives and activities to assess consequences and consider how to accomplish things, as well as to consider larger existential questions to find meaning and direction, and explore our relationships with institutions and society considering roles, position, context, power, and values. Utilising a similar concept for our professional lives can help us understand not only areas to develop but also what we already offer to our clients, cultivating a strengths-based perspective on our practice.

Adopt a growth mindset

Reflexivity also comes with a caution, we must '*be careful not to slide into a reflexive spiral where a preoccupation with self-obscures the phenomenon of interest*' (Gough, 2016, p. 1). Through reflexivity and listening to ourselves we may become aware of areas of our life that we feel are 'lacking'; that nagging inner critic – you are not perfect enough, smart enough, therapeutic enough, worthy enough and on and on it goes. This 'deficit' can impact how we manage several areas in our lives such as trauma, connection, negative emotions, uncertainty and powerlessness, establishing and maintaining boundaries, being assertive and saying 'no' – ultimately our genuine authentic 'this is me' self. However, at this point where we feel vulnerable, we also have opportunities to lean into the discomfort and grow, this is what is known as our growth edge – the point that we feel vulnerable and have opportunity to change it. Dweck notes that those who have a growth mindset are keen to receive feedback, are more resilient with setbacks and perform better, and rather than a 'can't do' attitude would use language such as 'yet' and 'not yet' (TED, 2014); '*I am not good enough at listening – yet,*' '*I do not yet understand the impact of living with a disability*', '*I can't offer CBT – yet*'. This awareness that we are on the edge of a potential growth can motivate us to enter back into training, supervision, personal development, and deliberate practice. Particular themes and moments to reflect on are offered (adapted from McLeod, 2017; Kagan, 1973; Cashwell, 1994):

- Moments of change – *What did I do/offer to facilitate this change?*

    - Are there any skills/methods that contributed to this change?
    - Would this change be likely without these?
    - Are these unique to me or generic within helping professions?

- Theories and interventions (including skills) – *What do I have to offer?*

    - What am I currently doing with client(s) and how do I understand them?
    - Why am I drawn to using these theories/interventions?
    - What theories/interventions am I not using and why might that be?

- Preference and goals – *What does the client want?*

    - Do I have any wishes for the client that I have not communicated?
    - What do I think/feel/believe about these goals and preferences?
    - Does this challenge me in anyway?

- Transference – *How does the client relate to me?*

    - Is this like other important people in, or aspects of, their life?
    - Is the emotion displayed relative to the work we are doing?

- Parallel processing and countertransference – *Is how I am acting/ responding typical or atypical?*

    - Are there characteristics that are like the client's story?
    - What do I think/feel/believe about the client?
    - What do I think/feel/believe when I am acting/responding at that time?
    - Does the client remind me of anyone?

- Who was the client for me at that moment?
- Points of feeling stuck – *What am I stuck with at this time?*
  - If I could say anything, what would I say?
  - Did something prevent me from sharing my thoughts or feelings at the time?
  - If I was a fly on the wall in our last session, what would I notice about the relationship?

38 If I want to work pluralistically, do I need a pluralistic supervisor?

Many practitioners find that, despite their affinity for and training in pluralistic therapy, they are unable to access supervision from someone experienced in the approach – this is a pipeline problem that will hopefully resolve over time. Many supervisors are already working with integrative models and are open and willing to oversee pluralistic work, and many of the distinctive features of pluralistic therapy are utilised by supervisors to facilitate an open and collaborative space – whether or not they are pluralistic themselves. Other practitioners find themselves in supervisory relationships with those who are new to the pluralistic approach, and some find that their supervisor is unwilling to work with them using the model. There are two aspects of supervision to consider for a pluralistic practitioner when choosing a supervisor – the first is whether their supervisor is willing and able to work with them using the approach, and the second is whether the supervisor is able to deliver pluralistic supervision.

If we use the pluralistic framework to conceptualise the supervisory role, the key aspects of the work are to create a collaborative space with the supervisee, to establish their goals and how these can be met, to share a conceptualisation of how the work of the therapist is undertaken, and to support the therapist's strengths and resources. These address the goals, tasks, and bonds identified by Bordin (1979, 1983), and Hawkins and Shohet (2006) consider that the supervision should have *developmental* [understanding the client, the supervisee, the relationship, and interventions], *resourcing* [ensuring the emotional needs of the supervisee are catered for to prevent burn-out], and *qualitative* [ensuring ethics and standards of counselling are adhered to] functions. A supervisor in these circumstances is best placed to recognise their own knowledge and skills and deploy them according to the need of the therapist. There are some topics that a pluralistic therapist may specifically want to talk

DOI: 10.4324/9781003305736-42

about in supervision, and it is worth examining these as a supervisor and practitioner:

Therapist actions

The ways in which the pluralistic framework is operationalised can create challenges for the practitioner; the articulation and evolution of goals, tasks, and methods (see Chapters 16 and 17) within the relationship can be both tricky in terms of conceptualisation, and how they are spoken about and undertaken in practice. The basis for this is the collaborative case formulation (see Chapters 14 and 15) which itself can cause concerns for supervisees, in that they feel, for example, that it is too soon, too presumptive, too therapist driven, and not meaningful enough for the client – and a supervisor should be closely monitoring how this is done to ensure that there is an emergent shared understanding of therapy. Some supervisees will seek to use the supervision space to-play at how they might present their case formulation to the client, to 'test out' how it feels, while or whilst others may work with the supervisor on its initial creation before sharing with the client for reviewing and amending. This also supports a therapist's ability to begin to evidence what they are doing and, importantly, why, as many supervisees early in their training struggle to articulate this, their 'evidence-based practice' (Bieling and Kuyken, 2003, p. 53); for example, '*I am doing C [intervention] with the client because I understand A [the issues] through the lens of B [the theories]*'. Discussing the multiple ways of knowing (see Chapter 12) can be a useful position to take:

- What do you know?
- How do you know this?
- What other sources of knowledge might be relevant?
- What are the different perspectives opened up by other ways of knowing?
- What are the intersections/tensions between different ways of knowing?

A further challenge faced by therapists is the integration and making sense of formal feedback, more of which is discussed in Chapter 20.

Client responses

Some supervisees, once they have ensured a good forum for feedback, may wish to process and understand the responses given by their clients, consider how they might be able to respond to preferences and engage in dialogue – particularly when they are finding open communication with their client difficult. This can also be reflected in the way that a supervisee structures, or changes the structure of, their sessions and views the options available for delivery.

Consideration must also be given to the socio-cultural context of the client, and the impact of this on the therapeutic work. A risk in all therapy work is that there are seen and unseen aspects of the clients' lives, and that what is experienced in therapy is merely a window into their lived experience. Does the therapist have the capacity for bridging and broaching difference, for example?

Therapist resourcing

Other areas that supervisees may also need support with are developing methodological skills sets, understanding research and theory to appreciate their clients experience and bring this back to the clients for discussion. The supervisor may also take an active role in ensuring the therapist's frame of reference and client lens are broad enough to incorporate a full view of client strengths and resources and help them in identifying appropriate cultural resources.

This can also be true for the supervisee who may need help to identify and develop their own cultural resources and strengths. Useful questions might include:

- What have you learned about yourself from your work with this client?
- How have you managed...(typical themes for example) Your openness to feedback? Your self-belief? The risk of being in the present moment? Engaging in dialogue?
- What are the implications for your on-going personal and professional development (see Chapter 37 for the deliberate practice model)?
- What are the implications for how we work together in supervision?

Yet regardless of supervisory functions, tasks, distinctive features, or theoretical orientation, supervisees, like clients and supervisors, are also unique in who they are, the work they do and their preferences for supervision (Wallace and Cooper, 2015). Finding a supervisor who fosters and maintains the supervisory working alliance (SWA) and can promote professional development (Enlow et al., 2019) is important, regardless of whether they are pluralistic. One tool which may help is the supervisory preference form (Wallace and Cooper, 2015), but we also propose several important considerations when choosing a supervisor:

- Do they have conceptual knowledge of pluralistic practice, and can they effectively interpret the collaborative relationship, shared decision-making, and other key aspects of practice?
- Is the supervisor able to own their own theoretical position in a way which complements or even benignly contrasts with pluralism – are they willing to de-centre from their belief systems and accept and work positively with other 'truths'?
- Is the supervisor open to, and supportive of, consultation, collaboration, preference accommodation, and feedback from their supervisees?
- Is the supervisor able to adopt different positions in their relationship with the therapist? For example, can they undertake dialogue around different conceptual understandings of what might be going on for the client (both formal-theoretical and emergent-client-focused)? Are they willing to support the deployment of different methods and interventions which are felt to suit the current interpretation of the client problems?
- Can they tolerate and support the idea of 'not knowing' in therapy?
- Are they willing to be flexible and creative in their work?
- Can they support and validate the therapist, recognise challenges, work with personal and professional growth needs?
- Would they welcome being taught about the pluralistic framework by the supervisee? This can tell you a lot about their openness to learning and ability to hold a pluralistic stance!

Overall, the short answer is no, you do not need a pluralistic supervisor if you want to work pluralistically. There are many aspects of good quality supervision that align with pluralistic principles. However, there are some key concerns and challenges that pluralistic practitioners face and it is therefore recommended that due care and consideration is given to finding the right supervisor who can support your individual and practical needs. It would also be important, but not essential, that your supervisor had some knowledge of more than one theoretical orientation, integration model, or pluralism itself but nevertheless, if they are open to learning about it, then it may be helpful to share reading material, particularly about the distinctive features (McLeod, 2018a).

39 Is pluralism a concept relevant to other disciplines in mental health/therapy?

A response to a pluralistic world needs to speak to each part of it, the notion of pluralism is one which is already used extensively in other fields, and it means something very similar in therapy. It is about the consideration of other perspectives, and the intentional incorporation of these in practice – so *medical pluralism*, for example, is the use of mainstream and complementary interventions to improve health outcomes (note here however the implications of thinking in terms of mainstream and 'other' treatment options). Within *religious pluralism*, the focus is on the tolerance of other beliefs, and in doing so providing impetus for bridging these, garnering the capacity to reduce friction and conflict between firmly held beliefs which transcend the everyday. Pluralistic thinking can therefore be usefully applied in a range of contexts and areas such as social work, education, and nursing, which have already moved organically along their own paths towards creating pluralistic approaches. This chapter offers an examination of some other professions who are 'thinking pluralistically' in terms of mental health.

Mental health nursing

In the United Kingdom, and internationally, mental health nursing is sometimes thought to be an uncomfortable fit to the more medical nursing professions. It is a primarily relational practice in which mental health nurses increasingly find themselves at a counterpoint with the systems within which they work. Notwithstanding the historic context of the psychiatric movement, the tensions to be found in work on anti-psychiatry (Nasrallah, 2011; Nasser, 1995), and questions around the validity of diagnostics in mental healthcare (e.g. Allsopp et al., 2019), mental health nurses often find themselves within a system where their work can be seen as quietly subversive in striving for a more empowering

DOI: 10.4324/9781003305736-43

relational approach in state-funded systems. Explaining why in-patient care warrants spending time 'simply' undertaking activities with the companionship of a nurse, or that the sources of change must lie in the broader socio-political context (e.g. the role of poverty in creating and maintaining mental health problems), is one which is difficult to justify to the holders of budgets and an outcome focused system. In his work which aimed to aid understanding of service-user experience, and how nurses can engage with the recovery journey, mental health nurse Phil Barker defined the influential Tidal Model of mental health recovery, describing it as,

> *a philosophical approach to the discovery of mental health. It emphasises helping people reclaim the personal story of mental distress, by recovering their voice. By using their own language, metaphors and personal stories people begin to express something of the meaning of their lives. This is the first step towards helping recover control over their lives.*
>
> (Barker, 2001, p. 234)

The recovery model assumes that an individual's mental well-being is dependent on their individual life experiences, including their sense of self, perceptions, thoughts, and actions. The 'recovery' movement in nursing (Trenoweth, 2016) includes initiatives and methods which focus on patient-defined outcomes rather than, necessarily, a cessation of symptoms. Within this work is the idea that people are best aided by building a life that is meaningful to them, to promote empowerment, choice, responsibility, and control, guided by a principle of 'person-centredness' (not Rogerian person-centredness but rather a healthcare term used commonly to prioritise the needs of the patient). Despite the use of slightly different terms (e.g. 'patient'), a powerful resonance with the pluralistic framework is seen in the philosophical assumption provided by Barker (2001):

- A belief in the virtue of *curiosity*.
- Recognition of the power of *resourcefulness*, instead of focusing on problems, deficits, or weaknesses.
- *Respect for the patient's wishes* instead of being paternalistic.
- Acceptance of the paradox of crisis as opportunity.
- Acknowledging that all *goals must belong to the individual patient*.
- The virtue of pursing elegance – the simplest possible means should be sought.

Contemporary mental health nurses often find themselves in situations where the ambition to align to the recovery model is counteracted by the systems in which they function and, compared to pluralistic therapists, may have far fewer choices in responding to patients. In their work lives, mental health nurses must often hold dissonant 'truths' around the range of explanatory models which are provided for their patients, so working in a medicalised context but holding a belief in the recovery model is likely to reflect decisions made on the basis of ethical principles rather than professional guidelines. Something of an enforced pluralism in this context! An example of this might be a practitioner who works with someone who carries a diagnosis of borderline personality disorder, is at risk of self-harm, and understands the root of their problems to be the injustices presented by the world. In response to being sectioned under the mental health act, the person may have been stigmatised by the care system where the use of the term 'Personality Disorder' renders them subject to suspicion of their motives and potential for recovery, disempowered by their ability to make choices and engaged, sometimes unwillingly, in therapeutic interventions. The opportunity for a nurse in this context is to offer a boundaried, role-driven, yet potentially congruent relationship with the person. Whilst holding an acceptance of the imposed requirements (of 'risk-management', medication regimes, and the socio-cultural stigma impacting on the person), it is possible to relate to the person as an individual, to understand how they may be constructing their understanding of the world, and seek to find ways of working, ultimately rendering changes that stem from the *individual in the relationship* and not the *individual within the system*. This final point is becoming increasingly pertinent in discussion across the profession, with mental health nurses increasing drawing on socio-cultural and socio-economic causes of mental health challenge, this too is an area of growth for pluralistic practice. It is fair to say that it may be easier for a mental health nurse to work from a pluralistic *perspective*, acknowledging the reality of the persons context, than use pluralism in *practice* (see Chapter 7), by working to find goals, tasks, and methods (see Chapter 17), although these may be helpful for the person.

Clinical psychology

The work of clinical psychology is often impacted by its centralisation within medical health services, and whilst practitioners work in therapeutic contexts, they may be more constrained by practice guidance, client presentation severity, and research-evidenced practice requirements, than counsellors and psychotherapists, throughout both training and practice. They are also more likely to practice in multi-disciplinary teams involving psychiatry and social work. But, unlike many mental health nurses, they can be fairly autonomous in their work, and a contemporary revision of thinking around how to respond to mental health problems has recently challenged the status quo.

A new, relatively contentious (Johnstone et al., 2019), non-diagnostic framework for working in mental health psychology was published by the British Psychological Society in 2018. This collaboratively produced Power-Threat-Meaning (PTM) framework (Boyle and Johnstone, 2020; Johnstone and Boyle, 2018; BPS, 2018) has considerable overlap with the pluralistic framework, and as such presents evidence that non-medicalisation and individuation of distress is not simply a phenomenon grown from counselling and psychotherapy. The framework itself asks practitioners to work with three core questions for the client in mind, and it is clear that the client-centred collaboration and construction of meaning seen in the PTM framework, links to the notion of pluralism:

1. What happened to you?
2. What meaning did you make of it?
3. What did you have to do to survive?

Philosophically speaking, the imposition of any consistent theoretical framework for practice is contrary to a pluralistic philosophy, however, whilst proposing some cause-and-effect assumptions (such as attachment theory, trauma responses, and externally identifiable distress patterns), the PTM framework does not impose structures of meaning on individuals, nor proscribed practice methods on therapy. Holding roles in healthcare, similar to those of clinical psychologists, the growth of pluralistic counselling psychology has its own challenges, as psychology aligns to empiricism and evidence-based practice so, whilst philosophically the programme may teach pluralism, it is in the context of a professional body which is, at times, heavily aligned to positivism.

What will be interesting in the future is whether cross-fertilisation of ways of working and ways of understanding these can build bridges between the professions.

40 As an agency, how can we work pluralistically if some of our therapists are not pluralistic?

Valuing pluralism as a framework for delivering community based mental health can have many advantages, such as having a breadth of options for responding, and a flexibility in practice delivery, but it is complicated by the fact that not all therapists will be trained in, or believe in, pluralistic therapy. So, can an agency identify as pluralistic whilst some of those who work within it are not? Pluralism emphasises that '*knowledge, experience, and awareness of values are always limited, open, and incomplete*' (Yumatle, 2015, p. 8) and holds an appreciation and affirmation of diversity and openness to other, including the truths held by non-pluralists. Groups of therapists can maintain a stable framework, whilst allowing new perspectives, truths, and people, to enter and leave the open system. Whilst it is unlikely any organisation can exist as completely closed, there are degrees as to how open an agency strives to be, and this is further dependent on the employees within, creating a point of tension for some agencies with therapists who hold more rigid or monist perspectives while working within the pluralistic service. It is important that an agency considers the standards, ethos, and culture of the organisation, and establishes management to support these aims and the staff working within. It is perhaps prudent to note that many have sought to identify a best practice model for community based mental health however, it is apparent that, again, there are multiple 'truths' and no single formula (Flannery et al., 2011) for this. Therefore, this chapter will focus on commonly shared perspectives, in addition to those held by a pluralistic model, and will cover some key principles which can lead to a pluralistic ethos within an agency, no matter what the theoretical background of the therapists employed within.

DOI: 10.4324/9781003305736-44

Point of entry preference accommodation and breadth of opportunity

The first consideration for a pluralistic agency is, 'What are we offering and how are we offering this?'. Ideally, an agency can adopt a strengths and resource ethos, with the benefits of creating, and working with, a diverse range of employees with varying cultural and ethnic backgrounds, specialised areas of expertise, and a broad spectrum of knowledge, beliefs and values. Being able to draw from this pool of expertise, and working to their strengths, supports the likelihood of resilience and job satisfaction (Harzer and Ruch, 2015) and places the agency is a better position to match clients with their preferred supports, which ultimately improves engagement, outcomes (Swift and Callahan, 2009), fosters collaboration, and satisfaction with therapy (Vollmer et al., 2009). It is therefore essential to build an understanding with and between therapists about who they are and the skills they offer, and develop a system that responds to preferences on 'point of entry' for the clients. Whilst these may typically include modality, language, gender, religion, and cost, short preference interviews or questionnaires could also begin to explore whether the client would like certain process factors such as focus on their past or present, emotions of thoughts or relational factors (for example, support, challenge, humour). We know that it is impossible to meet all preferences (see Chapter 22) and services are under time constraints to deliver a service, but an agency can both encourage growth, through deliberate practice in the areas that are not available, and communicate to clients and therapists that, whilst preferences will be considered, they are not guaranteed. Being able to work in a manner that supports strengths, resources, and preferences offers an ethical service which is tailored to the individuals involved and, insofar as possible, utilises and models the pluralistic principle of collaboration.

Collaboration within and across agencies

Collaborative working relationships can support the growth and development of the service and is considered an important component of many models of mental health care (Ee et al., 2020; NHS, 2014; Gov. Wales, 2019) with some studies finding collaborative care is more beneficial than treatment as usual (Sighinolfi, 2014). Collaboration should also extend to other agencies, hosts, communities, stakeholders, and clients, in order to maintain a high standard and range of services and promote a diverse, equal and inclusive environment. Along with mutual respect and understanding, a commitment to collaboration and a shared understanding of goals (NHS, 2014) between agencies, inviting feedback as well as the sharing of information, can aid a more coherent response for clients engaging in services.

Feedback to enhance practice and demonstrate agency impact

Feedback is incorporated in agency work to support evidence-based practice, quality assurance, quality enhancement, and reporting, which is particularly important for funding as many agencies are dependent on grants (Garland et al., 2003). It can also be utilised to determine whether clients are satisfied with their care and whether the support they receive is helping them. However, for those who have not been trained in the use of feedback and outcome measures, there can be a considerable amount of reluctance, including fears that their personal performance will be monitored (Unsworth et al., 2011), concerns over time constraints and paperwork (Boswell et al., 2013) and a belief that the clients will not like the use of a 'bureaucratic' tool within their session (see Chapter 21). It is therefore essential that agency staff have adequate time for discussion of their concerns and any scope for flexibility, as well as comprehensive training. Fundamentally, there will need to be some level of openness by the end of the discussion and training for the measures to be appropriately and systematically implemented.

Demystification of services and information management

The sharing of information about the agency can include the provision of leaflets, websites, phone calls, and posters, which are applicable to all service users and stakeholders, including outside agencies, as well as through verbal discussion as part of the intake procedure for clients. Therapists should be provided with a therapist induction process coherently outlining ethical and best practice policy guidelines for the service, along with sharing the service's culture, ethos, and aims and objectives (Gov.Wales, 2019). Additionally, there are times that it may be helpful or necessary to share information specifically related to a client with other agencies; however, it is important to note that this should always be considered with the best interest of the client in mind and actioned within ethical guidelines ensuring confidentiality, and where necessary and possible the client's consent (Gov.Wales, 2019). Furthermore, this should form part of the informed consent agreement discussed at the beginning of therapy. Yet, ethical dilemmas are prevalent and lie in the grey area of beneficence and non-maleficence and, whilst therapists will have their own supervision process, it is also important that the agency is available to create transparent processes and support practitioners in managing the balance between both legal and agency requirements, and therapist and client autonomy.

Responsiveness to client needs

Referrals into and out of the service are a further point to aid the agency in working pluralistically, even with therapists who might be monist in their work or perspective. Having a clear referral process through which clients can self-refer, and also a way of informing choices and channels to access other agencies or supports, offers an empowering option for people experiencing problems in living. Clients often report feeling they are pushed from pillar to post (Parsonage et al., 2014) and having a direct line of transparent communication between the agency, therapist and themselves can provide the client with a high degree of autonomy and agent for change.

One important consideration is whether therapy is the right path for the client; not all clients are suitable for therapy, and not all therapists have the skills to work with every client. Additionally, whilst clients may be accepted for therapy based on the therapist's ability to work with the presenting problem, quite often a client's perceptions of problems, goals, and tasks evolve over time. It is therefore essential to support therapists and clients in re-referral to additional agencies, or to therapists with other skills. This can be difficult for any therapist, especially for those whose self-efficacy is low, and particularly for those who come from a monist background with a one-size fits all approach. It is therefore important to instil the pluralistic stance that different people need different things at different times (Cooper and McLeod, 2011), to empower the therapist to refer on and to enable the client to make a choice to see someone else (see Chapter 44).

The key principles discussed to create a pluralistic agency that welcomes therapists who practice from different perspectives, involve a culture of working with transparent, user-friendly information, an emphasis on creating collaboration across the agency, encouraging appropriate sharing of information and feedback, the incorporation of preferences, and taking a strengths-based approach. It is essential that these are always underpinned by ethics and available best practice guidelines. Through these practices, there can be a sharing and distribution of power between several experts, rather than being led from the top.

41 How can pluralism influence approaches to research in psychotherapy?

Many students and academics, but sadly very few practitioners and clients, get involved in research, and the bulk of research in counselling and psychotherapy stems from individuals and collaborations housed within traditional higher education institutions. This often means that it is undertaken within the context of convergent pressures of timeframe, funding, and the merit of publishing in peer-reviewed journals, where the acceptability of research is measured within the constraints of traditional methodological and epistemological approaches. Alongside this sits an imposed research value system where population-level comparative studies, designed to elucidate commonalities [e.g. a randomised control trial (RCT) which might involve randomly assigning 500 therapy clients to one of two therapy interventions, and the performance of the interventions are compared depending on how the clients score on a questionnaire measuring emotional distress], are favoured over more nuanced inquiries which represent individual experience and difference.

Counselling and psychotherapy research tends to sit within the field of psychology, which is subject to a few problems in terms of validity. In psychology, striving for impactful 'headline' results, is an unfortunate side-effect of this research environment, with the effect that data which support a null hypothesis (i.e. the expected effect is not seen) are significantly less likely to reach publication (Hopewell et al., 2009; Rosenthal, 1979), and many research findings have been found to be irreplicable despite being accepted on the basis of statistical significance (Ioannidis, 2005). Therapy research, on the other hand, tends towards more qualitative and case-study methodologies, which are often considered less 'valuable' and generalisable. Overall, whilst there is merit in all research traditions, there is perhaps too little critique of the impact of these biases, particularly when seeking knowledge to inform real-world

DOI: 10.4324/9781003305736-45

situations. This is a problem that a pluralistic approach to research has the potential to address.

Pluralism is not a new concept in research (Downing, 2004; Howard, 1983; Omer and Strenger, 1992; Samuels, 1995) however, the research cultures which we draw from to support our work, and the way it is used to develop practice, would still benefit from epistemological change towards a more pluralistic frame. An approach to research using the principles of pluralistic therapy was first mooted by Hanley and Winter (2016), and in their recent paper on the nature of research evidence in counselling and psychotherapy, Smith and colleagues (2021) highlight the systematic problems with the current research methods. Within this paper (Smith et al., 2021), the authors define a pluralistic stance on research, which would allow the current reliance on traditional research approaches to evolve into more meaningful activities, supporting the elucidation of client experience and multiple-perspectives involvement in the process.

The adoption of a pluralistic perspective on research design is embedded in an epistemic justice agenda, drawing on practices of inclusivity, dialogue, collaboration, co-creation, and the recognition of multiple sources of valid (but sometimes conflicting) knowledge. This involves:

- Recognising ways of knowing and how these may be enhanced or diminished by research activity.
- Thinking about the purpose of the research activity and the research questions asked.
- Fitting the methodology to the research question to ensure it is giving a meaningful response.
- Examining processes of data collection and considering triangulation of multiple sources of data.
- Conducting the analysis whilst sustaining an interest in difference, rather than the convergence of findings (e.g. different perspectives on the interpretation process).
- Disseminating findings to those on which it has the greatest meaning and significance.
- Considering the impact of being involved in research; that it can be empowering, and insight driven for participants, researchers, and the chosen audience.

An example of the impact of this work can be imagined if we consider a project designed to examine the best way to respond therapeutically to people presenting with a diagnosis of depression. Alongside a range of other treatments, including medication, the United Kingdom has recognised counselling as one of a number of interventions that can be useful for this group (NICE, 2022) but now needs better evidence for what it does. Before we apply a pluralistic approach to the work, we might first consider that behind this quest for evidence might be a series of assumptions, for example:

- That depression is a unitary experience and, at a population level, it is likely that interventions shown to be helpful for the majority of people will be helpful for everyone.
- That the focus of the intervention is the person rather than the socio-cultural or economic context (which may ultimately be the cause of the problem).
- That provision of interventions should stem from healthcare/therapy.

They also propose that the research itself might best be undertaken using a research stakeholder team including:

- People with lived experience of holding a diagnosis of depression.
- Therapists working with these people.
- Healthcare services who will fund interventions.
- Researchers who wish to facilitate the process and have methodological knowledge.
- Those who wish to disseminate and/or use the findings and those who have a vested interest in them.

The stakeholder group can then engage in discussions about what they want to find out (the research questions), and how they would like to go about it (the research methods). These choices are often framed by knowledge, experience, and perspective, and this speaks to the need for multiple lenses in the team. Some important questions might include:

- How is the experience of depression conceptualised?
- What do people with depression find helpful in terms of managing their depression?
- How effective are current treatments and how are they measured?
- What happens to people for whom the current interventions are not effective?

But for others there may be questions around '*what does it feel like to not be depressed?*', or '*how can we drive efficiency so more people can be helped?*'. Whilst some answers may already exist in published literature, it is also important to consider that not all questions can be answered. Methodologically, once the focus of the research, and its related questions, are agreed, the research can be addressed in a variety of ways. To enhance the richness of the response though, it is preferable that the voice of the people carrying a diagnosis of depression should be prioritised and recognition given to the uniqueness of each person involved. Regarding the impact of the research, generalisability may be considered a priority, in which case a 'breadth and challenge' case can be constructed, such as thinking about how wide reaching the results can be, for example. Alternatively, the focus may be more concerned with uncovering the lived experience of the individuals seeking help. The pluralistic lens is also useful when thinking about the results:

• Does it 'buck the trend', what is the novelty of what has been found?
• Is this different from that already out there?
• Are there opportunities stemming from the data to render change in practice?
• How has the understanding of each stakeholder evolved because of being involved in the process and the emergent results?

In parallel with pluralistic therapy practice, knowledge is distributed through the group. It may be that some of those involved in the example research project provided here will have better knowledge of the structuring and organisation of the research process, whilst others will have far deeper knowledge of the experience of depression, or the systems in which support is delivered. Recognising and valuing these perspectives in an open and accepting frame would increase the chance that the research itself will be useful. The challenge of undertaking such an endeavour is that it relies on inspiring the engagement of communities beyond academia, and to do this, it is likely that the kinds of research questions that are asked are both directly socially relevant and also have the ability to harness enough purpose and passion in stakeholders to gain real commitment to the process.

42 Where is pluralism going?

Interest in pluralism, as both a stance and as a practice framework (see Chapter 7), has grown enormously since its inception. Because the practice tends to involve a personal and professional alignment and adoption of a set of principles and ways of working in practice (see Chapters 5 and 13), 'wearing the badge' does not require re-training, or necessarily any formal work to shift from a particular school of therapy or integrative framework (this is discussed in Chapter 8). It is fair to say that the popularity of the approach and discussions around it (including challenges, see Ong et al., 2020) are increasing with the legitimisation of the framework stemming from practitioners, academics, and membership bodies. Additionally, as it is based on the principles of building a collaborative community, there are practitioner groups that have grown up through the central steering group, and the annual conference is a well-attended and optimistic event (for more on this, see Chapter 43).

Alongside this, pluralistic practice can be seen as developing specifically in a number of ways, each bringing challenges and a broadening of understanding of how the framework can be applied. The growth of '*pluralistic therapy for children and young people*' is discussed in Chapter 33; and here we will look at the development of a '*pluralistic model for specialist areas*', the demand for *pluralistic supervision* (see Chapter 38), the use of '*pluralism cross-culturally*' (see Chapter 36), and finally we give some reflections on the growth of pluralism as it might sit alongside '*different schools of therapy*'.

Specialist models in pluralism – the example of bereavement counselling

As discussed in Chapter 18, pluralism lends itself to creating specific models for responding to clients with shared lived experiences and it

DOI: 10.4324/9781003305736-46

is worth focusing on how these are developing. Some of these models have been developed using a pluralistic frame, whilst others have adopted pluralism as a stance because of the resonance between what is known and what the philosophy offers. An example of this work is that which has been developed by John Wilson (2013, 2020) who has created an evidence and experience-based framework for bereavement counselling. Wilson's work stems from practice and research in bereavement services, and a critique of the existing theoretical and practice frameworks for bereavement interventions - in particular, the position of 'expertise' and limited cultural frame of reference seen in grief-work models highlighted by Rosenblatt (2020). The model now being taught by Wilson, emphasises the need to collaborate on creating a new narrative for the person, as well as sustaining a relational space for self-healing, meaning making, and adjustment to loss, and some aspects of these can be found in Chapter 18.

Supervision in pluralism

Supervision is an essential aspect of therapeutic practice and, for those using the pluralistic framework, there is a perception that there are insufficient supervisors with good knowledge of the model and, at the time of writing, a movement towards the establishment of more access to pluralistic supervision. In a similar way to therapists who encounter pluralism and find that their approach already aligns with the framework, there are many aspects of supervision which align with the principles of pluralism (Creaner and Timulak, 2016) and some might argue that it is 'pluralistic enough' without the need to formalise this (see Chapter 38). For pluralistic supervision to be effectively undertaken there are however factors that require emphasis and, potentially, adjustments for supervisors who have trained in different therapeutic perspectives. Cooper and McLeod (2011) and McLeod (2018a) highlight the need to encourage a pluralistic stance from supervisors and proposals for how supervision might be structured tend towards reducing, or removing, the barriers to collaborative learning and shifting the frame towards a consultative relationship, rather than one of oversight and guidance. Pluralistic supervision aims to meet the therapist's learning needs, empower autonomy by focusing on strengths and resources (Ladany et al., 2013), and draw on knowledge from theory, and personal and professional experience within a responsive collaboration. Importantly there is an emphasis both on using research evidence and external sources of knowledge to enhance practice, and a sensitivity to how process and outcomes are monitored effectively to identify what is, and what is not, helping the client.

Cross-cultural working in pluralism

Cross-cultural working is discussed further in Chapter 36 and is deemed to be a potential area of huge significance for the use of pluralistic practice, not simply in its alignment to a social justice agenda, but because it is structured as an open system, within which all socio-cultural traditions and beliefs can be accommodated. It is therefore worth considering whether pluralism can exist within different cultures or merely sit within a Euro-centric viewpoint and allow inclusion of other beliefs within an already established value system (Goodman and Gorski, 2015). Whilst not hegemonic, this would present a challenge to the settlement of pluralistic practice in other cultures. Other points for consideration may also include that there are different systems of mental health care, different expectations of the therapist, and different cultural understandings of what it means to be in the place of a client, which could disrupt the open-handed power sharing approach when culturally sanctioned interventions require an expert to intervene.

The application of pluralism cross-culturally will involve therapists becoming better informed of the context of the client in seeking help, examples of this might include knowing how acceptable it might be to admit and articulate distress, the construction of language (for example, what it might mean to use terms common in therapy like 'mental health'), and the extent to which individuals consider themselves as components of family or social systems, rather than being individuals within these. These would further impact on the ways a person might speak of the reasons for entering therapy, and their goals. Cross-cultural and inclusive working is the ambition of the pluralistic community, but the impact of this is yet to be seen.

Theoretical development in pluralism

In the 'Handbook of Pluralistic Therapy' (Cooper and Dryden, 2016), there are a number of chapters discussing the resonance between the approach and various schools of therapy, highlighting similarities and areas of practice that can benefit the approach. Despite this, there is always a question of how, and whether, pluralism can be adopted within different schools as easily as it has been with the humanistic approaches. Pluralistic practice is developed from a humanistic origin and, as a result, has been adopted with greater ease by people trained in person-centred therapies and those who believe it 'makes sense' to them and their theoretical approach to therapy. But there are different touchpoints and core understandings in schools of therapy which facilitate and create barriers to the adoption of pluralism.

In cognitive-behavioural schools of thought, the assumption of collaboration is already present (although see Proctor, 2017 for a refutation of this), the ethical framework for CBT therapies encourages the client to progressively take charge of their own responses to the world with deepening insight into their own thoughts and behaviour – ultimately becoming their own therapists. This notion is at a slight contrast to pluralism because firstly, the understanding initially provided by the therapist (the links between cognitive 'givens' like unhelpful thinking styles and underlying beliefs which can be adjusted to create more functional thinking and responding) has an apparently unrefutably fixed position of a universal experience. This may not be in line with the client's position and a CBT therapist would need to understand, and believe, that client resistance is not a barrier but a choice which is important to support. Similarly, the psychodynamic reliance on unconscious processes and defences influencing client experience would need to be set aside in favour of encouraging and trusting client 'knowing'. Even in pluralistic trainees there is a sense of frustration that clients do not see something which feels obvious and 'true' to the therapist (see Chapter 49 for a discussion on this).

To adopt pluralism, a therapist from any school would have to actively de-centre themselves from a belief set and choose whether they can allow alternative explanations and truths to emerge for the client. This is because the ideas presented by their own training, and the methods by which they attempt to aid the client, would need to be set within a far broader frame. It is not yet clear how therapists go about this de-centring of their beliefs, either to allow alternative ways of thinking to be included or whether they can be independently flexible in their own beliefs to accommodate the clients. Pluralistic practice is about holding theories lightly and deploying them when helpful, being fully transparent about aims, and using methods only when they fit with an agreed change process, rather than having them as essential ingredients for therapy.

43 Pluralism is still so new, what support is out there if I want to work pluralistically?

The pluralistic philosophy of openness and respect for others has resulted in an open system of sharing and dialogue around practice and research, and it is not surprising that a vibrant community has built up around the approach. Pluralistic therapy has a network of academics, therapists, students, and associates who are interested in developing and supporting both the concept of pluralistic therapy and people who would like to work in this way. A key feature of pluralism that runs through the network is collaboration, and anyone can join the community and conversations through the pluralistic practice website, https://pluralisticpractice.com/. The site offers signposts to blogs, resources for practice, and research that further supports practitioners and encourages a conversation around core aspects of this framework through comment boxes throughout the site. This can aid therapists in critically analysing their existing knowledge and starting to formulate their opinions and questions in a constructive manner, which not only develops the individual's knowledge but also helps pluralism to develop. It builds a collective knowledge base and reciprocal responsibility for the development and maintenance of pluralistic therapy. Some of this development can be further enhanced within working groups (see https://pluralisticpractice.com/get-involved) of likeminded professionals across a range of activities, all of which are important aspects of the work we do, including:

- Creativity and storytelling group – an open space (including therapists from any modality, whether qualified or in training) to exchange ideas and gain inspiration about creative approaches to therapy through sharing stories, ideas, images, and techniques.
- Research group – a space to engage in research, through discussing your own project, research in general, connect with other researchers and become more involved with research. This group is the

DOI: 10.4324/9781003305736-47

platform for the development of a practitioner research network, and the development of the open access journal, *Pluralistic Practice*.

- Inclusivity and diversity group – a space to explore inclusivity and diversity within counselling and psychotherapy primarily, but also concerned with the wider social context and how pluralistic therapy may aid this work.
- Interdisciplinary group – a space to discuss pluralism across other disciplines and professions such as social work, supervision, education, and community development.
- Supervision group – a space to explore the role of pluralism within the context of supervision.
- Pluralistic encounter group – a space to develop self-awareness within relational interactions, these groups can involve working with the edge of awareness and so mutual growth can occur (Moloney, 2021).

One of the key feasible and cost-effective ways to support yourself in working pluralistically is through the growing number of texts, including research which describes, explores, and supports pluralism – either as a whole or specific components. Obviously, we hope this book is a useful resource in supporting therapists, and other professionals, who wish to take a pluralistic stance or perspective. However, other important and useful texts might include:

- Cooper, M., and Dryden, W. (Eds.). (2016). *Handbook of Pluralistic Counselling and Psychotherapy*. London: Sage.
- Cooper, M., and McLeod, J. (2010). Pluralism: towards a new paradigm for therapy. *Therapy Today*, 21(9), 10–14.
- Cooper, M., and McLeod, J. (2011). *Pluralistic Counselling and Psychotherapy*. London: Sage.
- McLeod, J. (2013b). Developing pluralistic practice in counselling and psychotherapy: Using what the client knows. *The European Journal of Counselling Psychology*, 2(1), 51–64.
- McLeod, J. (2018). *Pluralistic Therapy: Distinctive Features*. Abingdon, Oxon: Routledge.
- Smith, K., and de la Prida, A. (2021). *The Pluralistic Therapy Primer*. Monmouth: PCCS Books.

This is not an exhaustive list of useful reading material-further articles, books and research related to pluralism can be found at, https://plural isticpractice.com/pluralistic-bibliography and through our reference list.

Research coming from the field of pluralistic therapy is beginning to emerge, for example, one such study conducted by Cooper and colleagues (2015), found that pluralistic therapy was effective in reducing symptoms and meeting the client's goals for therapy for the majority of clients with anxiety and depressive symptoms. Furthermore, the results indicate that there were lower levels of disengagement after assessment (only 7.1%) average levels of drop out (38.5%) and higher rates of recovery (40.4%) than previous studies of these phenomena, particularly within IAPT therapies. Clients reported to find pluralistic therapy helpful, citing both technical and relational aspects, in addition to specific pluralistic tools such as the goals forms. Whilst unhelpful factors were not frequently reported on, some clients stated they would have liked more guidance on the particular method of treatment (see Chapter 6 for more about pluralistic therapy's evidence base).

However, it is also important, as a pluralistic therapist, that we don't just draw from in-house literature but are able to critically read outside of the framework, considering some of the underlying philosophies and concepts. Pluralism is perhaps unique in that it does not contend to be a 'better' or more 'superior' therapy, although benchmarking studies like the one above, are useful to explore. Instead, as this book has discussed, pluralism offers a framework from which to utilise evidence-based, common factors, and well-established theories – which have, over the years, demonstrated similar potential in helping clients. Of particular interest to pluralistic therapists, and those who wish to work pluralistically, would be exploring literature on setting goals (see Chapter 16), and breaking these into tasks and methods (see Chapter 17), collaboration (see Chapter 11) and shared decision making and preferences (see Chapter 22). Furthermore, it would be beneficial to consider skills in communication, case conceptualisation (see Chapters 14 and 15) and the use of outcome and process measures (see Chapter 20), as well as how to implement the common factors. One of the important aspects of the community is that it is a platform for a growing understanding of how pluralism functions in practice; how individual practitioners internalise and deploy the framework, and where the challenges lie. Conversations with therapists indicate that the adoption of pluralism happens when it 'makes sense' to them, and this is an important reflection for those interested in the approach – it is hard to operationalise if it doesn't make sense!

There are also annual conferences, which have run annually since 2018 and moved online during the Covid-SARS pandemic. This flexibility allowed us to reach a broader network base and we have seen contributions from both inside and outside of the pluralistic field, including keynote speakers:

- 2022, David Denborough discussing narrative processes;
- 2021, Tony Rousmaniere and Alexandre Vaz who shared deliberate practice knowledge, and Andrew Reeves from a background in social work and counselling, with a keen interest in collaboration and pluralism;
- 2020, Lucy Johnstone, who co-created the Power-Threat-Meaning (PTM) framework;
- 2019, John Norcross who is an expert on psychotherapy relationships; and
- 2018, Mick Cooper co-creator of pluralistic therapy, who spoke about directionality.

This addition of knowledge from 'outside' again supports the collaboration of building knowledge and openness to other perspectives and methods for both understanding and working with clients.

For those who wish to formally train in pluralistic therapy, there are currently seven training institutes that include pluralistic modules as part of their programme, or specialise in pluralism as the degree, within their bachelor qualification (IICP, Dublin; University of East London; University of South Wales), masters (Abertay Univeristy; IICP, Dublin; Metanoia Institute, London), and doctoral programme (University of Manchester), and there are a number of other programmes of study who offer training aligning with pluralistic perspectives and principles. Seeking continual professional development to enhance and support self-development, and supervision (see Chapter 38) aligned with pluralistic concepts would also be advantageous in supporting someone on their early journey with pluralism. Once you think you have the hang of it, it might be helpful to head over to Chapter 37 to understand more about how you can retain and maintain what you have developed!

Section 5

Critiques of pluralistic counselling and psychotherapy

44. What happens if the therapist's approach doesn't meet the client's needs in practice?
45. If you can do anything in therapy, can pluralistic clients become overwhelmed with choice?
46. You are asking a lot of clients, do they like it?
47. Is a collaborative therapy approach suitable for everyone?
48. How can outcomes be defined when client goals are so unique and personal?
49. What happens if the client can't see or understand the problem, and what if it is a result of something outside their awareness?
50. Is a pluralistic therapist a 'Jack of all trades and master of none'?

DOI: 10.4324/9781003305736-48

44 What happens if the therapist's approach doesn't meet the client's needs in practice?

Given the way that pluralistic therapists endeavour, from the outset, to establish client empowerment and choice (whilst acknowledging their own limitations in what they offer), it is not surprising that sometimes a client will discover needs that are not being met – because they have been given the space and empowerment to recognise and voice these - and so, it is likely that the therapist will need to respond to this knowledge. This may simply be a case of the client telling the therapist that what they are doing could be more helpful if done differently, or is not going to help, and could they assist in finding someone or something that might be a better fit. However, even in doing so, a client will usually feel reticence, and research has shown that clients will accommodate their therapist pragmatically to get their needs partially met (Rennie, 1994). More troubling is a situation where the client minimises, or tries to ignore, their needs to maintain the therapists good will. As discussed in Chapter 11, a good pluralistic and collaborative relationship would function to prevent this happening. Opportunities for direct (in conversation), and indirect (through feedback forms and review), feedback (see Chapter 20) should allow conversations around what the client wants, in terms of therapist relational style and methods undertaken, and the therapist can then discuss the ways and extent to which they can accommodate these.

Despite working towards preference accommodation (see Chapter 22), in practice, disjoints still happen on *theoretical* (how to understand the client experience), *formulation* (how we prioritise what we do to understand and address the client problems), *relational* (how we interact and undertake the work), and *methodological* (what can the therapist and client do together) levels. Therefore, situations do arise where the therapist or client (or both) acknowledge that, despite their best efforts,

DOI: 10.4324/9781003305736-49

the therapist is not able to offer what the client needs. Sometimes this will be based on a knowledge of alternative therapeutic options, better suited to the client needs, for example, a client seeking CBT-type interventions with lots of coaching and structure might not have their needs met with someone who works almost exclusively from a Rogerian person-centred perspective. It may be that the client is seeking someone with a particular socio-cultural background or lived experience, but there is always the possibility of the therapist and client simply not 'bonding'. Some indication of preference from clients gives clues as to where this might occur (Swift et al., 2018). Client drop-out from therapy, whilst sometimes framed as a 'life factor' or even as a failing in the person, '*they just weren't ready*', is an indication that their needs are not being met, and research has indicated that therapists are not all that good at knowing this (Murdoch et al., 2010; Norcross and Lambert, 2019; Roos and Werbart, 2013). If a rupture in the relationship is detected, evidence points to the link between rupture repair and positive therapeutic outcomes (Eubanks et al., 2018), through examination of what has happened, what can be changed, the therapist and client experience, and how these might provide a source of insight.

Any therapist who recognises, is told directly, or detects through process feedback such as the C-NIP (Cooper and Norcross, 2016), that there is a misalignment and the client is not getting what they need, or that they feel the therapy is a poor fit, should consider if they can tailor their work to meet the client. However, if, on reflection and evaluation, the therapist believes they cannot meet the client's preferences or needs, then they should consider how the client might get their needs met elsewhere, via an onward referral. Often both therapists and clients are concerned that a referral to better meet the client's therapeutic needs is reflective of a poor performance of the therapy in hand. In pluralistic therapy, there is a pre-established understanding that the scope is broad and flexible for trying new or different things, because there are multiple potential routes for meeting client need, and a range of cultural resources which are available to the client. Maintaining a porous boundary, between what is happening in therapy and what is happening elsewhere, mitigates concerns that progression for the client to a more helpful space is in some way a negative reflection on what has already been achieved, and a therapist and client can keep in mind that the goal for a pluralistic therapy is to help the client to *find* their way forward, not that therapy *must* be the way forward.

In cases where a client is moving on to a new therapist, there are several therapeutic tasks to consider, these are also useful if the client is simply leaving therapy and trying something else.

- Framing the referral as a positive step and ensure the reasons for the change are understood.
- Planning the transition to be integrated into the therapeutic process using tasks such as:

  - Finding and evaluating referral options together.
  - Managing the timing of the ending and the new therapy, with consideration of important factors such as aspects of the client's life which might impact on the transition.
  - Discussing any formal referral information and offer to co-create a referral letter.
  - Reflecting with the client on the anticipated transition, asking them to think about (for example):

    - How will this transition feel?
    - How would you like the new therapy to be different and how might you get this need met?
    - What are you hoping to achieve?
    - What learning will you take with you?
    - What do you need the new therapist to know?
    - Is there any feedback that you'd like to give about how we've worked together?

  - Planning and undertaking a 'good ending' (see Chapter 27)– consider ending activities such as a letter to the client.

Generally, it is a good idea to agree with the client how the change will happen, and whilst this may reflect the clients' preferences in terms of their 'attachment' and sense of security in relationships, it is important for the subsequent therapist to understand the transition – so, for example, a request from the client that they can 'return' to you for a check-in at some point might be contracted. Imagery can also provide a useful tool to externalise the process of therapy and review what has been gained and what is still to be achieved, the example of 'The Suitcase' highlights this further:

> *When I decided to leave my first therapist and started working with someone who could offer me a more trauma-focused approach, we talked about my suitcase, she said that if I thought about the move like I was moving house*

and was taking a suitcase with me what would I pack and what would I leave. I said I'd like to take my case formulation and the way we could sit together and remember my mum. What wasn't going in the suitcase were the times when we'd gone round and round getting nowhere trying to change how I felt about the assault – this is what I was seeking from my new therapist.

Following the transition of a client to another therapist, or indeed another source of therapeutic work (some clients will decide that counselling is not for them but will undertake other activities – I once had a client leave to start a new life in a Buddhist commune), there is an opportunity for a pluralistic therapist to self-evaluate their work and manage any sense of loss. Keeping in mind that pluralism is about finding the right route for a client and that the therapist should strive to support this.

45 If you can do anything in therapy, can pluralistic clients become overwhelmed with choice?

Whilst it is viewed that having a toolkit from which to offer clients a choice in the way they think therapy should be done is essential in pluralistic practice, naturally there is a shadow-side of being able to potentially undertake any activity in therapy, such as the risk of the client and therapist making un-informed or ill-informed choices, or of the therapist attempting too many or unhelpful ways of approaching the client process. In practice, choices are based on the shared understanding developed within the therapeutic relationship, too many simplistic overt offers of, '*do you want to do X or Y*' can be unsettling for a client, and an over reliance on clients choosing every aspect of therapy can result in them feeling overwhelmed and may reduce their faith in the therapist's competence (Thompson and Cooper, 2012). It is therefore important to recognise that pluralistic therapy is not the injudicious presentation of a menu of decontextualised choices to a client who may have nothing to aid their decisions. It is the development of a collaborative dialogue where client and therapist are known to one another, where knowledge and expertise are shared together, and the goals and preferences of the client are prioritised, whilst the therapist does their best to respond. Across therapy, the choices made by clients tend to focus on:

- How therapy is structured, for example, the frequency and location of therapy.
- The nature of the therapeutic interaction, for example, pace, directionality, mood.
- The approach and presence of the therapist, including things like self-disclosure and challenge.
- The ways that the client's experience is interpreted and understood.
- The formulation of goals and tasks which can be undertaken.
- The ways that tasks are undertaken using particular methods.

DOI: 10.4324/9781003305736-50

The principles of pluralism prioritise client choice, so it is perhaps useful here to think about what choice represents. First, it's fair to say that individualism and choice are fairly Westernised notions of what it means to be a person, and sit within a particular cultural understanding, and so the idea of choice may need a different approach, depending on the cultural context and personality of the client. Even within some client's familial and medical environments choice might not have been an option and can therefore be alien. The 'choice in what degree of choice' might feel tautological but is worth holding at the back of a therapist's mind. Choice is often linked to directionality and purpose for the client and having a sense of this will help the process of therapy.

It is important to recognise that choices and preferences do not usually arrive fully formed with the client (see Chapter 22), and whilst initial preferences might be shared, pluralistic therapy involves a parallel process of discovery and direction. If purpose is constructed during therapy, then choices and preferences will be an emergent quality of the experience and it would be unwise to assume any objectivity in either the client or the therapist – because choices are made from within the process. The way this happens in therapy can be reflected by the evolution of goals, the changing focus of the dialogue and activities, and the moments of realisation and deep shifts in client experience that can occur. The therapist is involved in these, not as an observer and catalyser of the client process, but as an integral part of their reality, and this means that choices are made collaboratively, with the therapist taking some responsibility for their impact on the client, '*I hadn't realised how important it was until you spoke about it, but I see now that what I need is to grieve for the children I did not conceive*'. In practice, the choices are therefore limited by the shared experience of therapy, but in more practical terms, the things that inform and optimise the way choices are undertaken and how clients are increasingly empowered to make choices includes:

- The therapist tending to take responsibility for establishing the mechanisms and processes for choice, initially deciding what choices are offered, and when. This can allow the therapist to manage any overwhelm for the client, but also requires awareness of when decisions are being made for the client.
- Clients may not know, or recognise, what choices they have, and in the early stages of therapy the premise of choice is made clear, whilst 'when' and 'how' choices tend to be orchestrated by the therapist. This is a temporary situation, as therapy progresses clients become

increasingly able to respond in a highly engaged way to the question, '*do you have a sense of what you'd like to do with today's session?*'

- There is no hard-and-fast rule as to who decides how much information is needed to make the right decisions in therapy. The therapist may supply choice-making information, reviewing and offering the options to the client, but anticipating that the client would then become an active partner in sharing ideas, knowledge, and opinions as therapy progresses.

Notwithstanding this issue, choice of some kind is fundamental to pluralism and actions are taken to accommodate preference and offer choice to a client wherever possible. Opportunities for choice are therefore woven into the fabric of the therapy, within the pre-therapy information, and during the early sessions, and pluralistic therapists will take responsibility for introducing the ideas of choice and ensuring that opportunities for feedback are presented (and responded to). Once the rhythm of therapy has been established, and collaboration becomes standard, the ambition is that the client is empowered to indicate choices and preferences. The use of feedback practices (see Chapter 20), meta-communication, and 'choice-points', combine to help fit the therapy to the client, with good choice-facilitation reducing the potential for overwhelm. These are constructed through several tasks, starting with creating an open culture of choice-making, preference accommodation, and meta-communication including:

- Working in the context of client preferences such as the degree of choice and the pace of change.
- Recognising the choices available and evaluating them with the client.
- Recognising the timing of choices and being able to explore them with the client.

Creating an open culture is imperative because it can reassure the therapist that, if they have taken a 'wrong-turn' or made a choice based on their perceived idea of a shared decision, the client will feel able to bring them back to what they need. A further systemic aspect of therapy, which might be helpful in developing this culture of choice, is for the therapist to be able to transparently reflect to the client when they are considering choices, facilitating openness to recognising how choices might come about, referencing directionality and acknowledging changes and poor outcomes of their own decisions around choices, so the shared process of choice-making is apparent – '*I had thought I would offer you some ideas about how we might look at this last session but chose not to because we were working on what came up for you at work, I think now it might have been helpful*'.

The ability to discerningly include a wide range of therapeutic activities into practice is both a creative and flexible stance that allows client needs to be responded to, but there is no denying that it is also a challenge for therapists, particularly those new to practice. However, in answer to the question of whether choice can become overwhelming, it is apparent that there is a difference between having a framework with limitless options and a client being given limitless options in the room (which would be unachievable!).

46 You are asking a lot of clients, do they like it?

Pluralistic therapy was designed in response to what clients have been saying to researchers over many years (see Chapter 6), the ideas around how they wish the therapy to respond to their needs, align to their ideas, and be 'done with' not 'done to' are clear. But this does not necessarily mean that the application of the pluralistic framework to therapy gets it right. It is worthwhile thinking about clients who have undertaken it, for example, do they appreciate the level of meta-communication? Do they want to have their preferences accommodated? Do they want to share decisions? Does this lead to better outcomes and reduced drop-out? In simple terms, do they like it?

Let's start with that idea of it being a 'demanding' therapy for the client, and what things might influence pluralistic therapy's expectations of clients. Many clients will come to therapy to initially 'get things off their chest', to talk about things that have no other place for expression and are likely to simply feel relieved that there is someone who will listen and strive to understand. This process can be so important (and sometimes entirely sufficient) for change to take place and it may feel that the navigation of information sharing, setting of meta-communication and process monitoring, even formulation, are just barriers to what is really needed. In essence, some clients may prefer to be provided with a service without knowing the nuts-and-bolts of what is going on, hear therapist reflections without knowing their context, and be free to cry, rage, or process uninterrupted. They may find that the therapist making choices for them in terms of the direction, focus, and methods used is a relief and they really don't want to think about preferences or choice-points.

This begs the question of whether clients want to be active participants and have influence on what is done in therapy? Firstly, we have plenty of evidence to support the individual concepts which can

DOI: 10.4324/9781003305736-51

be found throughout this book, particularly within collaboration (see Chapter 11), goals (see Chapter 16), and monitoring feedback (see Chapters 20 and 48). Anecdotally, we also have good evidence for clients finding the approach useful and meaningful, but the pluralistic framework is relevantly new, so the extant research does not provide a comprehensive overview of client experiences of being in pluralistic therapy. However, two useful studies (Antoniou et al., 2017; Gibson et al., 2020) provide indications that the combination of a good quality therapeutic relationship, and the development of processes for shared decision making in pluralistic therapy, are well-received.

In their pilot study examining client experiences of pluralistic counselling for depression, Antoniou and colleagues (2017) discovered, through interviews with 18 clients post-therapy, that the helpful aspects of the therapy aligned with the intentions of the approach, and found being both comfortable and being challenged, within an empowering relationship and alongside having the opportunity to share the decision-making process, were important. They were also able to clearly identify what had changed for them and that they were the active agents in this. There was also good evidence for the common factors being essential for change, and the helpfulness of the therapy appears to be based in an established and trusting relationship, which can be both predicted, that is, '*what I wanted was*', but was also often a retrospective understanding, '*it was helpful that we did this*'. This indicates that clients appreciated therapists making time to evaluate how helpful something *was*, and that this is as important as trying to find and offer what *might* be helpful. In essence, clients seem to want the feedback loop for both them and the therapist.

Additionally, research into the experience of shared decision-making in pluralistic therapy has been carried out by Gibson and colleagues (2020) with clients who had undergone therapy for depression. Participants were asked to recall their experiences of events where discussion occurred around therapy aims, goals, preferences, methods, or therapeutic contracting. Picking up on the subtleties of shared decision-making, the author identified both therapist-led, client-led, and shared decisions, but when focusing on only the shared decisions this resulted in a dimension from more therapist-led to more client-led sharing, where clients still felt active engagement in the former but were aware of taking the primary role in the latter. The daunting nature of asking clients to take part in the decision-making process was identified in subsequent interviews of participants (Gibson, 2020), but it was clear that it was a valuable aspect of therapy, both in the way it allowed goals and activities to be targeted to needs, and in the therapeutic nature of the consultation itself. Clients recognised that the underlying framework to support the decisions was coming from therapists, and that this included:

• The creation of space for the client to offer input.
• Directly referring to clients or inviting them to have input.
• Helping clients to frame suggestions during difficulty.
• Acknowledging and reassuring the client after they made suggestions.
• Encouraging further contributions.

Ultimately this highlighted the process nature of shared decision-making which was useful but also required active participation and therapist actions to support the process.

So how might pluralistic practitioners balance the demands on clients in therapy? It is important to recognise that within the collaborative relationship there will be times when decisions are made explicitly and times when things are taken on trust (the use of intuition in this is discussed in Chapter 25), clients cannot be asked to confirm all their preferences throughout a session, and excessive demands for feedback are likely to both stall the process, and make the therapist appear unprofessional. Practitioners address this in a number of ways, the first is to set the scene with the client at the start of therapy; that there is an openness to dialogue, feedback, and preferences, and try and support any opportunity the client takes to voice their perspective or comment on what is being done in therapy. Alongside this, the therapist and client are also likely to have a keen sense of how the therapy is progressing (see Chapters 20 and 48), and any sense of 'stuckness' or jarring with the client can be observed and resolved once the importance of open dialogue is understood.

It is also worth noting that the client themselves might not find their active role in being a co-therapist arduous. The relationship and process of therapy is negotiated, and it is important to recognise the need for both therapist and client to remain aware of the tasks and methods that are undertaken. Some unanswered questions remain in pluralistic therapy around this process, such as, whether clients prefer to have their therapy coming from one school and if they perceive shifts and differences when working on new tasks or with different understandings. Whilst it has not been subject to significant inquiry, it is likely that concerns about the clunkiness of task and method shift, and the mental energy involved in being meta-aware of the therapy process, are not as apparent in the room as they are when described in theory. In our experience, tasks and methods flow, evolve, and merge within the conversation, which itself may change in tone and pace according to the focus of the session. It's also important to remember that whilst clients may grow and develop their understanding of themselves, they are unlikely to undergo a fundamental shift in the way they understand change to happen (Kühnlein, 1999; Valkonen et al., 2011), and this limits the degree to which activities range. The pluralistic therapy process enables the fitting of therapy to the client belief system and in comparison to introducing, either explicitly or implicitly, a whole new belief system, pluralism is perhaps less demanding for some clients as it does its best to fit to what they prefer and believe will help.

47 Is a collaborative therapy approach suitable for everyone?

Collaboration is the cornerstone that runs right through therapy in terms of goals, tasks, and bonds (Bordin, 1979), and underpins the therapeutic alliance, which is widely reported to enhance outcomes (Ribeiro et al., 2012; Wampold, 2015), motivation, and confidence (Bachelor et al., 2007; Ahmad et al., 2014), and is desired by many clients (Bachelor et al., 2007). So powerful is the role of collaboration, that Norcross and Lambert note, '*If we are even a little bit successful as a task force, then . . . psychotherapists from all camps will increasingly collaborate and our patients will benefit from the most efficacious treatments and relationships available*' (2011, pp. 7–8). However, it is important to consider when collaborative therapy might not be suitable, or even preferred. There is an over-riding consensus that collaboration alludes to a working together, involving '*the sharing of information, ideas, opinions, resources, activities, power, rewards, accountability and responsibility*' (Shoesmith et al., 2019, p. 6). In examining these concepts of collaboration, we can begin to understand why collaboration may not be a suitable approach for all, and how the therapist may be able to adapt to maximise the potential for collaboration.

In deciphering the difference between 'mundane' collaboration and 'creative' collaboration, it has been thought that the latter requires an exchange of ideas to problem solve and find novel solutions that neither party would have necessarily managed alone (Chua et al., 2012), supporting the necessity of sharing information, ideas, activities, resources, and opinions. Yet Bachelor and colleagues (2007) view that for this to be significant, it must involve the client's ability to self-disclose in a deep and meaningful manner and express intensity of affect. Herein lie two 'potential' barriers to collaboration, the first being the client's ability to connect with their own inner world; either because of an intellectual capacity or because of protective strategies

DOI: 10.4324/9781003305736-52

against psychological pain and the second being the ability to express this, in a meaningful way, to the therapist. For example, in a bid to stay psychologically 'safe', clients may struggle to trust the practitioner to such an extent that they feel able to self-disclose (Chua et al., 2012; Shoesmith et al., 2019). Whilst there are techniques that the therapist can utilise to develop and enhance trust, including communication, boundary setting, making personal and emotional connections, there is no guarantee that the client will develop a felt-sense of trust.

A sense of trust can further be moderated by the power dynamic and, whilst the therapist may strive to equalise the power (see Chapter 31), the client and therapist exist within larger social, political and health systems which can result in the service user feeling disempowered. Hierarchical cultures, such as those found within medical systems, family structures, or mandated therapy, can leave clients and service users feeling frustrated and lacking in motivation. This in turn results in poorer communication such as awkwardness in turn-taking and the sharing of 'information' rather than personally significant opinions and ideas necessary for collaboration (Shoesmith et al., 2019). The client's ability to be autonomous is also seen as an important factor in collaboration (Bachelor et al., 2007), and whilst some cultures value psychological autonomy (towards internal values, emotions, and wishes) others value relatedness which results in autonomy being responsible and obligated to the communal system (Keller, 2016).

Autonomy can be further impacted by both the client's legal and psychological capacity (see Chapter 29). It requires the client (if in therapy) to understand the relevance of the decision in relation to their own value system including the risk, benefits, and alternative options, and whether they can retain this knowledge long enough to make a voluntary choice and be able to communicate this (Citizens Information Board, 2016; Health Service Executive, 2005). It is possible, however, to maximise capacity through delivering the necessary information in a format that is accessible to the individual, which can aid collaboration. Therefore it is not appropriate to judge a client to be lacking in capacity based on superficial factors such as age, disability, or behaviour (Health Service Executive, 2005). Even those who lack capacity will still have preferences (Health Service Executive, 2005), and it is important that these are considered in the decisions to be made, bearing in mind that collaboration (but not consent unless there are legal responsibilities) can be extended to close friends, family, and other professionals who the client considers as helpful in making a decision (Citizens Information Board, 2016; Health Service Executive, 2005). It has also been discussed that psychological capacity to engage in collaborative work, such as working toward shared goals, can be affected by the service user's symptomology (Gaston, 1991), it may be useful to read more about this in Chapter 29. Despite this, and as Bowlby (1988) notes, through providing a secure base, with understanding and involvement, we can support the working relationship. This is akin to collaboration being on a spectrum, varying from no/ low client involvement with high therapist participation, whereby the therapist assumes the main responsibility for the working relationship, to high/active client involvement and low therapist participation, whereby clients view themselves as the main change agent, and joint involvement in the middle, providing shared responsibility (Bachelor et al., 2007). In our experience, this continuum can often be observed as clients come in seeking a greater degree of direction and, as they build trust and autonomy, they begin to take a greater share of the responsibility and we step back. Therefore, even with lower psychological capacity, efforts can still be made to achieve a collaborative relationship.

Most importantly, not all clients desire a collaborative relationship, for a variety of potential reasons including, but not limited to, personal preference and cultural expectations. Older people, for example, have, in some cases, been found to prefer not to be as involved in their care, particularly regarding decision making processes, and prefer a more Rogerian style of care and support (Bunn et al., 2018). Perhaps it can be useful to consider a social-cultural perspective on age, as, at the time of writing, this generation's core experience of health systems was during an era of 'expert-layperson' and therefore providing feedback and involvement may feel counterintuitive. Other cultural considerations may include that inter-personal styles differ between cultures and may affect their perception, and desire, of how to collaborate; some studies have found that Asian clients prefer a 'non-directive' approach compared to American clients who mostly liked the directive style of therapy (D'Rozario and Romano, 2000). However, there is usually considerable diversity within cultural groups (D'Rozario and Romano, 2000), some Chinese clients recognise the need to take responsibility for the therapeutic process including motivation, a key component of collaboration (Ng and James, 2013), and the desire to be involved in care may be part-mediated by the individuals current need for care, and health literacy (Kiselev et al., 2018). Therefore, a need to tailor 'the work' and be responsive to the client's preferences for their involvement, whether collaborative or otherwise, is paramount (Bastiaens et al., 2007).

When considering collaboration, including trust, capacity, preference, and culture, it is important to recognise the risk versus benefit nature of collaboration. As collaboration is a key component of shared goals, a client's goal that is harmful to themselves or someone else can fall outside of a therapist's ability to collaborate fully, because ultimately the therapist must take account of risk and put the necessary safety measures in place. There are legal obligations that enable the therapist to conduct a risk assessment (see Chapter 29), however, they may also have value judgements that they are unable to leave to one side, which can act as a barrier to maintaining a collaborative relationship with their client. In both of these scenarios, it is possible for the therapist to attempt a collaborative safety plan or make a referral to other services (see Chapter 44). Ultimately, we would argue that collaborative therapy has the *potential* to be suitable for everyone, although it will be dependent on the client's preferences, ability to build trust in the relationship enough to communicate meaningful aspects of themselves, and the therapist's ability to adapt their style and communication of information to their client's capacity, cultural, and preference needs. The sharing of information, and eliciting the client's choice and perspective about the style of therapy, will attend to the client's preference for therapy, which has the potential to enhance the relationship as well as outcomes.

48 How can outcomes be defined when client goals are so unique and personal?

The evidence of change processes in therapy is monitored and recorded for a range of different reasons. A service may wish to evidence the outcomes for the group they are supplying therapy to in order to secure funding, a researcher may wish to gather evidence for one intervention compared to another, whilst therapists may wish to track changes through therapy for a single client (see Chapter 20). The challenge for practitioners is the tension between nomothetic 'routine outcome measures' and the idiographic 'client desired outcomes of therapy', as the latter is usually of more interest and relevance to our work.

In a bid to evidence the effectiveness of the profession and offer clients the highest level of care, monitoring standardised outcomes can demonstrate effectiveness (Evans et al., 2002; Gondek et al., 2016; Boswell et al., 2013), improvements in quality of life, identification and reduction of deterioration and risk of premature termination (Lambert, 2013), ensuring early risk detection and management (Lambert, 2013; Donnelly et al., 2011; Gondek et al., 2016). Whilst it is acknowledged that there are limitations in published psychometric evidence (Donnelly et al., 2011; Coster, 2013), outcome measures have been found to be a cost-effective and feasible tool to aid client engagement, collaborative practice, and encourage client autonomy and self-confidence (Joosten et al., 2011). Clients may be encouraged and motivated by improving scores or feel better understood when the therapist discusses their responses.

Outcome measurement in mental health is linked to the idea of 'recovery', a metaphoric and relative term used to signify a return or improvement to a state of well-being. It represents the complex and nuanced pathways that individuals take to improve their mental well-being (Slade, 2009; Trenoweth, 2016). However, for many therapists,

DOI: 10.4324/9781003305736-53

the term still reflects a tradition of medicalisation of emotional and psychological well-being and implies that a person can either be in a state of psychological 'wellness' or 'illness'. This hits upon the problem with standardised routine outcome measures – 'averaging' well-being across a population. Commonly used scales, such as the Beck Depression Inventory (Beck et al., 1996), are based on psychiatric symptom presence and severity over fixed periods of time. Even the CORE-OM (Evans et al., 2002), a well-being measure frequently used in counselling, is subject to predefined questions of risk, symptoms, function, and well-being, which may not be meaningful to the client and can be open to interpretation. There is a risk that we can conflate a client response to a well-being measure with reference to the population for whom it was developed. In practice, the value of these standard questionnaires is not necessarily the ability to track objective improvement but to (i) provide a meta-communicative reference point for discussions around areas of concern and (ii) to engage clients in thinking about their progress.

Outcomes of therapy are inherently subjective, and this raises the question of whose idea of recovery is being measured. Some of the most successful working relationships we have had with clients have been when we renegotiated the initial goal of symptom reduction (or eradication) for goals of managing their symptoms, or finding a different frame of reference for well-being. They identified that whilst they would rather not have symptoms (avoidant goal), what they wanted more is to live their life regardless of their symptoms. Yet, everyone's idea of a 'fulfilling' life is unique, for one, it may be climbing Mount Everest and sailing the world, whereas for others, it could be 'simply' functioning day-to-day without overwhelming distress. The concept of goals in therapy is explored in Chapter 16 and is closely linked to outcome monitoring.

Pluralistic therapists might use nomothetic measures within their work context to track outcomes across clients or the service, but they also utilise quantitative forms to stimulate a conversation to effectively gather qualitative information, for example, to understand the client's goals (Philpot et al., 2017). They can provide an opportunity to track symptom reduction, highlighting 'off-track' moments, alerting the therapist to clients who are getting worse which, if this continues, might signify the need to alter therapy. It is important to note the tentative language here, it can be extremely harmful to merely use a score which resulted from predefined 'symptom' questions, without seeking our client's understanding about both the questions and results. To illustrate the importance of this, and the dialogue around it, we offer a synopsis of the case study 'Minding Mom' (Brown, 2018, 2019),

> *Molly (16), reported she wanted to work on her anxiety so she could man-age daily living (friendships, school, self-esteem) and work on communication with her mam. At the end of twelve weeks, when she closed the work, her YP-CORE score indicated there was moderate levels of distress, as there had been when she started. When enquiring about her understanding of this, Molly explained that the raised anxiety was because she was out at a fair and, whilst she still has anxiety, she believed she had addressed her goal; she had made plans for college, written a CV to apply for work, had a better relationship with mam, and was doing more for herself, mam also echoed this.*
> (Brown, 2018, 2019)

This example highlights the discrepancy between the outcome meas-urements and goals, despite overlaps existing. In practice, pluralism seeks to address the client's desired outcomes of therapy, and so idiographic process and outcome monitoring is often of more value. The use of idiographic Patient Generated Outcome Measures or iPROMS (Sales et al., 2022) helps pluralistic therapists bridge the gap between gath-ering depersonalised and standardised outcomes, and monitoring and evaluating the client's unique desired outcomes. Whilst iPROMS have traditionally been based on either 'avoidance', that is, a cessation, or reduction in difficulties, and 'approach' outcomes, something which the client is striving towards, they are reflective of the constructionist philosophy of pluralism, and many practitioners and clients find them more meaningful in aiding alignment to what the client really wants. In their recent review of the use of iPROMS, Sales and colleagues (2022) argue that these instruments improve patient outcomes through indi-viduation of therapy and assist the client in identification and resolu-tion of problems, they also represent a less challenging instrument to operationalise in practice. Through collaboration iPROMS aid clients in understanding and defining, or redefining, their outcomes but also in helping them to recognise accomplishments which might meet, or work towards, their goals. Sometimes when small tasks are completed clients can find them negligible, but by holding these in the frame-work of their desired outcome they can see progress (examples of some iPROMS are given in Appendix II).

We can all be guilty of the 'happiness pursuit' and can locate evidence for our well-being in external indicators (like mood measures) and, even if symptoms have been alleviated or goals have been achieved, we can feel there is more to do. Referring to the client's pre-defined idea of what their preferred outcome is can help to structure therapy and identify when these have been met, but in therapy these desires can evolve, and pluralistic therapy can be flexible in accommodating this.

49 What happens if the client can't see or understand the problem, and what if it is a result of something outside their awareness?

Dryden (2012) highlighted that, in some of the literature on pluralism, the term 'comfortable' brings an implication that comfort should be given primacy over insight and change. Furthermore, he offered that an unquestioning acceptance of client perspectives and choice in pluralistic therapy can risk leaving the client in a position of being comfortable – when it may actually be helpful for them to be moved towards something which is uncomfortable but ultimately transformational. The role of client insight is vital and, during therapy, there are times when it is appropriate for both the therapist and the client to bring into awareness aspects of experience or interpretations of which the other is unaware (Castonguay and Hill, 2007). In fact, research tells us that clients often want their therapist to share their ideas, encourage them to look at things differently, or have their assumptions challenged (Norcross and Lambert, 2019). What can be problematic is that, once raised, the other person may not agree with the observation or inference of the observation. So, is it useful to pursue the subject when met with misalignment?

The idea of the unseen or unacknowledged interpretation was touched upon in Chapter 42, where we introduced the idea of how psychodynamic therapists might become pluralistic (see also Spurling, 2016). Sometimes clients will have ideas, perceptions, and beliefs, which therapists find hard to understand or align with (and vice versa), especially when they are interpreted to be part of the problem. For example, the cause of anxiety can produce several plausible rationales:

- External factors.
- Cognitive filters and core beliefs.
- Relationship patterns.
- Trauma.

DOI: 10.4324/9781003305736-54

- Biological imbalance.
- Lack of meaning and purpose.

The therapist and client can take quite different perspectives and the conversion of the therapist's interpretation to that of the client, or vice versa, can feel intrusive and unhelpful. On one hand, the therapist might believe that the client is at best 'unaware' and at worst 'resistant' to useful information that can lead to insight. On the other hand, the client might be striving, in the best way they can, to understand the world. Theorists such as Ribeiro and colleagues (2014) suggest that client denial or resistance is in fact due to them not yet being at a place where the information is within their *'therapeutic zone of proximal development'*, and it is down to the therapist to re-align, but effectively not give up on, their interpretation. However, whilst a therapist may draw from a 'dominant theory', a pluralistic therapist allows themselves to *'include other realities'* (Gergen, 2000, p. 367) and amend their understanding in dialogue (Gergen, 2000). It may be that clients will benefit from alternative narratives and ideas of the therapist, but in a context where they have autonomy and a right to choose not to align with them.

However, in therapeutic relationships there are power dynamics (discussed in Chapter 31) which, if not addressed, can silence both therapist and client, and often therapists will decide not to share potentially useful information and insights out of concern for influencing the process in unhelpful ways. In pluralistic therapy, establishing the ideal environment to enable a consideration of different viewpoints requires steps to be taken in the early stages of therapy in the form of:

- Open invitations to the client, coming from a place of therapist humility, to comment on the therapy process, *'I might sometimes suggest ideas that don't make sense or aren't helpful for you . . . as part of the therapy it might be useful for you to tell me how you feel if I say things you might disagree with.'*
- An open ability to reflect on the fallibility of the therapist, *'I wonder if I can check something out'* rather than, *'what I think is . . .'*
- Getting a sense of client preference for challenge, *'would it be helpful if I share ideas about how I see things, even if I see them differently from you . . .'* even, *'I am not sure how you would like me to raise ideas with you about what is going on'.*
- Asking permission to give an interpretation and build a meaning bridge, if one is possible, *'when you are talking, I get a sense that we*

maybe see things a bit differently . . . are you okay for me to share my thoughts?'

Despite therapist's fears of the impact of challenge, and the risk of imposing an interpretation, clients have reported that getting another perspective from their therapist is useful to them (Timulak and McElvaney, 2013), if they are permitted to reject the ideas presented. Additionally, if over-arching ideas or goals have been agreed, that promote the deepening or broadening understanding and insight, this helps provide 'permission' to share ideas. For example, if the client holds a belief in the concept of avoidance, or they are purposefully engaged in the discovery of unseen or unknown aspects of their experiences, then they may be more willing to discuss other perspectives. Indeed, if the needs and preferences of the client to engage in discovery (however uncomfortable this may be) are not met, then they may feel dissatisfied and that there was an opportunity missed (Lilliengren and Werbart, 2005; Lindhiem et al., 2014).

So, with this knowledge-sharing, there must be a context where the therapist and client can respect and disagree with the ideas they each hold. Clients are often highly aware and sensitive to what is said, and not said, in therapy, holding their own interpretations of therapist endeavours. When a therapist decides that a perspective or idea should be pursued, even in the light of a client not wishing to, then clients tended to simply quit therapy because they did not believe that uncovering the unseen would be helpful – whilst the therapist did (Philips et al., 2007).

The risk of the client withdrawing, either by becoming silent on the subject or from therapy completely, is always present if a therapist is working on a different values base, or beliefs around what therapy should be about (McLeod, 2013b). This can relate to what goes on in the relationship when managing different perspectives, but can also relate to the attitude of the client from the outset, and some evidence points to the impact of preconceptions of clients on drop-out (Bennemann et al., 2022; Philips et al., 2007); if a therapist's perspective diverges from the clients too much, they simply don't come back!

Here we offer some suggestions for how divergence in understanding and interpretation can be managed in practice:

- A therapeutic relationship is more effective when the role of the therapist has already been sketched, for example, by stating what might happen if the therapist has interpretations and ideas, and how the client might like to deal with these if they disagree.

- Therapists must be humble and know that their ideas are no truer than anyone else's (which can feel counterintuitive), holding a curiosity about aspects of client experience, that they do not yet fully understand, can help.
- Remember that the purpose of therapy is not the discovery and validation of objective truths, but rather the development of meaning for the client.
- Prioritising therapist truths, over the client, risks rupture, disengagement, and disempowerment, and should be avoided. Understanding what the client desires, and flexibility in accommodating perspectives, helps guide the dialogue.
- Therapists might like to examine why they need their perspective to take precedence to that of their client with their supervisor. Supervision is the place where contrasting ideas can be explored, and decisions made as to how clients' perspectives might be understood, alongside consideration of impact of the difference on the client journey.

A consideration of the client's frame of reference is essential, meaning is always in context, and the most acceptable interpretations of experience are likely to come from the client lifeworld. It is possible for a pluralistic therapist to use their knowledge (see Chapter 12), intuition (see Chapter 25), and experience to make interpretations with the purpose of aiding the client in their meaning-making of situations. What is not helpful is the potential divergence in understanding, leading from perspectives that neither fit with the client's worldview nor facilitate ways of moving forward.

50 Is a pluralistic therapist a 'Jack of all trades and master of none'?

A common challenge put to therapists training in, and undertaking, pluralistic practice, is that being able to provide a wide range of ways of working means that no single one is done very well. The rather derogatory term 'Jack of all trades' indicates that first, therapy is undertaken in an ad hoc and overly opportunistic way, '*I have an idea what needs to be done and I can give it a go*', but secondly, that somehow each therapeutic modality or method available is a 'trade' effective for every client who undertakes it and so distinct that they cannot be deployed in combination with other modalities. It can be an irksome metaphor for many, because, whilst in practice, integrative variability is a characteristic of the way a pluralistic therapist undertakes their work, this is practised with self-awareness, skill, and expertise. Additionally, it is also worth noting that some pluralistic therapists, whilst having a pluralistic stance, may practice a single modality, either due to client preference or through their own style/training (see Chapter 7).

One of the most important things to remember is that the rationale for adopting pluralism is based on a philosophical stance, with the assumption that multiple valid truths can exist in parallel (see Chapter 2). The implication of this is that there is a moral and ethical obligation to respond to clients within their frame of understanding, in combination with our own. This dismantles the validity of theoretical assumptions based within schools of therapy, and therefore the need to apply practice in particular ways. This deployment of a constructionist understanding on how meaning is created in therapy does not negate the benefits of knowledge, but rather requires the focus of skill on the ability to use it to best effect, and flex according to the client and context of therapy and the problem being addressed. So, pluralistic therapy strives to establish practice in a set of foundations, not based on a theoretical 'truth' or 'truths', but based within a set of principles (see

DOI: 10.4324/9781003305736-55

Chapter 5). These principles both guide the ethical judgements of therapists, but equally require them to value and promote client well-being above allegiance to theoretical (or even their own) beliefs and respond to the best of their abilities. These judgements draw on a number of competencies and practice conditions, an understanding of research evidence, recognition of commonalities of all therapeutic approaches, and an ethic of client empowerment, along with guiding structures to manage practice and an emphasis on therapist reflexivity and competence in offering choice. Although much of this is covered elsewhere in the book, it is perhaps worth examining these more closely in direct response to the question.

The first thing to note is that when the frame of reference transitions from a theoretical perspective to one which privileges the client, there is a need to anchor practice in a knowledge base (how do you justify what you are doing?) (see Chapter 12). We know that client knowledge and pre-existing ideas have a huge impact on their experience and outcomes for therapy (McLeod, 2013b). For pluralistic practice this is situated in a combination of empirical research, for example, knowledge of effectiveness of a range of foundational skills (see Chapter 13), interventions including the use-of-self (see Chapter 10), goals (see Chapters 16–17), the use of feedback (see Chapter 20), and client experiences of what helps and when (see Chapter 6). This portfolio of knowledge provides a menu of what is likely to be helpful for clients, and pluralism has established a framework for practice that optimises the use of this. Pluralistic therapy also invites clients into an environment infused with meta-communication and a shared monitoring of the process and outcome of the therapy, in this way a pluralistic therapist commits to responding and adapting to the client's experience of therapy, almost moment-to-moment, which is a demanding process.

The 'Jack' metaphor tends to imply a position where the therapist is doing things 'to' the client rather doing things 'with' the client. This directly conflicts with the principles of the approach, the reliance on client choice, the position a therapist takes on the client strengths, resourcefulness, and understanding of their situation. Thus, there is a need to actively engage clients in their therapeutic process, which occurs both at an operational and a relational level.

The 'Jack' metaphor additionally infers that pluralistic therapists act in isolation from all other aspects of the person's life. Conversely, rather than creating or deploying therapeutic interventions, which act to create a space for change in order to return a client to some socially acceptable point of 'normal' function, pluralism aims to create a highly porous boundary between 'in therapy' and 'outside therapy'. This enables the client to draw on cultural resources (see Chapter 23) and recognise that therapy is not an isolated process, but something which is woven into their lives. The impact of therapy is on the lifeworld of the client, and therefore the work undertaken within it is carefully constructed around other influential factors such as social and cultural context, ability and disability, client's philosophical and ethical stance, and of course their hopes and ambitions. Ultimately, pluralistic therapists strive towards the empowerment of the client to function in the real world, and this bridge is often neglected in therapy.

The final challenge coming from the metaphor concerns being a 'master of none'. The first contention to this is that therapists do not begin their training cobbling together odd bits of theories and interventions. They often begin rigorous training within a single, or integrative (two or more) theories, gaining core counselling skills therefore becoming 'experts', in-so-far as possible, in these disciplines and develop a pluralistic stance from this base. Furthermore, pluralistic therapy recognises, and commits to, the need for ongoing professional and personal training and for practitioners to continually work at their practice through feedback (see Chapter 20), supervision (see Chapter 38), and deliberate practice (see Chapter 37). The term 'master of none' further implies that pluralistic therapists draw on multiple schools of thought, and therefore work with incomplete conceptualisations of client process, and an inexpert application of methods and activities which have been developed in single schools. The implication that being a 'master' of one therapy is that the resonance with the client's lifeworld is of little importance when the therapist is an expert. In response to this, we would say that a theory, concept, or intervention is only complete when it sustains a 'fit' with client experience and understanding. If not, then it is a disjointed application, perhaps based on the beliefs of the therapist, or even the person who trained the therapist. Pluralistic therapists build and sustain complex work using their clients frame of understanding and preferences, and the idea that this bespoke structuring is *ad hoc* is a derogation of the therapist's capacity. The developmental track of pluralistic therapists is an ongoing striving to broaden their portfolio of responses, deepen their knowledge of client experience, and recognise that it is they, as people, and the way they respond (not necessarily the additional methods they deploy), that are truly valued by clients. For this reason, they use deliberate practice, self-directed learning, and training to fill gaps in their application of skills (see Chapter 37).

Ultimately, we would argue that, if anything, pluralistic therapists are 'masters' at getting it right for the client – which few would contest is a worthy pursuit.

Appendix I

The 'Ways Paradigm' of Frankie

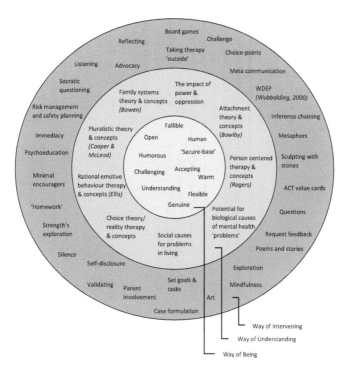

This is not an exhaustive list. Cheston's Ways Paradigm (2000) as taught by Finnerty et al (2016) enables me to consider my toolkit. In practice Pluralism, and the concepts within, supports me to draw from these in collaboration with the client

Figure AI.1 An example of the Ways Paradigm of Frankie

Appendix II
Which Measure and When?[1]

Table AII.1 A guide to choosing a measure of outcome, process, or preference

Outcome measures (to begin the session in order to understand how well someone is doing)	Process measures (to end the session in order to check on the relationship and process)	Preference measures (to understand what clients want, which is useful prior to therapy or at a review)
CORE package (OM, 10, 5, YP, LD): Clinical Outcome in Routine Evaluation. Exploring risk, functioning, wellbeing and problems (Evans et al., 2002).	**WAI:** Working Alliance Inventory consists of 12 questions to explore the relationship (Horvath and Greenberg, 1989).	**C-NIP:** Cooper–Norcross Inventory of Preferences. 18 questions under four sections on directiveness, warm support, emotional intensity, or past/present. Plus further qualitative preferences of modality, length, medication, etc. (Cooper and Norcross, 2016).
ORS: Outcome Rating Scale. Four scale lines to explore individual, interpersonal, social and overall factors of wellbeing (Miller et al., 2003).	**SRS:** Session Rating Scale. Four scale lines to explore relationships, goals, methods and overall factors of therapy (Duncan et al., 2003).	**TPF:** Therapy Personalisation Form. 20 scaled questions based on focus of session, roles, and characteristics (Bowen and Cooper, 2012).
BDI: Becks Depression Inventory. To explore depression (Beck et al., 1996).	**ARM5 or 12:** Agnew Relationship Measure. To assess confidence, openness, support and collaboration (Cahill et al., 2012 adapted from Agnew-Davies et al., 1998).	**TPI:** Treatment Preference Interview. Qualitative exploration across three domains such as bonds (relationship), goals, tasks and methods. (Vollmer et al., 2009).

BAI: Becks Anxiety Inventory. To explore anxiety (Beck et al., 1988).

HAT: Helpful Aspects of Therapy. Seven qualitative and quantitative questions to understand what did, or did not, work well in session (Llewelyn, 1988).

HAM-A: Hamilton Anxiety Rating Scale. To explore anxiety (Hamilton, 1959).

GAD-7: Generalised Anxiety Disorder. To assess if anxiety is present and the severity of symptoms (Spitzer et al., 2006).

HDRS: Hamilton Depression Rating Scale. To explore depression (Hamilton, 1960).

PHQ-9: Patient Health Questionnaire. To explore depression (Kroenke et al., 2001).

FEQ: Family Expressiveness Questionnaire. To understand the family environment as positive or negative, submissive or dominant (Halberstadt, 1986).

SDQ: Strengths and Difficulties Questionnaire. For young people, parents, and/or teachers (Goodman et al., 2004).

Session Bridging Worksheet: Multiple versions available but designed for the client to report on the process of their session and review how their week was prior to the next session (Tsai, 2009).

1   This is not a complete list but offers some common tools that you may come across. The important part of any form is how you use (introduce and discuss) this with your client.

References

Adler, J.M., Harmeling, L.H., and Walder-Biesanz, I. (2013). Narrative meaning making is associated with sudden gains in psychotherapy clients mental health under routine clinical conditions. *Journal of Consulting and Clinical Psychology*, 81(5), 839–845. https://doi.org/10.1037/a0033774.

Agnew-Davies, R., Stiles, W.B., Hardy, G.E., Barkham, M., and Shapiro, D.A. (1998). Alliance structure assessed by the Agnew Relationship Measure (ARM). *British Journal of Clinical Psychology*, 37, 155–172.

Ahmad, N., Ellins, J., Krelle, H., and Lawrie, M. (2014). *Person-Centred Care: From Ideas to Action. Bringing Together the Evidence on Shared Decision Making and Self-Management Support*. London: ICF GHK.

Ahsan, S. (2022). *I'm a Psychologist – and I Believe We've been Told Devastating Lies about Mental Health*. The Guardian.

Allsopp, K., Read, J., Corcoran, R., and Kinderman, P. (2019). Heterogeneity in psychiatric diagnostic classification. *Psychiatry Research*, 279(15). https://doi.org/10.1016/j.psychres.2019.07.005.

Al-Roubaiy, N.S., Owen-Pugh, V., and Wheeler, S. (2017). Iraqi refugee men's experiences of psychotherapy: clinical implications and the proposal of a pluralistic model. *British Journal of Guidance and Counselling*, 45(5), 463–472.

American Psychiatric Association. (2013). *Diagnostic and Statistical Manual of Mental Disorders* (5th ed.). Washington, DC: American Psychiatric Association.

American Psychological Association. (2017). *Multicultural Guidelines: An Ecological Approach to Context, Identity, and Intersectionality*. Retrieved September 4, 2022, from www.apa.org/about/policy/multicultural-guidelines.pdf

Antoniou, P., Cooper, M., Tempier, A., and Holliday, C. (2017). Helpful aspects of pluralistic therapy for depression. *Counselling and Psychotherapy Research*, 17(2), 137–147. https://doi.org/10.1002/capr.12116.

Aponte, H., and Kissil, K. (2012). "If I can grapple with this I can truly be of use in the therapy room": using the therapist's own emotional struggles to facilitate effective therapy. *Journal of Marital and Family Therapy*. https://doi.org/10.1111/jmft.12011.

Arendt, H. (1963). *On Revolution*. London: Penguin Classics.

Ayala, E., Hage, S., and Wilcox, M. (2011). Social justice theory. In R.J.R. Levesque (Ed.), *Encyclopedia of Adolescence*. New York: Springer.

Aylesworth, G. (2015). Postmodernism. In E.N. Zalta (Ed.), *The Stanford Encyclopedia of Philosophy*. Stanford: Metaphysics Research Lab, Stanford University.

Bachelor, A., Laverdière, O., Gamache, D., and Bordeleau, V. (2007). Clients' collaboration in therapy: self-perceptions and relationships with client psychological functioning, interpersonal relations, and motivation. *Psychotherapy* (Chicago, IL), 44, 175–192. https://doi.org/10.1037/0033–3204.44.2.175.

BACP. (2022). www.bacp.co.uk/membership/registered-membership/guide-to-cpd/.

Bados, A., Balaguer, G., and Saldañ, C. (2007). The efficacy of cognitive – behavioral therapy and the problem of drop-out. *Journal of Clinical Psychology*, 63(6).

Balbuena Rivera, F. (2018). In honor of Jurgen Ruesch: remembering his work in psychiatry. *The International Journal of Social Psychiatry*, 64(2), 198–203. https://doi.org/10.1177/0020764017752020

Barker, P. (2001). The tidal model: developing an empowering, person-centred approach to recovery within psychiatric and mental health nursing. *Journal of Psychiatric and Mental Health Nursing*, 8(3), 233–240.

Bastiaens, H., Van Royen, P., Pavlic, D.R., Raposo, V., and Baker, R. (2007). Older people's preferences for involvement in their own care: a qualitative study in primary health care in 11 European countries. *Patient Education and Counseling*, 68(1), 33–42. https://doi.org/10.1016/j.pec.2007.03.025.

Bauminger, N., Finzi-Dottan, R., Chason, S., and Har-Even. (2008). Intimacy in adolescent friendship: the roles of attachment, coherence, and self-disclosure. *Journal of Social and Personal Relationships*, 25, 409–428. https://doi.org/10.1177/0265407508090866.

Beck, A.T., Epstein, N., Brown, G., and Steer, R. (1988). *Beck Anxiety Inventory* [Database Record]. APA PsycTests. https://doi.org/10.1037/t02025-000.

Beck, A.T., Steer, R.A., and Brown, G.K. (1996). *Manual for the Beck Depression Inventory-II*. San Antonio, TX: Psychological Corporation.

Bell, V., Wilkinson, S., Greco, M., et al. (2020). What is the functional/organic distinction actually doing in psychiatry and neurology? *Wellcome Open Research*, 5, 138. https://doi.org/10.12688/wellcomeopenres.16022.1.

Bennemann, B., Schwartz, B., Giesemann, J., and Lutz, W. (2022). Predicting patients who will drop out of out-patient psychotherapy using machine learning algorithms. *British Journal of Psychiatry*, 220(4), 192–201.

Berger, P.L., and Luckmann, T. (1966). *The Social Construction of Reality: A Treatise in the Sociology of Knowledge*. Garden City, NY: Anchor Books.

Bieling, P., and Kuyken, W. (2003). Is cognitive case formulation science or science fiction? *Clinical Psychology: Science and Practice*, 10(1), 52–69.

Biringer, E., Davidson, L., Sundfør, B., et al. (2016). Experiences of support in working toward personal recovery goals: a collaborative, qualitative study. *BMC Psychiatry*, 16, 426. https://doi.org/10.1186/s12888-016-1133-x.

Blanchard, M., and Farber, B.A. (2016). Lying in psychotherapy: why and what clients don't tell their therapist about therapy and their relationship.

Counselling Psychology Quarterly, 29(1), 90–112. https://doi.org/10.1080/09
515070.2015.1085365.

Blanchard, M., and Farber, B.A. (2020). "It is never okay to talk about suicide":
patients' reasons for concealing suicidal ideation in psychotherapy. *Psychotherapy Research*, 30(1), 124–136. https://doi.org/10.1080/10503307.2018.1
543977.

Bohart, A. (1999). Intuition and creativity in psychotherapy. *Journal of Constructivist Psychology*, 12, 287–311.

Bohart, A. (2000). The client is the most important common factor: clients'
self-healing capacities and psychotherapy. *Journal of Psychotherapy Integration*.
https://doi.org/10.1023/A:1009444132104.

Bolton, J. (2018). Deliberate practice for psychologists, psychotherapists and psychiatrists part 1. *Journal of Psychology & Clinical Psychiatry*, 9(1). https://doi.
org/10.15406/jpcpy.2018.09.00491.

Bordin, E.S. (1983). Supervision in counseling: II. Contemporary models of
supervision: a working alliance based model of supervision. *The Counseling
Psychologist*, 11(1), 35–42. https://doi.org/10.1177/0011000083111007.

Bordin, E.S. (1979). The generalizability of the psychoanalytic concept of the
working alliance. *Psychotherapy: Theory, Research and Practice*, 16(3), 252–260.
https://doi.org/10.1037/h0085885

Boswell, J., Kraus, J., Miller, S., and Lambert, M. (2013). Implementing routine
outcome monitoring in clinical practice: benefits, challenges, and solutions.
Psychotherapy Research. https://doi.org/10.1080/10503307.2013.817696.

Bowen, M., and Cooper, M. (2012). Development of a client feedback tool: a
qualitative study of therapists' experiences of using the therapy personalisation
forms. *European Journal of Psychotherapy and Counselling*, 14, 47–62.

Bowie, C., McLeod, J., and McLeod, J. (2016). 'It was almost like the opposite
of what I needed': a qualitative exploration of client experiences of unhelpful
therapy. *Counselling and Psychotherapy Research*, 1–9. https://doi.org/10.1002/
capr.12066.

Bowlby, J. (1988). *A Secure Base: Clinical Applications of Attachment Theory*. London: Routledge.

Boyle, M. (2022). Power in the power threat meaning framework. *Journal of
Constructivist Psychology*, 35(1), 27–40.

Boyle, M., and Johnstone, L. (2020). *A Straight Talking Introduction to the Power
Threat Meaning Framework: An Alternative to Psychiatric Diagnosis*. Monmouth:
PCCS Books.

Bradby, H. (2010). Institutional racism in mental health services: the consequences of compromised conceptualisation. *Sociological Research Online*, 15,
8–19.

British Psychological Association BPS. (2018). *Power Threat Meaning Framework –
The British Psychological Society*. Retrieved August 25, 2022, from bps.org.uk.

Brown, C., and Augusta-Scott, T. (2007). *Narrative Therapy: Making Meaning,
Making Lives*. London: Sage.

Brown, F. (2018). *"Minding Mom": A Study of Pluralistic Therapy with an Adolescent Girl, Molly, Who Has Anxiety, and the Counter-Transference of the Therapist.* Presented as part of a Symposium at SEPI Conference, New York.

Brown, F. (2019). *"Minding Mom": A Study of Pluralistic Therapy with an Adolescent Girl, Molly, Who has Anxiety, and the Counter-Transference of the Therapist.* Presented at ICPCP, Roehampton.

Brown, L.S. (1994). *Subversive Dialogues: Theory in Feminist Therapy.* New York: Basic Books.

Brown, L.S. (2018). *Feminist Therapy* (2nd ed.). Theories of Psychotherapy Series. Washington: American Psychological Association.

Buber, M. (1947). Dialogue. In R.G. Smith (Trans.), *Between Man and Man* (pp. 17–59). London, England: Fontana.

Bunn, F., Goodman, C., Russell, B., Wilson, P., Manthorpe, J., Rait, G., Hodkinson, I., and Durand, M.A. (2018). Supporting shared decision making for older people with multiple health and social care needs: a realist synthesis. *BMC Geriatrics*, 18(1), 165. https://doi.org/10.1186/s12877-018-0853-9.

Butler, J. (1997). *The Psychic Life of Power.* Stanford, CA: Stanford University Press.

Cabral, R.R., and Smith, T.B. (2011). Racial/ethnic matching of clients and therapists in mental health services: a meta-analytic review of preferences, perceptions, and outcomes. *Journal of Counseling Psychology*, 58(4), 537–554. https://doi.org/10.1037/a0025266.

Caetano, A. (2019). Designing social action: the impact of reflexivity on practice. *Journal for the Theory of Social Behaviour*, 49(2), 146–160. https://doi.org/10.1111/jtsb.12196.

Cahill, J., Stiles, W.B., Barkham, M., Hardy, G.E., Stone, G., Agnew-Davies, R., and Unsworth, G. (2012). Two short forms of the Agnew relationship measure: the ARM-5 and ARM-12. *Psychotherapy Research*, 22(3), 241–255.

Cairns, A., Kavanagh, D., Dark, F., and Mcphail, S. (2019). Goal setting improves retention in youth mental health: a cross-sectional analysis. *Child and Adolescent Psychiatry and Mental Health*, 13. https://doi.org/10.1186/s13034-019-0288-x.

Cambridge. (n.d.). Assessment. In *Cambridge.org Dictionary*. Retrieved June 26, 2022, from https://dictionary.cambridge.org/dictionary/english/assessment.

Campitelli, G., and Gobet, F. (2011). Deliberate practice: necessary but not sufficient. *Current Directions in Psychological Science*, 20(280). https://doi.org/10.1177/0963721411421922.

Cashwell, C. (1994). *Interpersonal Process Recall.* Greensboro, NC: ERIC Digest.

Castelnuovo, G., Pietrabissa, G., Cattivelli, R., Manzoni, G.M., and Molinari, E. (2016, May 9). Not only clinical efficacy in psychological treatments: clinical psychology must promote cost-benefit, cost-effectiveness, and cost-utility analysis. *Frontiers in Psychology*, 7, 563. https://doi.org/10.3389/fpsyg.2016.00563. PMID: 27242562; PMCID: PMC4860399.

Castonguay, L., Eubanks, C., Goldfried, M., Muran, J., and Lutz, W. (2015). Research on psychotherapy integration: building on the past, looking to the future. *Psychotherapy Research*, 25(3), 365–382. https://doi.org/10.1080/1050 3307.2015.1014010.

Castonguay, L., and Hill, C. (2007). *How and Why Are Some Therapists Better Than Others? Understanding Therapist Effects* (pp. 71–84). Washington, DC: American Psychological Association. http://dx.doi.org/10.1037/0000034-005.

Chater, N., and Loewenstein, G. (2016). The under-appreciated drive for sense-making. *Journal of Economic Behavior and Organization*, 126(B), 137–154.

Cheston, S. (2000). A new paradigm for teaching counseling theory and practice. *Counselor Education and Supervision*, 39. https://doi.org/10.1002/j.1556-6978.2000.tb01236.x.

Chibucos, T., Leite, R., and Weis, D. (2004). *Readings in Family Theory*. London: Sage Publications. https://uk.sagepub.com/sites/default/files/upm-assets/4991_book_item_4991.pdf.

Chow, D.L., Miller, S.D., Seidel, J.A., Kane, R.T., Thornton, J.A., and Andrews, W.P. (2015). The role of deliberate practice in the development of highly effective psychotherapists. *Psychotherapy*, 52, 337–345.

Chua, R., Morris, M., and Mor, S. (2012). Collaborating across cultures: cultural metacognition and affect-based trust in creative collaboration. *Organizational Behavior and Human Decision Processes*, 118(2), 116–131.

Citizens Information Board. (2016). Assisted Decision Making Act (2015). *Relate The journal of Developments in Social Services, Policy and Legislation in Ireland*, 43(4). ISSN 0790–4290.

Clamp, M. (2022). *What Outcome Goals Do Young People Aged 16 to 20 Years Who Self-Harm Have for Therapy and What in Therapy Helped or Hindered Them in Achieving These Goals?* (Unpublished thesis). Lancaster University, Lancaster.

Clare, L., and Woods, B. (2001). A role for cognitive rehabilitation in dementia care. *Neuropsychological Rehabilitation*, 11(3–4), 193–196.

Clarke, S.P., Crowe, T.P., Oades, L.G., and Deane, F.P. (2009). Do goal-setting interventions improve the quality of goals in mental health services? *Psychiatric Rehabilitation Journal*, 32(4), 292–299. https://doi.org/10.2975/32.4.2009.292.299 training in goal setting is important.

Cooper, M. (2008). *Essential Research Findings in Counselling and Psychotherapy: The Facts are Friendly*. Los Angeles, CA: British Association for Counselling and Psychotherapy Content Provider; London, England: Sage.

Cooper, M. (2009). Welcoming the other: actualising the humanistic ethic at the core of counselling psychology practice. *Counselling Psychology Review*, 24.

Cooper, M. (2018). The psychology of goals: a practice friendly review. In M. Cooper and D. Law (Eds.), *Working with Goals in Counselling and Psychotherapy*. Oxford: Oxford University Press.

Cooper, M. (2020). *Person-Centred Therapy Is Not One Thing: An Introduction to the Tribes*. Retrieved February 7, 2023, from https://mick-cooper.squarespace.com/new-blog/2020/1/29/person-centred-therapy-is-not-one-thing-an-introduction-to-the-tribes

Cooper, M. (2021). *The Existential Counselling Primer* (2nd ed.). Monmouth: PCCS books.

Cooper, M. (2023). *Psychology at the Heart of Social Change: Developing a Progressive Vision for Society.* Bristol: Bristol University Press.

Cooper, M., and Dryden, W. (2016). *Handbook of Pluralistic Counselling and Psychotherapy.* London: Sage.

Cooper, M., and Law, D. (2018). *Working with Goals in Counselling and Psychotherapy.* Oxford: Oxford University.

Cooper, M., and McLeod, J. (2007). A pluralistic framework for counselling and psychotherapy: implications for research. *Counselling and Psychotherapy Research*, 7(3), 135–143. ISSN1473–3145.

Cooper, M., and McLeod, J. (2011). *Pluralistic Counselling and Psychotherapy.* London: Sage.

Cooper, M., and McLeod, J. (2012). From either/or to both/and: developing a pluralistic approach to counselling and psychotherapy. *European Journal of Psychotherapy and Counselling.* https://doi.org/10.1080/13642537.2012.652389.

Cooper, M., and Norcross, J.C. (2016). A brief, multidimensional measure of clients' therapy preferences: the Cooper-Norcross inventory of preferences (C-NIP). *International Journal of Clinical and Health Psychology*, 16(1), 87–98. https://doi.org/10.1016/j.ijchp.2015.08.003.

Cooper, M., Norcross, J.C., Raymond-Barker, B., and Hogan, T. (2019). Psychotherapy preferences of laypersons and mental health professionals: whose therapy is it? *Psychotherapy*, 56. https://doi.org/10.1037/pst0000226.

Cooper, M., van Rijn, B., Chryssafidou, E., and Stiles, W.B. (2021). Activity preferences in psychotherapy: what do patients want and how does this relate to outcomes and alliance? *Counselling Psychology Quarterly*, 35(3), 503–526. https://doi.org/10.1080/09515070.2021.1877620.

Cooper, M., Wild, C., van Rijn, B., Ward, T., McLeod, J., Cassar, S., Antoniou, P., Michael, C., Michalitsi, M., and Sreenath, S. (2015). Pluralistic therapy for depression: acceptability, outcomes and helpful aspects in a multisite study. *Counselling Psychology Review*, 30(1), 6–20.

Cooper, M., and Xu, D. (2022). Goals form: reliability, validity, and clinical utility of an idiographic goal-focused measure for routine outcome monitoring in psychotherapy. *Journal of Clinical Psychology*, 1–26. https://doi.org/10.1002/jclp.23344.

Corrigan, F.M., Fisher, J.J., and Nutt, D.J. (2011). Autonomic dysregulation and the window of tolerance model of the effects of complex emotional trauma. *Journal of Psychopharmacology*, 25(1), 17–25.

Coster, W.J. (2013). Making the best match: selecting outcome measures for clinical trials and outcome studies. *The American Journal of Occupational Therapy: Official Publication of the American Occupational Therapy Association*, 67(2), 162–170. https://doi.org/10.5014/ajot.2013.006015.

Creaner, M., and Timulak, L. (2016). Clinical supervision and counseling psychology in the Republic of Ireland. *The Clinical Supervisor*, 35(2), 192–209. https://doi.org/10.1080/07325223.2016.1218812.

Davis, D., and Younggren, J. (2009). Ethical competence in psychotherapy termination. *Professional Psychology: Research and Practice*, 40(6). https://doi.org/10.1037/a0017699.

Denborough, D. (2014). *Retelling the Stories of Our Lives: Everyday Narrative Therapy to Draw Inspiration and Transform Experience*. New York: W.W. Norton & Company.

De Witte, M., Orkibi, H., Zarate, R., Karkou, V., Sajnani, N., Malhotra, B., . . . Koch, S. (2021). From therapeutic factors to mechanisms of change in the creative arts therapies: a scoping review. *Frontiers in Psychology*, 12, 678397.

Di Malta, G., Oddli, H.W., and Cooper, M. (2019). From intention to action: a mixed methods study of clients' experiences of goal-oriented practices. *Journal of Clinical Psychology*, 75(10), 1770–1789. https://doi.org/10.1002/jclp.22821.

Diamond, G., Wintersteen, M., Brown, G., Diamond, G., Gallop, R., Shelef, K., and Levy, S. (2010). Attachment-based family therapy for adolescents with suicidal ideation: a randomized controlled trial. *Journal of the American Academy of Child and Adolescent Psychiatry*, 49(2), 122–131. http://dx.doi.org/10.1016/j.jaac.2009.11.002.

Dickson, J., Moberly, N., O'Dea, C., and Field, M. (2016). Goal fluency, pessimism and disengagement in depression. *PLoS One*, 11(11). https://doi.org/10.1371/journal.pone.0166259.

Dobud, W. (2017). Towards an evidence-informed adventure therapy: implementing feedback-informed treatment in the field. *Journal of Evidence-Informed Social Work*, 14(3), 172–182. https://doi.org/10.1080/23761407.2017.1304310.

Donnelly, M., Scott, D., McGilloway, S., O'Neill, T., Williams, J., and Slade, M. (2011). Outcome and process measures appear adept at capturing client information patient outcomes: what are the best methods for measuring recovery from mental illness and capturing feedback from patients in order to inform service improvement? *Bamford Implementation Rapid Review Scheme*.

Douglas, E., and Bushardt, W. (1988). Interpersonal conflict: strategies and guidelines for resolution. *Journal of the American Medical Record Association*, 56(18).

Downing, J.N. (2004). Psychotherapy practice in a pluralistic world: philosophical and moral dilemmas. *Journal of Psychotherapy Integration*, 14(2), 123–148. https://doi.org/10.1037/1053-0479.14.2.123.

D'Rozario, V., and Romano, J.L. (2000). Perceptions of counsellor effectiveness: a study of two country groups. *Counselling Psychology Quarterly*, 13(1), 51–63. https://doi.org/10.1080/09515070050011060.

Dryden, W. (2012). Pluralism in counselling and psychotherapy: personal reflections on an important development. *European Journal of Psychotherapy and Counselling*, 14(1), 103–111.

Dryden, W. (2020). Single-session one-at-a-time therapy: a personal approach. *Australian and New Zealand Journal of Family Therapy*, 41(3), 283–301. https://doi.org/10.1002/anzf.1424.

Duncan, B.I., and Miller, S. (2008). Supershrinks: What is the secret of their success? Psychotherapy.net.

Duncan, B.I., Miller, S.D., and Sparks, J.A. (2004). *The Heroic Client: A Revolutionary Way to Improve Effectiveness Through Client-Directed, Outcome-Informed Therapy*. San Fransisco: Jossey-Bass.

Duncan, B.L. (2015). The person of the therapist: one therapist's journey to relationship. In K.J. Schneider, J.F. Pierson, and J.F.T. Bugental (Eds.), *The Handbook of Humanistic Psychology: Theory, Research, and Practice* (pp. 457–472). Thousand Oaks, CA: Sage Publications, Inc.

Duncan, B.L., Miller, S.D., Sparks, J.A., and Claud, D.A. (2003). The session rating scale: preliminary psychometric properties of a "working" alliance measure. *Journal of Brief Therapy*, 3(1), 3–12.

Ee, C., Lake, J., Firth, J., Hargraves, F., De Manincor, M., Meade, T., . . . Sarris, J. (2020). An integrative collaborative care model for people with mental illness and physical comorbidities. *International Journal of Mental Health Systems*, 14(1), 1–83.

Eells, T.D., Kendjelic, E.M., and Lucas, C.P. (1998). What's in a case formulation? Development and use of a content coding manual. *The Journal of Psychotherapy Practice and Research*, 7(2), 144–153.

Ekhtiari, H., Rezapour, T., Aupperle, R., and Paulus, M. (2017). Chapter 10 – neuroscience-informed psychoeducation for addiction medicine: a neurocognitive perspective. In T. Calvey and W. Daniels (Eds.), *Progress in Brain Research* (vol. 235, pp. 239–264). Elsevier. https://doi.org/10.1016/bs.pbr.2017.08.013.

Ellen, P., Lukens, E., and McFarlane, W. (2004). Psychoeducation as evidence-based practice: considerations for practice, research, and policy. *Brief Treatment and Crisis Intervention*, 4(3). https://doi.org/10.1093/brief-treatment/mhh019.

Elliot, A.J., and Church, M.A. (2002). Client articulated avoidance goals in the therapy context. *Journal of Counseling Psychology*, 49(2), 243–254. https://doi.org/10.1037/0022-0167.49.2.243.

Elliott, R., Bohart, A.C., Watson, J.C., and Greenberg, L.S. (2011). Empathy. *Psychotherapy*, 48, 43–49. https://doi.org/10.1037/a0022187.

Enlow, P.T., McWhorter, L.G., Genuario, K., and Davis, A. (2019). Supervisor – supervisee interactions: the importance of the supervisory working alliance. *Training and Education in Professional Psychology*, 13(3), 206–211. https://doi.org/10.1037/tep0000243.

Enright, J. (1972). Thou art that: projection and play in therapy and growth. *Psychotherapy* (Chicago, IL), 9(2), 153–156.

Ericsson, K., Krampe, R., and Tesch-Roemer, C. (1993). The role of deliberate practice in the acquisition of expert performance. *Psychological Review*, 100, 363–406. https://doi.org/10.1037//0033-295X.100.3.363.

Eubanks, C.F., Muran, J.C., and Safran, J.D. (2018). Alliance rupture repair: a meta-analysis. *Psychotherapy*, 55, 508–519. http://dx.doi.org/10.1037/pst0000185.

Evans, C. (2012). Cautionary notes on power steering. *Canadian Psychological Association*, 53(2), 131–139.

Evans, C., Connell, J., Barkham, M., Margison, F., McGrath, G., Mellor-Clark, J., and Audin, K. (2002). Towards a standardised brief outcome measure: psychometric properties and utility of the CORE – OM. *British Journal of Psychiatry*, 180(1), 51–60.

Evans, C., Connell, J., Barkham, M., Marshall, C., and Mellor-Clark, J. (2003). Practice-based evidence: benchmarking NHS primary care counselling services at national and local levels. *Clinical Psychology & Psychotherapy*, 10, 374–388. http://doi.org/10.1002/cpp.384.

Everall, R.D., and Paulson, B.L. (2002). The therapeutic alliance: adolescent perspectives. *Counselling and Psychotheraphy Research*, 2. https://doi.org/10.1080/14733140212331384857.

Feltham, C., and Dryden, W. (2006). *Brief Counselling A Practical, Integrative Approach* (2nd ed.). Buckingham: Open University Press.

Finnerty, M., Kearns, C., and O'Regan, D. (2018). Pluralism: an ethical commitment to dialogue and collaboration. *Irish Journal of Counselling and Psychotherapy*, 18(3).

Finnerty, M., McLeod, J., Kearns, C., O'Neill, D., and O'Regan, D. (2016). *Teaching Integration through the Ways Paradigm.* Paper Presented at 2016 SEPI Annual Conference, Dublin.

Flannery, F., Adams, D., and O'Connor, N. (2011). A community mental health service delivery model: integrating the evidence base within existing clinical models. *Australasian Psychiatry: Bulletin of Royal Australian and New Zealand College of Psychiatrists*, 19, 49–55. https://doi.org/10.3109/10398562.2010.539220.

Flaskas, C., and Humphreys, C. (1993). Theorizing about power: intersecting the ideas of Foucault with the "problem" of power in family therapy. *Family Process*, 32, 35–47. https://doi.org/10.1111/j.1545-5300.1993.00035.x.

Fleet, D. (2022). *Pluralistic Sand-Tray Therapy: Humanistic Principles for Working Creatively with Adult Clients.* Abingdon: Routledge.

Foerschner, A.M. (2010). The history of mental illness: from skull drills to happy Pills." *Inquiries Journal/Student Pulse*, 2(9). www.inquiriesjournal.com/a?id=1673.

Fonseca-Pedrero, E., Al-Halabí, S., Pérez-Albéniz, A., and Debbané, M. (2022). Risk and protective factors in adolescent suicidal behaviour: a network analysis. *International Journal of Environmental Research and Public Health*, 19(3), 1784. https://doi.org/10.3390/ijerph19031784.

Fox, J., Hagedorn, W., and Sivo, S. (2016). Clinical decision-making and intuition: a task analysis of 44 experienced counsellors. *Counselling and Psychotherapy Research*, 16(4), 244–255.

Freedman, J., and Combs, G. (1996). Narrative therapy: the social construction of preferred realities. *Psyccritiques*, 42.

Freud, S. (1959). Future prospects of psychoanalytic psychotherapy. In J. Strachey (Ed.), *Standard Edition of the Complete Psychological Works of Sigmund Freud* (vol. 20, pp. 87–172). New York, NY: Basic Books.

Gabriel, L., and Casemore, R. (Eds.). (2009). *Relational Ethics in Practice: Narratives from Counselling and Psychotherapy*. London: Routledge.

Garland, A., Kruse, M., and Aarons, G. (2003). Clinicians and outcome measurement: what's the use? *The Journal of Behavioral Health Services & Research*, 30(4), 393–405.

Garland-Thomson, R. (2002). Integrating disability, transforming feminist theory. *NWSA Journal*, 14, 1–32. https://doi.org/10.1353/nwsa.2003.0005.

Gaston, L. (1991). Reliability and criterion-related validity of the California psychotherapy alliance scales-patient version. *Psychological Assessment: A Journal of Consulting and Clinical Psychology*, 3, 68–74. https://doi.org/10.1037/1040–3590.3.1.68.

Gaudiano, B., Brown, L., and Miller, I. (2011). Let your intuition be your guide? Individual differences in the evidence-based practice attitudes of psychotherapists. *Journal of Evaluation in Clinical Practice*, 17(4), 628–634.

Geller, J., Fernandes, A., Srikameswaran, S., et al. (2021). The power of feeling seen: perspectives of individuals with eating disorders on receiving validation. *Journal of Eating Disorders*, 9. https://doi.org/10.1186/s40337-021-00500-x.

Gergen, K. (1994). *Realities and Relationships: Soundings in Social Constructionism*. Cambridge, MA: Harvard University Press.

Gergen, K. (1999). *An Invitation to Social Construction*. London: Sage.

Gergen, K. (2000). Creative confluence. *Psychotherapy*, 37(4).

Gibson, A., Cooper, M., Rae, J., and Hayes, J. (2020). Clients' experiences of shared decision making in an integrative psychotherapy for depression. *Journal of Evaluation in Clinical Practice*, 26, 559–568. https://doi.org/10.1111/jep.13320.

Gibson, K., Cartwright, C., Kerrisk, K., Campbell, J., and Seymour, F. (2016). What young people want: a qualitative study of adolescents' priorities for engagement across psychological services. *Journal of Child and Family Studies*, 25. https://doi.org/10.1007/s10826-015-0292-6.

Glass, C., Arnkoff, D., and Shapiro, S. (2001). Expectations and preferences. *Psychotherapy: Theory, Research, Practice, Training*, 38, 455–461. https://doi.org/10.1037/0033–3204.38.4.455.

Glasser, W. (2003). *For Parents and Teenager: Dissolving the Barrier Between You and Your Teen*. New York: Harpercollins.

Goldberg, S., Babins-Wagner, R., Rousmaniere, T., Berzins, S., Hoyt, W., Whipple, J., Miller, S., and Wampold, B. (2016). Creating a climate for therapist improvement: a case study of an agency focused on outcomes and deliberate practice. *American Psychological Association*, 53(3), 367–375. http://dx.doi.org/10.1037/pst0000060.

Gondek, D., Edbrooke-Childs, J., Fink, E., Deighton, J., and Wolpert, M. (2016). Feedback from outcome measures and treatment effectiveness, treatment efficiency, and collaborative practice: a systematic review. *Administration and Policy in Mental Health*, 43(3), 325–343. https://doi.org/10.1007/s10488-015-0710-5.

Goode, J., Park, J., Parkin, S., Thomkins, K., and Swift, J. (2017). A collaborative approach to psychotherapy termination. *Psychotherapy*, 54(1). https://doi.org/10.1037/pst0000085.

Goodman, R. (2001). Psychometric properties of the strengths and difficulties questionnaire. *Journal of the American Academy of Child and Adolescent Psychiatry*, 40(11), 1337–1345. https://doi.org/10.1097/00004583-200111000-00015.

Goodman, R., Ford, T., Corbin, T., and Meltzer, H. (2004). Using the strengths and difficulties questionnaire (SDQ) multi-informant algorithm to screen looked-after children for psychiatric disorders. *European Child & Adolescent Psychiatry*, 13(Suppl 2), II25–II31. https://doi.org/10.1007/s00787-004-2005-3.

Goodman, R., and Gorski, P. (Eds.). (2015). *Decolonizing "Multicultural" Counseling Through Social Justice. International and Cultural Psychology*. New York: Springer. https://doi-org.libproxy.abertay.ac.uk/10.1007/978-1-4939-1283-4_1.

Gough, B. (2016). Reflexivity in qualitative psychological research. *Journal of Positive Psychology*, 1–2. ISSN 1743–9760. https://doi.org/https://doi.org/10.1080/17439760.2016.1262615.

Gov.Wales. (2019). *School and Community-Based Counselling Operating Toolkit*. Retrieved August 31, 2022, from https://gov.wales/school-and-community-based-counselling-operating-toolkit

Griffiths, G. (2013). *A Systematic Review of Young People's Experiences of Helpful and Unhelpful Factors in School-Based Counselling* (Unpublished thesis). University of Strathclyde and Glasgow Caledonian University, UK.

Gu, J., Strauss, C., Bond, R., and Cavanagh, K. (2015). How do mindfulness-based cognitive therapy and mindfulness-based stress reduction improve mental health and wellbeing? A systematic review and meta-analysis of mediation studies. *Clinical Psychology Review*, 37, 1–12.

Gulliver, A., Griffiths, K., and Christensen, H. (2010). Perceived barriers and facilitators to mental health help-seeking in young people: a systematic review. *BMC Psychiatry*, 10, 106–113.

Gupta, N. (2022). Truth, freedom, love, hope, and power: an existential rights paradigm for anti-oppressive psychological praxis. *The Humanistic Psychologist*, 50(3), 460–475.

Halberstadt, A.G. (1986). Family socialization of emotional expression and non-verbal communication styles and skills. *Journal of Personality and Social Psychology*, 51(4), 827–836. https://doi.org/10.1037/0022-3514.51.4.827.

Hall, E., and Mufson, L. (2009). Interpersonal psychotherapy for depressed adolescents (IPT-A): a case illustration. *Journal Of Clinical Child and Adolescent Psychology*, 38(4), 582–593. http://dx.doi.org/10.1080/15374410902976338.

Hallam, R.S. (2013). Appendix – guidelines for assessment and constructing an individual case formulation (ICF). In *Individual Case Formulation* (pp. 175–257). Elsevier Inc. https://doi.org/10.1016/B978-0-12-398269-8.15001-X.

Hamilton, M. (1959). The assessment of anxiety states by rating. *British Journal of Medical Psychology*, 32, 50–55.

Hamilton, M. (1960). A rating scale for depression. *Journal of Neurology, Neurosurgery, and Psychiatry*, 23, 56. https://doi.org/10.1136/jnnp.23.1.56.

Hanley, T., and Winter, L. (2016). Research and pluralistic counselling and psychotherapy. In M. Cooper and W. Dryden (Eds.), *Handbook of Pluralistic Counselling and Psychotherapy* (pp. 337–349). London: Sage.

Harzer, C., and Ruch, W. (2015). The relationships of character strengths with coping, work-related stress, and job satisfaction. *Frontiers in Psychology*, 6. https://doi.org/10.3389/fpsyg.2015.00165.

Hawkins, P., and Shohet, R. (2006). *Supervision in the Helping Professions*. Berkshire, UK: Open University Press.

Health Service Executive. (2005). *Consent: A Guide for Health and Social Care Professionals*. www.hse.ie/eng/about/who/qid/other-quality-improvement-programmes/consent/guidehealthsocialcareprofdoc.html.

Hoener, C., Stiles, W.B., Luka, B.J., and Gordon, R.A. (2012). Client experiences of agency in therapy. *Person-Centred and Experiential Psychotherapies*, 11(1), 64–82.

Hogan, S. (2016). *Art Therapy Theories: A Critical Introduction*. Oxon: Routledge.

Hook, J., Davis, D., Owen, J., Worthington, E., and Utsey, S. (2013). Cultural humility: measuring openness to culturally diverse clients. *Journal of Counseling Psychology*, 60(3), 353–366.

Hopewell, S., Loudon, K., Clarke, M., Oxman, A., and Dickersin, K. (2009). Publication bias in clinical trials due to statistical significance or direction of trial results. *Cochrane Database of Systematic Reviews*, 2010(1), MR000006.

Horvath, A.O., and Greenberg, L.S. (1989). Development and validation of the working alliance inventory. *Journal of Counseling Psychology*, 36, 223–233.

Howard, G.S. (1983). Toward methodological pluralism. *Journal of Counseling Psychology*, 30(1), 19–21. https://doi.org/10.1037/0022-0167.30.1.19.

Hunsley, J., Aubry, T.D., Verstervelt, C., and Vito, D. (1999). Comparing therapist and client perspectives on reasons for psychotherapy termination. *Psychotherapy*, 36(4).

IACP. (2019). *IACP Continuing Professional Development Policy*. Retrieved September 4, 2022, from www.iacp.ie/Continuing-Professional-Development-Framework.

Inoue, T., Kimura, T., Inagaki, Y., and Shirakawa, O. (2020). Prevalence of comorbid anxiety disorders and their associated factors in patients with bipolar disorder or major depressive disorder. *Neuropsychiatric Disease and Treatment*, 16, 1695–1704. https://doi.org/10.2147/NDT.S246294.

The International Bateson Institute. (2018). *About | Gregory Bateson*. Retrieved August 25, 2022, from https://batesoninstitute.org/gregory-bateson/.

Ioannidis, J.P.A. (2005). Why most published research findings are false. *PLoS Medicine*, 2(8), e124. https://doi.org/10.1371/journal.pmed.0020124.

Jacob, J., Edbrooke-Childs, J., Lloyd, C., Hayes, D., Whelan, I., Wolpert, M., and Law, D. (2018). Measuring outcomes using goals. In M. Cooper and D. Law (Eds.), *Working with Goals in Psychotherapy and Counselling*. Oxford: Oxford University Press.

Janssen, M., Heerkens, Y., Kuijer, W., Van der Heijden, B., and Engels, J. (2018). Effects of mindfulness-based stress reduction on employees' mental health: a systematic review. *PLoS One*, 13(1), E0191332.

Jensen, S.B., Eplov, L.F., Mueser, K.T., and Petersen, K.S. (2021). Participants' lived experience of pursuing personal goals in the illness management and recovery program. *International Journal of Social Psychiatry*, 67(4), 360–368. https://doi.org/10.1177/0020764020954471.

Jessop, B. (2012). Marxist approaches to power. In E. Amenta, K. Nash, and A. Scott (Eds.), *Developments in Marxist Theory the Wiley-Blackwell Companion to Political Sociology* (pp. 3–14). Oxford: Blackwell.

Johnstone, L., and Boyle, M. (2018). The power threat meaning framework: an alternative nondiagnostic conceptual system. *The Journal of Humanistic Psychology*, 2216781879328.

Johnstone, L., Boyle, M., Cromby, J., Dillon, J., Harper, D., Kinderman, P., Longden, E., Pilgrim, D., and Read, J. (2019). Reflections on responses to the power threat meaning framework one year on. *Clinical Psychology Forum*, 313, 47–54.

Jones-Smith, E. (2012). *The Fourth Force in Psychotherapy in Theories of Counseling and Psychotherapy: An Integrative Approach*. Thousand Oaks, CA: SAGE Publications.

Joosten, E.A., De Jong, C.A., de Weert-van Oene, G.H., Sensky, T., and van der Staak, C.P. (2011). Shared decision-making: increases autonomy in substance-dependent patients. *Substance Use and Misuse*, 46(8), 1037–1038. https://doi.org/10.3109/10826084.2011.552931.

Jorm, A., Griffiths, K., Christensen, S., Parslow, R., and Rogers, B. (2004). Actions taken to cope with depression at different levels of severity: a community survey. *Psychological Medicine*, 34, 293–299. https://doi.org/10.1017/S003329170300895X.

Joyce, P., Cooper, M., McLeod, J., and Vos, J. (2023). Pluralistic counselling versus counselling as usual for young people presenting with addiction issues: a pilot randomised controlled trial. *Counselling and Psychotherapy Research*, 23(1), 74–83.

Kabat-Zinn, J. (1990). *Full Catastrophe Living: How to Cope with Stress, Pain and Illness Using Mindfull Meditation*. London: Piatkus.

Kagan, N. (1973). *Influencing Human Interaction – Eleven Years with IPR*. East Lansing: Michigan State University.

Källström, A., and Thunberg, S. (2019). "Like an equal, somehow" – what young people exposed to family violence value in counseling. *Journal of Family Violence*, 34(6), 553–563.

Karkou, V., Omylinska-Thurston, J., Parsons, A., Nair, K., Starkey, J., Haslam, S., . . . Marshall, L. (2022). Bringing creative psychotherapies to primary NHS Mental Health Services in the UK: a feasibility study on patient and staff experiences of arts for the blues workshops delivered at improving access to psychological therapies (IAPT) services. *Counselling and Psychotherapy Research*, 22(3), 616–628.

Kazdin, A. (1996). Dropping out of child psychotherapy: issues for research and implications for practice. *Clinical Child Psychology and Psychiatry*, 1(1), 133–156. http://dx.doi.org/10.1177/1359104596011012.

Keller, H. (2016). Psychological autonomy and hierarchical relatedness as organizers of developmental pathways. *Philosophical Transactions of the Royal Society of London. Series B, Biological Sciences*, 371(1686), 20150070. https://doi.org/10.1098/rstb.2015.0070.

Kellog, S. (2015). *Transformational Chairwork: Using Psychotherapeutic Dialogues in Clinical Practice*. Lanham: Rowman and Littlefield Publishers.

Kinderman, P. (2019). *A Manifesto for Mental Health: Why We Need a Revolution in Mental Health Care*. Liverpool: Palgrave Macmillan.

Kirmayer, L.J., Simpson, C., and Cargo, M. (2003). Healing traditions: culture, community and mental health promotion with Canadian Aboriginal peoples. *Australasian Psychiatry*, 11(S1), S15–S23.

Kiselev, J., Suija, K., Oona, M., Mellenthin, E., and Steinhagen-Thiessen, E. (2018). Patient involvement in geriatric care – results and experiences from a mixed models design study within project INTEGRATE. *International Journal of Integrated Care*, 18(1), 12. http://doi.org/10.5334/ijic.2517.

Kitwood, T. (1997). The experience of dementia. *Aging & Mental Health*, 1(1), 13–22.

Kleiman, E.M., and Liu, R.T. (2013). Social support as a protective factor in suicide: findings from two nationally representative samples. *Journal of Affective Disorders*, 150(2), 540–545. https://doi.org/10.1016/j.jad.2013.01.033.

Knox, S., Adrians, N., Everson, E., Hess, S., Hill, C., and Crook-Lyon, R. (2011). Clients' perspectives on therapy termination. *Psychotherapy Research*, 21(2), 154–167. https://doi.org/10.1080/10503307.2010.534509.

Koç, V., and Kafa, G. (2019). Cross-cultural research on psychotherapy: the need for a change. *Journal of Cross-Cultural Psychology*, 50(1), 100–115. https://doi.org/10.1177/0022022118806577.

Kolmanskog, V. (2018). *The Empty Chair: Tales from Gestalt Therapy*. Abingdon: Routledge.

Kotter, J., and Whitehead, L. (2010). *Buy-In: Saving Your Good Idea From Getting Shot Down*. Boston: Harvard Business School Press.

Kraft, Z. (2020). Metamodernism: historicity, affect, and depth after postmodernism. In R. van den Akker, A. Gibbons, and T. Vermeulen (Eds.). Lanham, Rowman and Littlefield, 2017. *C21 Literature*, 8(1).

Kroenke, K., Spitzer, R.L., and Williams, J.B.W. (2001). The PHQ-9 validity of a brief depression severity measure. *Journal of General Internal Medicine*, 16, 606–613. https://doi.org/10.1046/j.1525-1497.2001.016009606.x.

Kühnlein, I. (1999). Psychotherapy as a process of transformation: analysis of post-therapeutic autobiographical narrations. *Psychotherapy Research*, 9, 274–287. https://doi.org/10.1093/ptr/9.3.274.

Ladany, N., Mori, Y., and Mehr, K. (2013). Effective and ineffective supervision. *The Counseling Psychologist*, 41, 28–47. https://doi.org/10.1177/001100001 2442648.

Lambert, M. (2013). Outcome in psychotherapy: the past and important advances. *Psychotherapy*, 50(1), 42–41. https://doi.org/10.1037/a0030682.

Lambert, M., and Shimokawa, K. (2011). Collecting client feedback. *Psychotherapy*, 48(1). https://doi.org/10.1037/a0022238.

Laska, K.M., Gurman, A.S., and Wampold, B.E. (2014). Expanding the lens of evidence-based practice in psychotherapy: a common factors perspective. *Psychotherapy*, 51, 467–481. https://doi.org/10.1037/a0034332.

Law, D. (2014). Why use forms to measure outcomes and get service user feedback? In what young people say about outcomes and feedback tools. In D. Law and M. Wolpert (Eds.), *Guide to Using Outcomes and Feedback Tools with Children, Young People and Families*. London, UK: CORC Ltd.

Law, D., and Jacob, J. (2015). *Goals and Goal Based Outcomes (GBO's): Some Useful Information* (3rd ed.). London: CAMHS Press.

Lazarus, A.A., and Beutler, L.E. (1993). On technical eclecticism. *Journal of Counseling and Development*, 71, 381–385. https://doi.org/10.1002/j.1556-6676.1993.tb02652.x.

Lazarus, A.A., Beutler, L.E., and Norcross, J.C. (1992). The future of technical eclecticism. *Psychotherapy*, 29, 11–20.

Lee, E., Greenblatt, A., Hu, R., Johnstone, M., and Kourgiantakis, T. (2022). Developing a model of broaching and bridging in cross-cultural psychotherapy: toward fostering epistemic and social justice. *American Journal of Orthopsychiatry*, 92(3), 322–333.

Levitt, H.M., Pomerville, A., and Surace, F.I. (2016). A qualitative meta-analysis examining clients' experiences of psychotherapy: a new agenda. *Psychological Bulletin*, 142, 801–830.

Lilliengren, P., and Werbart, A. (2005). A model of therapeutic action grounded in the patients' view of curative and helping factors in psychoanalytic psychotherapy. *Psychotherapy* (Chicago, IL), 3, 324–399.

Lindhiem, O., Bennett, C., Trentacosta, C., and McLear, C. (2014). Client preferences affect treatment satisfaction, completion, and clinical outcome: a meta-analysis. *Clinical Psychology Review*, 34(6), 506–517.

Lipinska, D. (2009). *Making Sense of Self – Person Centred Counselling for People with Dementia*. London: Jessica Kingsley Publishers.

Llewelyn, S. (1988). Psychological therapy as viewed by clients and therapists. *British Journal of Clinical Psychology*, 27, 223–238.

Lloyd, C., Duncan, C., and Cooper, M. (2019). Goal measures for psychotherapy: a systematic review of self-report, idiographic instruments. *Clinical Psychology* (New York, NY), 26(3), N/a.

Lowndes, L., and Hanley, T. (2010). The challenge of becoming an integrative counsellor: the trainee's perspective. *Counselling and Psychotherapy Research*, 10(3), 167–172.

Lynass, R., Pykhtina, O., and Cooper, M. (2012). A thematic analysis of young people's experience of counselling in five secondary schools in the UK. *Counselling and Psychotherapy Research*, 12(1), 53–62.

Lyotard, J.-F. (1984). *The Postmodern Condition*. Minneapolis: University of Minnesota Press.

Mackrill, T. (2011). Differentiating life goals and therapeutic goals: expanding our understanding of the working alliance. *British Journal of Guidance and Counselling*, 39(1), 25–39. https://doi.org/10.1080/03069885.2010.531382.

Maguire, M. (2004). *Men, Women, Passion And Power: Gender Issues in Psychotherapy*. Abingdon, Oxfordshire: Brunner-Routledge.

Mapp, S., and Gatenio Gabel, S. (2019). The climate crisis is a human rights emergency. *Journal of Human Rights and Social Work*, 4(4), 227–228.

Marley, E. (2011). Self-help strategies to reduce emotional distress: what do people do and why? A qualitative study. *Counselling and Psychotherapy Research*, 11(4), 317–324. https://doi.org/10.1080/14733145.2010.533780.

Martinez, J., Lau, A., Chorpita, B., and Weisz, J. (2015). Psychoeducation as a mediator of treatment approach on parent engagement in child psychotherapy for disruptive behavior. *Journal of Clinical Child and Adolescent Psychology*, 1–15. http://dx.doi.org/10.1080/15374416.2015.1038826.

Marx, C., Benecke, C., and Gumz, A. (2017). Talking cure models: a framework of analysis. *Frontiers in Psychology*, 8. http://dx.doi.org/10.3389/fpsyg.2017.01589.

Maslow, A.H. (1954). *Motivation and Personality*. New York: Harper and Row.

May, R., Angel, E., and Ellenberger, H. (1958). *Existence: A New Dimension in Psychiatry and Psychology*. London: Simon and Schuster.

McArthur, K., Cooper, M., and Berdondini, L. (2016). Change processes in school-based humanistic counselling. *Counselling and Psychotherapy Research*, 16(2), 88–99.

McAteer, D. (2010). Philosophical pluralism: navigating the sea of diversity in psychotherapeutic and counselling psychology practice. In M. Martin (Ed.), *Therapy and Beyond: Counselling Psychology Contributions to Therapy and Social Issues*. New York: Wiley.

McElvaney, J., and Timulak, L. (2013). Clients' experience of therapy and its outcomes in 'good' and 'poor' outcome psychological therapy in a primary care setting: an exploratory study. *Counselling and Psychotherapy Research*, 13(4), 246–253.

McGillivray, L., Rheinberger, D., Wang, J., Burnett, A., and Torok, M. (2022). Non-disclosing youth: a cross sectional study to understand why young people do not disclose suicidal thoughts to their mental health professional. *BMC Psychiatry*, 22(1), 3.

McLeod, J. (1998). *An Introduction to Counselling*. Maidenhead: Open University Press.

McLeod, J. (2005). Counselling and psychotherapy as cultural work. In L. Tsoi Hoshman (Ed.), *Culture, Psychotherapy, and Counseling*. London: Sage Publications.

McLeod, J. (2012). What do clients want from therapy? A practice friendly review of research into client preferences. *European Journal of Psychotherapy and Counselling*, 14(1), 19–32.

McLeod, J. (2013a). *An Introduction to Counselling* (5th ed.). Berkshire, England: Open University Press.

McLeod, J. (2013b). Developing pluralistic practice in counselling and psychotherapy: using what the client knows. *The European Journal of Counselling Psychology*, 2(1), 51–64. https://doi.org/10.5964/ejcop.v2i1.

McLeod, J. (2013c). Process and outcome in pluralistic transactional analysis counselling for long-term health conditions: a case series. *Counselling and Psychotherapy Research*, 13(1), 32–43. https://doi.org/10.1080/14733145.2012.709873.

McLeod, J. (2015). Client preferences: building bridges between therapy and everyday life. *Psychotherapy and Counselling Federation of Australia Journal* (3). Retrieved from https://pacja.org.au/2015/07/client-preferences-building-bridges-between-therapy-and-everyday-life-2/

McLeod, J. (2017). *Using Personal Experience Research and Writing to Contribute to the Development of Therapy Theory and Practice*. IICP, Dublin.

McLeod, J. (2018a). Pluralistic therapy. In W. Dryden (Ed.), *Psychotherapy and Counselling Distinctive Features*. Oxon: Routledge.

McLeod, J. (2018b). *An Introduction to Counselling and Psychotherapy: Theory, Research, and Practice* (6th ed.). Milton Keynes: Open University Press.

McLeod, J., Lumsdaine, S., and Smith, K. (2021). Equipping students to be resourceful practitioners in community settings: a realist analysis. *European Journal of Psychotherapy & Counselling*, 23(4), 496–525.

McLeod, J., and Mackrill, T. (2018). Philosophical, conceptual, and ethical perspectives on working with goals in therapy. In M. Cooper and D. Law (Eds.), *Working with Goals in Counselling and Psychotherapy* (pp. 26–29). Oxford: Oxford University Press.

McLeod, J., and McLeod, J. (2011). *Counselling Skills: A Practical Guide for Counsellors and Helping Professionals*. Maidenhead: Open University Press.

McLeod, J., and McLeod, J. (2014). *Personal and Professional Development for Counsellors, Psychotherapists and Mental Health Practitioners*. New York: Open University Press.

McLeod, J., and McLeod, J. (2016). Assessment and formulation in pluralistic counselling and psychotherapy. In M. Cooper and W. Dryden (Eds.), *The Handbook of Pluralistic Counselling and Psychotherapy* (pp. 1–11). London: Sage Publications.

McLeod, J., McLeod, J., Cooper, M., and Dryden, W. (2013). Pluralistic therapy. In W. Dryden and A. Reeves (Eds.), *The Handbook of Individual Therapy* (vol. 6, pp. 547–574). London: Sage Publications.

Midgley, N., Holmes, J., Parkinson, S., Stapley, E., Eatough, V., and Target, M. (2014). "Just like talking to someone about like shit in your life and stuff, and they help you": hopes and expectations for therapy among depressed adolescents. *Psychotherapy Research*. https://doi.org/10.1080/10503307.2014.973922.

Miller, R.B. (1967). Task taxonomy: science or technology? *Ergonomics*, 10(2), 167–176.

Miller, S.D., Duncan, B.L., Brown, J., Sparks, J., and Claud, D. (2003). The outcome rating scale: a preliminary study of the reliability, validity, and feasibility of a brief visual analog measure. *Journal of Brief Therapy*, 2, 91–100.

Miller, S.D., Duncan, B.L., and Hubble, M.A. (2008). Supershrinks: what is the secret of their success? *Psychotherapy in Australia*, 14, 14.

Min, K., Liu, P., and Kim, S. (2018). Sharing extraordinary experiences fosters feelings of closeness. *Personality and Social Psychology Bulletin*, 44. https://doi.org/10.1177/0146167217733077.

Moerman, M.T. (2012). Working with suicidal clients: the person-centred counsellor's experience and understanding of risk assessment. *Counselling and Psychotherapy Research*, 12, 214–223.

Moloney, R. (2021). *Reflections on the First Pluralistic Encounter Group*. Retrieved August 28, 2022, from https://pluralisticpractice.com/2021/11/06/reflections-on-the-first-pluralistic-encounter-group/.

Morgan, C., and Cooper, M. (2015). Helpful and unhelpful aspects of counselling following breast cancer: a qualitative analysis of post-session helpful aspects of therapy forms. *Counselling and Psychotherapy Research*, 15(3), 197–206. https://doi.org/10.1002/capr.12028.

Motlova, L., Balon, R., Beresin, E., Brenner, A., Coverdale, J., Guerrero, A., . . . Roberts, L. (2017). Psychoeducation as an opportunity for patients, psychiatrists, and psychiatric educators: why do we ignore it? *Academic Psychiatry*, 41(4), 447–451. https://doi.org/10.1007/s40596-017-0728-y.

Muran, J.C., and Barber, J.P. (2010). *The Therapeutic Alliance: An Evidence-Based Guide to Practice*. London: Guilford Press.

Murdoch, N.L., Edwards, C., and Murdoch, T.B. (2010). Therapists' attributions for client premature termination: are they self-serving? *Psychotherapy: Theory, Research, Practice, Training*, 47, 221–234. https://doi.org/10.1037/a0019786.

Murphie, M-C., and Smith, K. (submitted). The effectiveness of pluralistic counselling in a primary counselling setting: a pilot study. *Counselling Psychology Review*.

Nadirshaw, Z. (2009). Race, culture and ethnicity in mental health care. In R. Newell and K. Gournay (Eds.), *Mental Health Nursing: An Evidenced-Based Approach* (pp. 39–55). London: Churchill Livingstone.

Nasrallah, H.A. (2011). The antipsychiatry movement: who and why. *Current Psychiatry*, 10(12), 4–53.

Nasser, M. (1995). The rise and fall of anti-psychiatry. *Psychiatric Bulletin*, 19(12), 743–746. https://doi.org/10.1192/pb.19.12.743.

Newman, M., Castonguay, L., Borkovec, T., and Molnar, C. (2004). Integrative psychotherapy. In R. Heimberg, C. Turk, and D. Mennin (Eds.), *Generalized Anxiety Disorder: Advances in Research and Practice*. Hove: Guilford Press.

Ng, C.T., and James, S. (2013). "Directive approach" for Chinese clients receiving psychotherapy: is that really a priority? *Frontiers in Psychology*, 4, 49. https://doi.org/10.3389/fpsyg.2013.00049.

NHS. (2014). *Building Collaborative Teams Presentation*. www.england.nhs.uk/improvement-hub/wp-content/uploads/sites/44/2019/01/Building-Collaborative-Teams-workshop-guide-2014-1.pdf.

NICE. (2022). *Overview Depression in Adults: Treatment and Management*. Guidance | NICE. Retrieved July 30, 2022, from https://NICE.org.uk/guidance/ng222

Nonini, D.M. (2006). Introduction: the global idea of "the commons." *Social Analysis: The International Journal of Social and Cultural Practice*, 50(3), 164–177. www.jstor.org/stable/23182116.

Norcross, J.C. (2005). A primer on psychotherapy integration. In J. Norcross and M. Goldfried (Eds.), *The Handbook of Psychotherapy Integration* (2nd ed.). New York: Oxford University Press.

Norcross, J.C., and James, J. (2013). Psychotherapist self-care checklist reproduced from Norcross. In J.C. Norcross and J.D. Guy (Eds.), *Leaving It at the Office: A Guide to Psychotherapist Self-Care*. New York: Guilford, 2007. Retrieved August 24, 2022, from 10.1093/med:psych/9780199845491.003.0144.

Norcross, J.C., and Lambert, M.J. (2011). Psychotherapy relationships that work II. *Psychotherapy*, 48(1), 4–8. https://doi.org/10.1037/a0022180.

Norcross, J.C., and Lambert, M. (2019). *Psychotherapy Relationships That Work: Volume 1: Evidence-Based Therapist Contributions*. Oxford: Oxford University Press.

Norcross, J.C., and Neman, C. (2003). Psychotherapy integration: setting the context. In J. Norcross and M. Goldfried (Eds.), *Handbook of Psychotherapy Integration* (pp. 3–35). Oxford: Oxford University Press.

Norcross, J.C., Zimmerman, B., Greenberg, R., and Swift, J. (2017). Do all therapists do that when saying goodbye? A study of commonalities in termination behaviors. *American Psychological Association*, 54(1). https://doi.org/10.1037/pst0000097.

Oddli, H., McLeod, J., Reichelt, S., and Rønnestad, M. (2014). Strategies used by experienced therapists to explore client goals in early sessions of psychotherapy. *European Journal of Psychotherapy & Counselling*, 16(3), 245–266. https://doi.org/10.1080/13642537.2014.927380.

Oeberst, A., Kimmerle, J., and Cress, U. (2016). What is knowledge? Who creates it? Who possesses it? The need for novel answers to old questions. In *Mass Collaboration and Education* (Computer-Supported Collaborative Learning Series, pp. 105–124). Cham: Springer International Publishing.

O'Hara, D. (2013). *Hope in Counselling and Psychotherapy*. London: Sage Publications.

O'Hara, D., and Schofield, M. (2008). Personal approaches to psychotherapy integration. *Counselling and Psychotherapy Research: Linking Research with Practice*, 8(1), 53–62.

Omer, H., and Strenger, C. (1992). The pluralist revolution: from the one true meaning to an infinity of constructed ones. *Psychotherapy Theory Research Practice Training*, 29, 253–261. https://doi.org/10.1037/0033-3204.29.2.253.

Omylinska-Thurston, J., Karkou, V., Parsons, A., Nair, K., Dubrow-Marshall, L., Starkey, J., . . . Sharma, S. (2021). Arts for the blues: the development of a new evidence-based creative group psychotherapy for depression. *Counselling and Psychotherapy Research*, 21(3), 597–607.

O'Neill, P. (1998). Review of: the law, standards of practice, and ethics in the practice of psychology. *Canadian Psychology = Psychologie Canadienne*, 39(3), 244–245.

Ong, W.T., Murphy, D., and Joseph, S. (2020). Unnecessary and incompatible: a critical response to Cooper and McLeod's conceptualization of a pluralistic framework for person-centered therapy. *Person-Centered and Experiential Psychotherapies*, 19(2), 168–182. https://doi.org/10.1080/14779757.2020.17 17987.

Oswald, U. (2015). 'A curious dance round a curious tree': agency and amusement in Victorian asylums. *VIDES, Volume of Interdisciplinary Essays in Literature and Arts*, 3, 93–102.

Oulanova, O., Stein, I., Rai, A., Hammer, M., and Poulin, P.A. (Eds.). (2009). *Within and Beyond Borders: Critical Multicultural Counselling in Practice*. Toronto: Centre for Diversity in Counselling and Psychotherapy.

Owen, J., and Hilsenroth, M.J. (2014). Treatment adherence: the importance of therapist flexibility in relation to therapy outcomes. *Journal of Counseling Psychology*, 61(2), 280–288. https://doi.org/10.1037/a0035753

Pacini, R., and Epstein, S. (1999). The relation of rational and experiential information processing styles to personality, basic beliefs, and the ratio-bias phenomenon. *Journal of Personality and Social Psychology*, 76(6), 972–987.

Palfrey, J. (2018). *Safe Space Brave Spaces: Diversity and Free Expression in Education.* Boston: MIT Press.

Papayianni, F., and Cooper, M. (2018). Metatherapeutic communication: an exploratory analysis of therapist-reported moments of dialogue regarding the nature of the therapeutic work. *British Journal of Guidance & Counselling*, 46(2), 173–184. https://doi.org/10.1080/03069885.2017.1305098

Parsonage, M., Hard, E., and Rock, B. (2014). *Managing Patients with Complex Need. Evaluation of the City and Hackney Primary Care Psychotherapy Consultation Service*. London, UK: Centre for Mental Health.

Parsons, A., Omylinska-Thurston, J., Karkou, V., Harlow, J., Haslam, S., Hobson, J., . . . Griffin, J. (2020). Arts for the blues – a new creative psychological therapy for depression. *British Journal of Guidance and Counselling*, 48(1), 5–20.

Pederson, A., Konadu Fokuo, J., Thornicroft, G., Bamgbose, O., Ogunnubi, O., Ogunsola, K., and Oshodi, Y. (2022). Perspectives of university health care students on mental health stigma in Nigeria: qualitative analysis. *Transcultural Psychiatry*. https://doi.org/10.1177/13634615211055007.

Pennebaker, J.W., and Evans, J.F. (2014). *Expressive Writing: Words That Heal*. Enumclaw, WA: Idyll Arbour.

Pereira, A., Muris, P., Mendonça, D., Barros, L., Goes, A., and Marques, T. (2015). Parental involvement in cognitive-behavioral intervention for anxious children: parents' in-session and out-session activities and their relationship with treatment outcome. *Child Psychiatry and Human Development*, 47(1), 113–123. http://dx.doi.org/10.1007/s10578-015-0549-8.

Pernet, C., Belov, N., Delorme, A., and Zammit, A. (2021). Mindfulness related changes in grey matter: a systematic review and meta-analysis. *Brain Imaging and Behavior*, 15(5), 2720–2730. https://doi.org/10.1007/s11682-021-00453-4.

Perren, S., Godfrey, M., and Rowland, N.D. (2009). The long-term effects of counselling: the process and mechanisms that contribute to ongoing change from a user perspective. *Counselling and Psychotherapy Research*, 9, 241–249.

Pert, R. (2013). 'There is no map and there is no road': theorising best practice in the provision of creative writing therapy. *American, British, and Canadian Studies*, 20(1), 160–172.

Philips, B., Wennberg, P., and Werbart, A. (2007). Ideas of cure as a predictor of premature termination, early alliance, and outcome in psychoanalytic psychotherapy. *Psychology and Psychotherapy*, 80, 229–245. https://doi.org/10.1348/147608306X128266.

Philpot, L., Barnes, S., Brown, R., Austin, J., James, C., Stanford, R., and Ebbert, J. (2017). Barriers and benefits to the use of patient-reported outcome measures in routine clinical care: a qualitative study. *American Journal of Medical Quality: The Official Journal of the American College of Medical Quality*, 33. https://doi.org/1062860617745986.

Piaget, J. (1980). The psychogenesis of knowledge and its epistemological significance. In M. Piatelli-Palmarini (Ed.), *Language and Learning* (pp. 23–34). Cambridge, MA: Harvard University Press.

Pourhosein Gilakjani, A., and Sabouri, N. (2016). How can students improve their reading comprehension skill? *Journal of Studies in Education*, 6, 229. https://doi.org/10.5296/jse.v6i2.9201.

Prior, S. (2012). Overcoming stigma: how young people position themselves as counselling service users. *Sociology of Health and Illness*, 34(5), 697–713.

Prochaska, J.O., and DiClemente, C.C. (1982). Transtheoretical therapy: toward a more integrative model of change. *Psychotherapy: Theory, Research and Practice*, 19(3), 276–288. https://doi.org/10.1037/h0088437.

Prochaska, J.O., and DiClemente, C.C. (2005). The transtheoretical approach. In J.C. Norcross and M.R. Goldfried (Eds.), *Handbook of Psychotherapy Integration* (pp. 147–171). Oxford University Press. https://doi.org/10.1093/med:psych/9780195165791.003.0007.

Proctor, G. (2017). *The Dynamics of Power in Counselling and Psychotherapy: Ethics, Politics and Practice*. Monmouth: PCCS Books.

Rao, D., Young, M., and Raguram, R. (2007). Culture, somatization, and psychological distress: symptom presentation in south Indian patients from a public psychiatric hospital. *Psychopathology*, 40(5), 349–355. https://doi.org/10.1159/000106312.

Rastogi, M., Feldwisch, R., Pate, M., and Scarce, J. (2022). *Foundations of Art Therapy: Theory and Applications.* Rochester, NY: Elsevier Academic Press.

Read, J., and Dillon, J. (Eds.). (2013). *Models of Madness: Psychological, Social and Biological Approaches to Psychosis.* Abingdon: Routledge.

Reeves, A. (2013). *Challenges in Counselling: Self-Harm.* London: Hodder Education.

Reeves, A. (2015). *Working with Risk in Counselling and Psychotherapy.* London: Sage.

Reeves, A. (2016). Helping clients who are suicidal or self-injuring. In M. Cooper and W. Dryden (Eds.), *Handbook of Pluralistic Counselling and Psychotherapy* (pp. 259–271). London: Sage.

Regev, D., and Cohen-Yatziv, L. (2018). Effectiveness of art therapy with adult clients in 2018-What progress has been made? *Frontiers in Psychology*, 9, 1531. https://doi.org/10.3389/fpsyg.2018.01531

Rennie, D. (1994). Clients' deference in psychotherapy. *Journal of Counseling Psychology*, 41(4), 427–437.

Rescher, N. (1993). *Pluralism Against the Demand for Consensus.* Oxford: Clarenden Press.

Reusch, J., and Bateson, G. (1951). *Communication: The Social Matrix of Psychiatry.* London: WW Norton.

Ribeiro, A., Ribeiro, E., Loura, J., Gonçalves, M.M., Stiles, W.B., Horvath, A.O., and Sousa, I. (2014). Therapeutic collaboration and resistance: describing the nature and quality of the therapeutic relationship within ambivalence events using the therapeutic collaboration coding system. *Psychotherapy Research*, 24(3), 346–359. https://doi.org/10.1080/10503307.2013.856042.

Ribeiro, E., Ribeiro, A., Goncalves, M., Horvath, A., and Stiles, W. (2012). How collaboration in therapy becomes therapeutic: the therapeutic collaboration coding system. *Psychology and Psychotherapy: Theory, Research and Practice*, 86, 294–314.

Richards, B.M. (2000). Impact upon therapy and the therapist when working with suicidal patients: some transference and countertransference aspects. *British Journal of Guidance & Counselling*, 28(3), 325–337. https://doi.org/10.1080/03069880050118975.

Rogers, C.R. (1961). *On Becoming a Person.* Boston: Houghton Mifflin Company.

Rogers, C.R. (1986). Client-centered therapy. In I.L. Kutash and A. Wolf (Eds.), *Psychotherapist's Casebook: Theory and Technique in the Practice of Modern Psychotherapy* (pp. 197–208). San Francisco: JosseyBass Publishers.

Rogers, C.R. (2020). *On Becoming a Person: A Therapist's View of Psychotherapy* (60th anniversary ed.). London: Robinson.

Roos, J., and Werbart, A. (2013). Therapist and relationship factors influencing dropout from individual psychotherapy: a literature review. *Psychotherapy Research*, 1–25. https://doi.org/10.1080/10503307.2013.775528.

Rose, G., and Smith, L. (2018). Mental health recovery, goal setting and working alliance in an Australian community-managed organisation. *Health Psychology Open*. https://doi.org/10.1177/2055102918774674.

Rosenblatt, P. (2020). Challenges to cultural outsiders from the culture of grief counseling/therapy. *Journal of Loss and Trauma*, 25(3), 207–223.

Rosenthal, H. (2011). *Favorite Counseling and Therapy Techniques* (2nd ed.). London: Routledge.

Rosenthal, R. (1979). The "file drawer problem" and tolerance for null results. *Psychological Bulletin*, 86(3), 838–641.

Rousmaniere, T. (2016). *Deliberate Practice for Psychotherapists: A Guide to Improving Clinical Effectiveness*. New York: Routledge.

Royce, J.R., and Mos, L.P. (1981). *Humanistic Psychology: Concepts and Criticisms*. New York: Springer.

Rupani, P., Cooper, M., McArthur, K., Pybis, J., Cromarty, K., Hill, A., et al. (2014). The goals of young people in school-based counselling and their achievement of these goals. *Counselling and Psychotherapy Research*, 14(4), 306–314. https://doi.org/10.1080/14733145.2013.816758.

Safran, J.D., and Muran, J.C. (2006). Has the concept of the therapeutic alliance outlived its usefulness? *Psychotherapy: Theory, Research, Practice, Training*, 43(3), 286–291. https://doi.org/10.1037/0033-3204.43.3.286.

Sales, C., Ashworth, M., Ayis, S., Barkham, M., Edbrooke-Childs, J., Faísca, L., . . . Cooper, M. (2022). Idiographic patient reported outcome measures (I-PROMs) for routine outcome monitoring in psychological therapies: position paper. *Journal of Clinical Psychology*, 79(3), 596–621.

Samuels, A. (1995). Pluralism and psychotherapy. *Australasian Journal of Psychotherapy*, 14, 31–44.

Sarkhel, S., Singh, O.P., and Arora, M. (2020). Clinical practice guidelines for psychoeducation in psychiatric disorders general principles of psychoeducation. *Indian Journal of Psychiatry*, 62(Suppl 2), S319–S323. https://doi.org/10.4103/psychiatry.IndianJPsychiatry_780_19.

Serrano-García, I. (1994). The ethics of the powerful and the power of ethics. *American Journal of Community Psychology*, 22(1).

Shearin, E.N., and Linehan, M.M. (1994). Dialectical behavior therapy for borderline personality disorder: theoretical and empirical foundations. *Acta Psychiatrica Scandinavica*, 89(379, Suppl), 61–68. https://doi.org/10.1111/j.1600-0447.1994.tb05820.x.

Sheldon, K.M., and Kasser, T. (1998). Pursuing personal goals: skills enable progress, but not all progress is beneficial. *Personality and Social Psychology Bulletin*, 24(12), 1319–1331. https://doi.org/10.1177/01461672982412006.

Shoesmith, W., Awang Borhanuddin, A., Pereira, E.J., Nordin, N., Giridharan, B., Forman, D., and Fyfe, S. (2019). Barriers and enablers to collaboration in the mental health system in Sabah, Malaysia: towards a theory of collaboration. *BJPsych Open*, 6(1), e4. https://doi.org/10.1192/bjo.2019.92.

Shukla, S. (2022). Role of cultural resources in mental health: an existential perspective. *Frontiers in Psychology*, 13. https://doi.org/10.3389/fpsyg.2022.860560.

Siegel, D.J. (1999). *The Developing Mind*. New York: Guilford.

Sighinolfi, C., Nespeca, C., Menchetti, M., Levantesi, P., Belvederi Murri, M., and Berardi, D. (2014). Collaborative care for depression in European countries: a systematic review and meta-analysis. *Journal of Psychosomatic Research*, 77(4), 247–263. https://doi.org/10.1016/j.jpsychores.2014.08.006.

Singer, R.R., and Tummala-Narra, P. (2013). 'White clinicians' perspectives on working with racial minority immigrant clients. *Professional Psychology, Research and Practice*, 44(5), 290–298. https://doi.org/10.1037/a0034299.

Slade, M. (2009). *Personal Recovery and Mental Illness: A Guide for Mental Health Professionals* (Values-Based Practice). Cambridge and New York: Cambridge University Press.

Slife, B.D., and Wendt, D.C. (2009). Editors' introduction: the modern legacy of William James' 'a pluralistic universe'. *Journal of Mind and Behavior*, 30, 103–106.

Smith, K., and de la Prida, A. (2021). *The Pluralistic Therapy Primer*. Monmouth: PCCS Books.

Smith, K., McLeod, J., Blunden, N., Cooper, M., Gabriel, L., Kupfer, C., McLeod, J., Murphie, M-C., Oddli, H.W., Thurston, M., and Winter, L.A. (2021). A pluralistic perspective on research in psychotherapy: harnessing passion, difference and dialogue to promote justice and relevance. *Frontiers in Psychology*, 12, 742676. https://doi.org/10.3389/fpsyg.2021.742676.

Smith, R. (2022). The politics of distress. *Journal of Philosophy of Education*, 56, 105–114. https://doi.org/10.1111/1467-9752.12659.

Snyder, C.R. (2002). Hope theory: rainbows in the mind. *Psychological Inquiry*, 13(4), 249–275.

Sparks, J., and Duncan, B. (2016a). Client strengths and resources: helping clients draw on what they already do best. In M. Cooper and W. Dryden (Eds.), *The Handbook of Pluralistic Counselling and Psychotherapy*. London: Sage Publications.

Sparks, J., and Duncan, B. (2016b). Systematic feedback through the partners for change outcome management system (PCOMS). In M. Cooper and W. Dryden (Eds.), *The Handbook of Pluralistic Counselling and Psychotherapy*. London: Sage.

Spijkerman, M.P., Pots, W.T., and Bohlmeijer, E. (2016). Effectiveness of online mindfulness-based interventions in improving mental health: a review and meta-analysis of randomised controlled trials. *Clinical Psychology Review*, 45, 102–114. https://doi.org/10.1016/j.cpr.2016.03.009.

Spitzer, R.L., Kroenke, K., Williams, J.B., and Löwe, B. (2006). A brief measure for assessing generalized anxiety disorder: the GAD-7. *Archives of Internal Medicine*, 166(10), 1092–1097.

Spurling, L. (2016). Psychodynamic approaches in pluralism. In M. Cooper and W. Dryden (Eds.), *Handbook of Pluralistic Counselling and Psychotherapy* (pp. 68–79). London: Sage.

Stevens, K., and McLeod, J. (2019). Yoga as an adjunct to trauma-focused counselling for survivors of sexual violence: a qualitative study. *British Journal of Guidance and Counselling*, 47(6), 682–697.

Stiles, W.B., Elliott, R., Llewelyn, S.P., Firth-Cozens, J., Margison, F.R., Shapiro, D.A., and Hardy, G. (1990). Assimilation of problematic experiences by clients in psychotherapy. *Psychotherapy* (Chicago, IL), 27(3), 411–420. https://doi.org/10.1037/0033-3204.27.3.411.

Stiles, W.B., and Horvath, A.O. (2017). Appropriate responsiveness as a contribution to therapist effects. In L.G. Castonguay and C.E. Hill (Eds.), *How and Why Are Some Therapists Better Than Others? Understanding Therapist Effects* (pp. 71–84). Washington, DC: American Psychological Association. https://doi.org/10.1037/0000034-005.

Storm, J.A.J. (2021). *Metamodernism: The Future of Theory*. Chicago: University of Chicago Press.

Sue, D.W., Arredondo, P., and McDavis, R.J. (1992). Multicultural counseling competencies and standards: a call to the profession. *Journal of Multicultural Counseling and Development*, 20(2), 64–88. https://doi.org/10.1002/j.2161-1912.1992.tb00563.x.

Sue, S. (1998). In search of cultural competence in psychotherapy and counseling. *The American Psychologist*, 53(4), 440–448.

Sundet, R. (2012). Therapist perspectives on the use of feedback on process and outcome: patient-focused research in practice. *Canadian Psychological Association*, 53(2), 122–130.

Swift, J.K., and Callahan, J.L. (2009). The impact of client treatment preferences on outcome: a meta-analysis. *Journal of Clinical Psychology*, 65, 368–381. https://doi.org/10.1002/jclp.20553.

Swift, J.K., Callahan, J.L., Cooper, M., and Parkin, S.R. (2018). The impact of accommodation client preferences in psychotherapy: a meta-analysis. *Journal of Clinical Psychology*, 74(11), 1924–1937. https://doi.org/10.1002/jclp.22680.

Swift, J.K., Callahan, J.L., and Vollmer, B. (2010). Preferences. In J. Norcross (Ed.), *Psychotherapy Relationships That Work: Evidence-Based Responsiveness*. New York: Oxford University Press.

Tao, K., Owen, J., Pace, B., and Imel, Z. (2015). A meta-analysis of multicultural competencies and psychotherapy process and outcome. *Journal of Counseling Psychology*, 62(3), 337–350. https://doi.org/10.1037/cou0000086.

TED. (2014). *Developing a Growth Mindset | Carol Dweck* [Video]. YouTube. www.youtube.com/watch?v=hiiEeMN7vbQ.

Thompson, A., and Cooper, M. (2012). Therapists' experiences of pluralistic practice. *European Journal of Psychotherapy and Counselling*, 14(1), 63–75. https://doi.org/10.1080/13642537.2012.652393.

Thorpe, M. (2013). The process of conducting qualitative research as an adjunct to the development of therapeutic abilities in counselling psychology. *New Zealand Journal of Psychology*, 42, 35.

Thrift, E., and Sugarman, J. (2019). What is social justice? Implications for psychology. *Journal of Theoretical and Philosophical Psychology*, 39(1), 1–17. https://doi.org/10.1037/teo0000097.

Thurston, M., McLeod, J., and Thurston, A. (2013). Counselling for sight loss: using systematic case study research to build a client informed practice model. *British Journal of Visual Impairment*, 31(2), 102–122.

Timulak, L. (2007). Identifying core categories of client-identified impact of helpful events in psychotherapy: a qualitative meta-analysis. *Psychotherapy Research*, 17(3), 305–314.

Timulak, L. (2010). Significant events in psychotherapy: an update of research findings. *Psychology and Psychotherapy*, 83(4), 421–447.

Timulak, L., and Keogh, D. (2017). The client's perspective on (experiences of) psychotherapy: a practice friendly review. *Journal of Clinical Psychology*, 73(11), 1556–1567. https://doi.org/10.1002/jclp.22532.

Timulak, L., and McElvaney, R. (2013). Qualitative meta-analysis of insight events in psychotherapy. *Counselling Psychology Quarterly*, 26(2), 131–150. https://doi.org/10.1080/09515070.2013.792997.

Tompkins, K., Swift, J., and Callahan, J. (2013). Working with clients by incorporating their preferences. *Psychotherapy Theory Research Practice Training*, 50(3), 279–283. https://doi.org/10.1037/a0032031.

Trenoweth, S. (2016). *Promoting Recovery in Mental Health Nursing*. London: Sage Publications.

Tryon, G., Birch, S., et al. (2018). Meta-analyses of the relation of goal consensus and collaboration to psychotherapy outcome. *Psychotherapy*, 55(4), 372–382.

Tsai, M., et al. (2009). *A Guide to Functional Analytic Psychotherapy: Awareness, Courage, Love and Behaviorism*. New York: Springer.

Twigg, E., Barkham, M., Bewick, B.M., Mulhern, B., Connell, J., and Cooper, M. (2009). The young person's CORE: development of a brief outcome measure for young people. *Counselling and Psychotherapy Research*, 9(3), 160–168. https://doi.org/10.1080/1473314090 2979722.

Unsworth, G., Cowie, H., and Green, A. (2011). Therapists' and clients' perceptions of routine outcome measurement in the NHS: a qualitative study. *Counselling and Psychotherapy Research*, 12(1), 71–80. https://doi.org/10.1080/14733145.2011.565125.

Vaculik, C.L., and Nash, G. (Eds.). (2022a). *Integrative Arts Psychotherapy: Using an Integrative Theoretical Frame and the Arts in Psychotherapy*. London: Routledge.

Vaculik, C.L., and Nash, G. (2022b). Introduction to integrative arts psychotherapy. In C.L. Vaculik and G. Nash (Eds.), *Integrative Arts Psychotherapy: Using an Integrative Theoretical Frame and the Arts in Psychotherapy* (pp. 1–8). London: Routledge.

Valkonen, J., Hänninen, V., and Lindfors, O. (2011). Outcomes of psychotherapy from the perspective of the users. *Psychotherapy Research*, 21(2), 227–240. https://doi.org/10.1080/10503307.2010.548346.

Van Dam, N.T., van Vugt, M.K., Vago, D.R., Schmalzl, L., Saron, C.D., Olendzki, A., Meissner, T., Lazar, S.W., Kerr, C.E., Gorchov, J., Fox, K., Field, B.A., Britton, W.B., Brefczynski-Lewis, J.A., and Meyer, D.E. (2018). Mind the hype: a critical evaluation and prescriptive agenda for research on mindfulness and meditation. *Perspectives on Psychological Science: A Journal of the Association for Psychological Science*, 13(1), 36–61. https://doi.org/10.1177/1745691617709589.

van den Akker, R., Gibbons, A., and Vermeulen, T. (2017). *Metamodernism: Historicity, Affect, and Depth After Postmodernism*. Lanham, MA: Rowman & Littlefield.

van Deurtsen, E., Carig, E., Laengle, A., Sneitder, K.J., Tatam, D., and du Plock, S. (2019). *The Wiley World Handbook of Existential Therapy*. Oxford: Wiley-Blackwell.

Vollmer, B., Grote, J., Lange, R., and Walker, C. (2009). A therapy preferences interview: empowering clients by offering choices. *Psychotherapy Bulletin*, 44(2).

Von Below, C. (2020). "We just did not get on". Young adults' experiences of unsuccessful psychodynamic psychotherapy – a lack of meta-communication and mentalization? *Frontiers in Psychology*, 11, 1243.

Wachtel, P.L. (2014). An integrative relational point of view. *Psychotherapy*, 51(3), 342–349. https://doi.org/10.1037/a0037219.

Walker, C., Hart, A., and Hanna, P. (2017). *Social Approached to Distress: From Enclosures to Fluid Spaces in Building a New Community Psychology of Mental Health*. London: Palgrave MacMillan.

Wallace, K., and Cooper, M. (2015). Development of supervision personalisation forms: a qualitative study of the dimensions along which supervisors' practices vary. *Counselling and Psychotherapy Research*, 15(1), 31–40.

Waller, G., and Turner, H. (2016). Therapist drift redux: why well-meaning clinicians fail to deliver evidence-based therapy, and how to get back on track. *Behaviour Research and Therapy*, 77, 129–137. https://doi.org/10.1016/j.brat.2015.12.005.

Wampold, B.E. (2015). How important are the common factors in psychotherapy? An update. *World Psychiatry: Official Journal of the World Psychiatric Association* (WPA), 14(3), 270–277. https://doi.org/10.1002/wps.20238.

Wang, M., Wong, Y., Nyutu, P., and Fu, C. (2020). Suicidality protective factors among black college students: which cultural and personal resources matter? *Journal of Multicultural Counseling and Development*, 48(4). https://doi.org/10.1002/jmcd.12198.

Ward, T., Hogan, K., and Menns, R. (2011). Perceptions of integration in counselling psychology training, a pilot study. *Counselling Psychology Review- British Psychological Society*, 26(3), 8–19.

Ward-Wimmer, D. (2003). Introduction: the healing potential of adults at play. In C. Schaefer (Ed.), *Play Therapy with Adults*. Hoboken, NJ: John Wiley & Sons.

Watsford, C., and Rickwood, D. (2015). Young people's expectations, preferences and actual experience of youth mental health care. *International Journal of Adolescence and Youth*, 20(3), 284–294. https://doi.org/10.1080/02673843.2013.799038.

Watts, N., Amann, M., Ayeb-Karlsson, S., Belesova, K., Bouley, T., Boykoff, M., . . . Costello, A. (2018). The lancet countdown on health and climate change: from 25 years of inaction to a global transformation for public health. *The Lancet* (British Edition), 391(10120), 581–630.

Weaks, D. (2006). *Living Within a Limited Freedom: The Perceptions and Experiences of Early Dementia From the Perspectives of People with the Diagnosis and the Diagnosticians* (Doctoral Thesis). University of Abertay, Dundee.

White, M., and Epston, D. (1990). *Narrative Means to Therapeutic Ends*. London: Norton.

Wilk, K. (2014). Using a pluralistic approach in counselling psychology and psychotherapy practice with diverse clients: explorations into cultural and religious responsiveness within a Western paradigm. *Counselling Psychology Review*, 29(1), 16–28.

Williams, D., and Levitt, H. (2008). Clients' experiences of difference with therapists: sustaining faith in psychotherapy. *Psychotherapy Research*, 18(3), 256–270.

Williams, J., Mcmahon, H., and Goodman, R. (2015). Eco-webbing: a teaching strategy to facilitate critical consciousness and agency. *Counselor Education and Supervision*, 54. https://doi.org/10.1002/ceas.12006.

Willig, C. (2019). Ontological and epistemological reflexivity: a core skill for therapists. *Counselling and Psychotherapy Research*, 19(3), 186–194. https://doi.org/10.1002/capr.12204.

Wilson, J. (2013). *Supporting People Through Loss and Grief: An Introduction for Counsellors and Other Caring Practitioners*. London: Jessica Kingsley Publishers.

Wilson, J. (2020). *The Plain Guide to Grief*. Self-Published.

Winnicott, D.W. (1968). Playing: its theoretical status in the clinical situation. *International Journal of Psychoanalysis*, 49, 591–619.

Winter, L.A., Guo, F., Wilk, K., and Hanley, T. (2016). Difference and diversity in pluralistic counselling and psychotherapy. In M. Cooper and W. Dryden (Eds.), *Handbook of Pluralistic Counselling and Psychotherapy* (pp. 275–287). London: Sage.

Woods, R. (2001). Discovering the person with Alzheimer's disease: cognitive, emotional and behavioural aspects. *Aging & Mental Health*, 5(1), S7–S16.

Woody, W.D., and Viney, W. (2009). A pluralistic universe: an overview and implications for psychology. *Journal of Mind and Behavior*, 30, 107–120.

Wright, K. (2011). *The Rise of the Therapeutic Society: Psychological Knowledge and the Contradictions of Cultural Change*. Washington, DC: New Academia.

Young, I.M. (1990). *Justice and the Politics of Difference*. Princeton, NY: Princeton University Press.

Yumatle, C. (2015). Pluralism. In M.T. Gibbons (Ed.), *The Encyclopaedia of Political Thought*. Wiley-Blackwell. https://doi.org/10.1002/9781118474396.wbept0771.

Zittoun, T., and Brinkmann, S. (2012). Learning as meaning making. In N. Seel (Ed.), *Encyclopedia of the Sciences of Learning* (pp. 1809–1811). Manhattan, NYC: Springer Reference.

Index

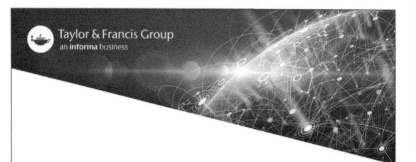

For Product Safety Concerns and Information please contact our
EU representative GPSR@taylorandfrancis.com Taylor & Francis
Verlag GmbH, Kaufingerstraße 24, 80331 München, Germany